Food Will Win the War

Food
THE POLITICS, CULTURE,
Will Win
AND SCIENCE OF FOOD ON
the War
CANADA'S HOME FRONT

Ian Mosby

UBC Press • Vancouver • Toronto

22 21 20 19 18 17 16   5 4 3

Printed in Canada on FSC-certified ancient-forest-free paper
(100% post-consumer recycled) that is processed chlorine- and acid-free.

Library and Archives Canada Cataloguing in Publication

Mosby, Ian, 1980-, author
    Food will win the war : the politics, culture, and science of food on Canada's
home front / Ian Mosby.

Includes bibliographical references and index.
Issued in print and electronic formats.
ISBN 978-0-7748-2761-4 (bound). – ISBN 978-0-7748-2762-1 (pbk.). –
ISBN 978-0-7748-2763-8 (pdf). – ISBN 978-0-7748-2764-5 (epub)

    1. World War, 1939-1945 – Food supply – Canada. 2. World War, 1939-1945 –
Social aspects – Canada. 3. Food supply – Canada – History – 20th century.
4. Food security – Canada – History – 20th century. 5. Nutrition policy – Canada
– History – 20th century. 6. Food habits – Canada – History – 20th century.
7. War and society – Canada – History – 20th century. 8. Food – Canada –
Historiography. I. Title.

HD9014.C32M73 2014   940.53'10971   C2014-901855-X
                                                   C2014-901856-8

Canadä

UBC Press gratefully acknowledges the financial support for our publishing program
of the Government of Canada (through the Canada Book Fund), the Canada
Council for the Arts, and the British Columbia Arts Council.

This book has been published with the help of a grant from the Canadian Federation
for the Humanities and Social Sciences, through the Awards to Scholarly Publications
Program, using funds provided by the Social Sciences and Humanities Research
Council of Canada.

UBC Press
The University of British Columbia
2029 West Mall
Vancouver, BC V6T 1Z2
www.ubcpress.ca

For Laural and Oscar

There is a communion of more than our bodies
when bread is broken and wine drunk. And that is
my answer, when people ask me: Why do you write
about hunger, and not wars or love?

— M.F.K. Fisher, *The Gastronomical Me* (1943)

A human being is primarily a bag for putting food into;
the other functions and faculties may be more godlike, but
in point of time they come afterwards. A man dies and is
buried, and all his words and actions are forgotten, but
the food he has eaten lives after him in the sound or rotten
bones of his children. I think it could be plausibly argued
that changes of diet are more important than changes of
dynasty or even of religion … Yet it is curious how seldom
the all-importance of food is recognized. You see statues
everywhere to politicians, poets, bishops, but none to
cooks or bacon-curers or market gardeners.

— George Orwell, *The Road to Wigan Pier* (1937)

Contents

Figures and Tables

Figures

Tables

Acknowledgments

Writing this book turned out to be a much more daunting undertaking than I'd anticipated, but it would have been impossible without the help of my amazing family, friends, and colleagues. She probably deserves at least a co-author credit, given the many years she's had to live in close quarters with this project, and I don't think it's an understatement to say that this book simply would not exist without Laural Raine. She's put up with a lot over the years as the long-suffering partner of a fledgling academic. Yet, somehow, she has always been there to read new drafts, listen to frequently tedious monologues about the history of food, and, most of all, help me get through some of the not-so-great times. This book and my life in general wouldn't be half of what they are without Laural's love and support, and I am forever grateful. I similarly owe a great debt to my parents, Rod and Pam Mosby, who never once told me that staying in university forever might not be the best career path but instead have given me nothing but encouragement and support. I hope you both – Mom with your passion for food, and Dad with your passion for politics – see something of yourselves in the chapters that follow.

I was extremely lucky to be surrounded by a group of truly fantastic scholars during my years as a graduate student at York University. In particular, I owe a profound debt to the late Gina Feldberg. Gina was a truly inspiring supervisor, mentor, and scholar whose unflagging enthusiasm for my project helped transform it from a series of half-formed and vague ideas into something that I was glad to have spent so many years working on and thinking about. I wish she could be here to read the finished product, but I feel lucky to have known her for the time that I did. I am also extremely lucky to have had a wonderful committee to support me through good times and bad. Kate McPherson, Molly Ladd-Taylor, and Marlene Shore all stepped in when I needed them and their comments, encouragement, and critical insights, all of which were invaluable, helped make this a much better book. I also want to thank Jeffrey Pilcher for his insightful feedback and much needed encouragement.

I was lucky to meet so many amazing friends and colleagues during my time at York. Jason Ellis and Christine Grandy both agreed to read far more drafts of my chapters, SSHRC applications, and cover letters than I would care to count, but I've also received substantial support for my work from my fellow history PhDs – Ben Lander, Jim Clifford, Beth Palmer, Laura Godsoe, Will Baker, Ian McPhedran, Val Deacon, Jenny Ellison, Joel Regehr, Ian Milligan, Jay Young, Andrew Watson, Sean Kheraj, Dan Bullard, Samira Saramo, Lisa Rumiel, Tom Peace, Eric Payseur, Lee Slinger, and Colin McCullough. Each one of you has become a lifelong friend, which is one of the best things to come out of my grad school experience. A special thanks also to Sarah Glassford for being the best unofficial guide to the Canadian Red Cross Society Archives that anyone could ask for and to everyone in the York Politics Reading Group for providing some excellent comments on early drafts of my work.

I've also had the extremely good fortune to spend the last two years as a SSHRC postdoctoral fellow in the Department of History at the University of Guelph. Catherine Carstairs has really gone above and beyond the call of duty in her role as my postdoc supervisor and, as a result, has had a hugely positive impact on my research, writing, and teaching over the past two years. I'm also hard-pressed to imagine a more collegial or welcoming history department in Canada, in large part because of great colleagues like Christine Ekholst, Peter Goddard, Alan Gordon, Matthew Hayday, Sofie Lachapelle, Stuart McCook, Susan Nance, Richard Reid, and Susan Armstrong-Reid – not to mention fellow postdocs Jennifer Bonnell and Cathryn Spence.

Finally, I would like to thank Darcy Cullen at UBC Press for being a truly fantastic editor – who somehow managed to see this book go from proposal to final draft in less than a year – and Graeme Wynn for encouraging me to submit my book to UBC Press in the first place. The research for this project was, in part, made possible by generous financial support from the Social Sciences and Humanities Research Council of Canada, the Province of Ontario, York University, and the Avie Bennett Historica Dissertation Scholarship.

Food Will Win the War

Introduction

Let every kitchen work for victory, for food will win the war
— Slogan of the Kingston Community Nutrition Council, 1942[1]

Canada has determined to change the eating habits of a nation, because she has learned that efficient production of food is only half the victory. It takes efficient consumption, too, to give full meaning to the slogan, "Food will win the war."
— *Saturday Night*, December 1942[2]

In November 1944, the Wartime Information Board (WIB) commissioned a poll that asked Canadians what they considered their country's greatest contribution to the war effort. They were given three possible choices: food, men, or munitions. If the work of later historians of Canada's Second World War is any guide, the answer should have been clear. Canada's military and its war industries dominate scholarly analyses of this country's wartime contributions. With the exception of the work of agricultural economists G.E. Britnell and V.C. Fowke in the early 1960s, the role of food in the history of the war effort is notable primarily for its absence.[3] Somewhat surprisingly, however, Canadians at the time appeared to have held a very different view. Food was selected by 30 percent of those surveyed as being Canada's most important wartime contribution – a finding that was fairly consistent across regions, occupations, income levels, and gender. In the same poll, 30 percent chose "men," and only 24 percent chose "munitions." In an earlier version of this survey, conducted in 1942, "food" actually trumped the other two choices, at 38 percent, beating "men" by a considerable margin.[4]

The WIB's question was no doubt leading and simplistic. Yet the fact that so many respondents in two separate polls gave Canada's food contribution the same weight as the lives of their friends, neighbours, and family members – especially given that the 1944 poll was conducted at the height of combat operations in Europe – suggests that at the very least, the impact of food on the Canadian experience of the Second World War needs to be revisited. During the 1940s, Canadians were well aware that there was much truth to the adage that "food is a weapon of war," and as we have since learned, the war for food had particularly devastating consequences. Historian Lizzie Collingham has estimated that a staggering 20 million people died of "starvation, malnutrition and its associated diseases" during the Second World War, a number equal in scale to the estimated 19.5 million military deaths. Collingham goes on to argue that the global struggle for food dictated military strategy and did much to decide the war's outcome – indeed, that it was "one of the driving forces behind some of the worst atrocities committed during the conflict."[5]

As one of the world's major food exporters, Canada played a crucial role in the war for food. In a September 1942 radio address, Prime Minister William Lyon Mackenzie King told Canadians it was "literally true that after Britain was cut off from European supplies in 1940, her people and her fighting men were saved from starvation by Canadian food."[6] While the British might not have *literally* starved without Canadian food exports, it was nonetheless very much true that their war effort would have been massively and perhaps even fatally hindered. By the end of the war, official estimates were that Canadian exports accounted for 57 percent of British wheat and flour consumption – down from its remarkable peak of 77 percent in 1941 – as well as 39 percent of bacon, 15 percent of eggs, 24 percent of cheese, and 11 percent of evaporated milk consumed in Britain.[7] In part, this was achieved through unprecedented state intervention in Canadian food production. The federal government had taken direct control over the bulk purchase, sale, and distribution of a range of basic commodities – including sugar, tea, coffee, wheat, and rice – and had also introduced a range of subsidies, price guarantees, and other controls to transform agricultural production. Between 1940 and 1943 alone, wheat acreage in the prairie provinces was reduced by 42 percent while areas sown for agricultural products needed to bridge gaps in Canada's domestic and export requirements saw dramatic increases. Feed grain production, for instance, increased by 72 percent over the prewar period while flaxseed production increased by 800 percent and hog production by 250 percent.[8]

All the while, journalists, food and nutrition experts, and government propagandists regularly reminded Canadians that the food front extended from field to table and depended as much on efficient consumption at home as it did on increased production.[9] To free up foods needed for export to Canada's overseas allies and soldiers while preventing unnecessary shortages and the inflationary spiral that had developed during the First World War, the federal government intervened directly in the operation of the nation's kitchens on an unprecedented scale. For example, it rationed meat, sugar, butter, tea, coffee, and preserves under a coupon system; by regulation, it mandated meatless days in restaurants, limited the types of canned goods that could be sold, and prohibited the sale of sliced bread, hot dog buns, and iced cakes. Meanwhile, its newly established Nutrition Division sent out the omnipresent message that more than half of Canadians were malnourished and that poor nutrition was sabotaging Canada's war effort. The government, in other words, set out to transform Canadians' dietary habits through a range of both voluntary and coercive means.

Canada's wartime mobilization on the home front not only led to very real changes in the ways Canadians shopped for, cooked, and consumed food but also transformed the broader symbolism of food and eating. Certain previously mundane or even unknown forms of food consumption and production became embodied with new meanings. Vegetable gardening became an act of solidarity with Canadian farmers and British civilians, while saving fats and bones transformed the kitchen into a munitions factory. Feeding one's family according to the newly created Canada's Official Food Rules emerged as a mother's wartime duty, while reporting the baker to the authorities for selling a loaf of Canada Approved Vitamin "B" Bread above its maximum ceiling price became an important patriotic act. At the same time, the language of food had taken on an increasingly political tone by the end of the war, particularly as more and more Canadians began to articulate a counter-discourse that stressed, not just their *obligation* to follow the rules of wartime eating, but also their *right* to adequate and nutritious food at a reasonable price both during and after the war.

Given the scale of these transformations in the material and symbolic realities of eating – and given the fact that the average Canadian household spent more than 30 percent of its income on food – it should come as no surprise that at the time, Canadians saw food as essential to both their

experience of the war and its eventual outcome. It is, therefore, these
broader changes in food *consumption* on the home front that are the focus
of the chapters that follow. While this book makes no attempt to reclaim
food as Canada's "greatest" contribution to the war effort – or even, like
Collingham, to offer a food-centred reinterpretation of the military history
of the war – it does attempt to use the seemingly mundane acts of shopping for, preparing, and eating food as a powerful and unique lens through
which to reinterpret the history of everyday life on the home front. This
is because, even though it is often overlooked by historians, food tends to
define the everyday. It is essential to our survival; more importantly, how
often and how well we eat has a profound effect on our health and well-
being. Because food is a biological necessity, it has therefore played a central
role throughout history in the functioning of family, regional, and national
economies, often determining the fate of governments, nations, and even
empires.[10] But food is also essential to our social, cultural, and spiritual
lives. A vast range of fundamentally important secular and religious rituals
have developed around food, and in nearly all societies food acts as an
essential site in which social distinctions based on region, religion, class,
ethnicity, age, and gender are both defined and maintained.[11] In other
words, because it is such a complex product of choice and coercion, necessity and pleasure, science and culture, food is an ideal avenue for exploring
the profound social, cultural, political, and scientific changes that characterized Canadians' everyday experience of the Second World War.[12]

The following chapters examine how the Second World War transformed
the politics, culture, and science of food on the Canadian home front.
They differ in their sources and approaches but are nonetheless united in
this common argument: food did not literally win the war, but it did much
to define the contours of everyday life on the home front, and more importantly, it became a central site where competing gendered visions of
the rights and responsibilities of Canadian citizenship were both articulated
and contested on a truly national scale. Reflecting this premise, the first
two chapters focus on what were, up to that point, two of the most significant attempts by Canada's federal government to intervene directly
in ordinary Canadians' eating habits. Chapter 1 examines how warnings
of a national malnutrition crisis made by the newly formed Canadian
Council on Nutrition led to an unprecedented response by the federal
government, one that included the founding of a national Nutrition
Services Division and the launch of the Canadian Nutrition Programme,
Canada's first large-scale national nutrition campaign. Through an examination of Canada's Official Food Rules (the predecessor to Canada's Food

Guide) and of other forms of wartime nutrition education and advice, this chapter focuses on how changes to the scientific consensus concerning the measurement of malnutrition not only transformed Canada's nutrition professions more broadly, but also became the basis for a public health program that was ultimately less concerned with preventing serious illness than with normalizing an unrealized physical and culinary ideal that prioritized the perceived industrial, military, and agricultural needs of a nation at war.

While Chapter 1 focuses mainly on the federal government's efforts to encourage Canadians to voluntarily change their eating habits, Chapter 2 examines a much more direct form of state intervention in Canada's kitchens. It does so by exploring the different ways in which ordinary Canadians responded to food rationing and price control, two of the main pillars of Canada's wartime command economy. Because coupon rationing was directed primarily at foodstuffs – and because food was the single largest expense for most families – it was at the kitchen table that Canadians most directly and regularly experienced the effects of centralized state control over the wartime economy. Both of these interventions, moreover, were without precedent. During the First World War, Canadians had been able to escape mandatory coupon rationing altogether, and wartime controls on food and other consumer goods were minimal and largely ineffective. The result was widespread shortages and a disastrous inflationary spiral that saw food prices increase by 128 percent over pre-war levels by 1920.[13] It was with this in mind that the Wartime Prices and Trade Board (WPTB) was established on 3 September 1939, only a few days after the passage of the War Measures Act and nearly a week before Canada officially declared war on Germany. The WPTB's mandate was "to provide safeguards under war conditions against any undue enhancement in the prices of food, fuel, and other necessaries of life, and to ensure an adequate supply and equitable distribution of such commodities."[14]

As Chapter 2 will show, fulfilling this mandate was a complex and uncertain enterprise that required an unprecedented level of voluntary cooperation from Canadian women in particular. By examining the major sources of popular support for and discontent with food rationing and price control, the chapter explores how the experience of both these programs transformed popular notions of social and economic citizenship by mobilizing consumers around the responsibilities of both citizens and the state to ensure a wartime marketplace governed by a common goal of "equality of sacrifice" and fairness. In particular, it argues that – contrary to the commonly repeated historical narrative[15] – these programs were remarkably popular and in fact made an important (and often unrecognized) contribution to Canadians' growing faith in the state's ability to intervene in and manage the postwar economy. Moreover, by rallying Canadian women around the need to protect their rights as both citizens and consumers through their cooperation with (and participation in) the government's wartime economic stabilization program, federal departments like the Consumer Branch of the WPTB actually helped politicize large numbers of Canadian women around issues such as the fair and equitable price and distribution of meat, milk, butter, and other foods. This in turn helped spark an unprecedented wave of consumer protest following the decontrol of food prices in the early postwar period.

Chapters 3 and 4 build on these broader examinations of state intervention into the Canadian diet by focusing on the ways in which the federal government's changing wartime priorities transformed the material realities of food consumption and culinary practice, as well as their symbolic and cultural meanings. Chapter 3 explores the ways in which ordinary Canadians rallied around household food production, conservation, and service on the home front in order to show their support for the larger war effort. Whether by salvaging fats and bones, planting victory gardens, operating active service canteens, or producing Red Cross prisoner-of-war parcels, millions of Canadians – and women in particular – mobilized their domestic space, labour, and skills to contribute to Canada's larger war production goals. Many of these activities rallied the private sphere and feminine domestic virtues in ways that reflected a pervasive and gendered propaganda discourse that stressed women's maternal obligations to nation and empire. But at the same time, such activities also often blurred the distinction between women's public and private roles in ways that highlighted the social and economic importance of women's domestic labour as a key component of the war effort. Chapter 3 therefore argues not only that the state mobilized women's unpaid labour on a scale that has gone largely unrecognized by historians, but also that food production, consumption, and service played an essential role in determining the boundaries of gendered notions of wartime citizenship.

Chapter 4 builds on many of the themes explored in the preceding three chapters by exploring how the larger forces driving Canadians to transform their eating habits were ultimately translated into the everyday language of food culture and culinary practice. In particular, it focuses on the multiple genres of wartime food writing that were produced during this period and ranged from ordinary Canadians' contributions to community cookbooks and the women's pages of their local newspapers to the avalanche of wartime prescriptive literature produced by food experts, government officials, and advertisers. This chapter explores the ways in which rationing and the identification of certain foods and culinary practices as "patriotic" created a space for a common, pan-Canadian wartime cuisine. At the same time, it examines how ordinary Canadians navigated the contradictions between a wartime discourse of home front sacrifice and the realities of material abundance – realities that became apparent as unemployment declined and disposable incomes grew. And, perhaps most importantly, the chapter argues that, through the production and use of wartime recipes and cookbooks, ordinary women were provided with a powerful and important means of articulating a number of very different visions of wartime citizenship and postwar reconstruction.

Finally, Chapter 5 situates all of these larger changes in the politics, culture, and science of food within broader debates surrounding Canada's plans for an expanded postwar welfare state. The "discovery" of a national malnutrition crisis by Canada's leading food and nutrition experts in the early years of the war led to a major expansion of nutrition-related initiatives in Canada. As a consequence, the nutrition question was put to increasingly political uses by a range of different groups. Many of the same scientific tools that had been used to measure malnutrition in Canadian cities, for instance, proved to be valuable resources for left-wing social critics of municipal and provincial welfare and relief policies. And, on a more national level, what we now often call *food security* – defined in part by the achievement of "physical, social and economic access to sufficient, safe and nutritious food that meets [a population's] dietary needs"[16] – was now being articulated by ordinary Canadians as well as by leading experts (such as Leonard Marsh and Harry Cassidy) as one of the most important pillars, if not *the* most important, of any postwar *social security* plan. The growing prominence of nutrition in these often heated wartime debates meant that divisions began to form among Canadian nutrition professionals, with some beginning to use their research to promote a more interventionist welfare state, and others defending the status quo. By examining how nutrition was used in political debates over unemployment relief rates and family allowances – as well as in efforts to establish a national school lunch program – the chapter shows how these debates exposed internal divisions among prominent nutrition experts, divisions that would, ultimately, help destroy the tenuous scientific consensus that had produced warnings of a wartime malnutrition crisis in the first place. This would have profound effects on the careers of many of Canada's leading nutrition professionals and, more importantly, on the direction of scientific research and popular nutrition education well into the postwar period.

This book is, first and foremost, a work of food history. Although long unfairly dismissed as a topic unfit for "serious" scholarly inquiry, the past two decades have seen an explosion of interest in food history of all kinds. Whether it has been through studies of individual commodities such as milk, sugar, or salt; examinations of concepts such as hunger and freshness; or much broader social histories focusing on everything from food and the making of national identity to the impact of nutritional science on culinary preferences and practices, recent scholarly work in food history has been impressive in its scope, quality, and interdisciplinary nature.[17] Inspired particularly by recent international scholarship on the social history of food consumption – and, more specifically, on the social history of food consumption during wartime – the research that went into this book used, as its starting point, the kinds of basic questions typically of interest to food scholars.[18] How, for instance, did Canadians' diets change over time? What forces drove these changes? And how did Canadians themselves respond to these dietary changes?

Until recently, these types of questions have rarely served as the starting point for scholarly inquiry among Canadian historians. Food has been an important component in a range of studies examining topics such as the role of agricultural staples in the consolidation of the national economy, the effects of industrialization on the family economy, and the state's policies of assimilating and economically marginalizing Aboriginal peoples.[19] Overall, however, the broader social relations of food and eating have tended to receive scant attention from Canadian historians, who have usually left such matters to popular historians, museum professionals, and antiquarians.[20] The recent publication of two edited collections on Canadian food history by McGill-Queen's and the University of Toronto presses are evidence that this is in the process of changing. But there still have not been any wide-ranging and foundational scholarly monographs on the social history of eating in Canada equivalent to, for instance, Jeffrey Pilcher's work on Mexico, John Burnett's work on England, or Harvey Levenstein and Donna Gabaccia's work on the United States.[21] In fact, very few scholarly monographs have been devoted to the social history of food in Canada, with Steve Penfold's *The Donut* and Diane Tye's *Baking as Biography* being two recent notable and impressive exceptions.[22]

This book, then, aims to fill at least a few of the many gaps that exist in the historiography of food and eating in Canada. At the same time, it engages with a broader international food studies literature – in particular, with the growing field of critical nutrition studies.[23] Although the twentieth century saw Canadians' nutritional status progressively improve from an apparent nadir during the early years of industrialization in the late nineteenth century – with the Second World War marking an important shift from the hunger and want of the Great Depression – this period was also marked by a scientific revolution in our understanding of the relationship between food and health.[24] This was spurred, specifically, by discovery in the 1910s and 1920s of the connection between what we now know as vitamins and minerals and a number of deficiency diseases, including scurvy, anemia, pellagra, beriberi, and rickets. These discoveries upended a number of long-held assumptions about what constituted human nutritional requirements, not to mention the very notion of what constituted healthy eating. But they also generated an emerging scientific consensus that deficiencies in these newly discovered vitamins and minerals were threatening the health, strength, and productivity of even the wealthiest and most industrially advanced nations.[25] These international developments led to the formation, in 1938, of the Canadian Council on Nutrition, a semi-official advisory body made up of the country's leading nutrition experts, whose warnings of a national wartime malnutrition crisis would result in the establishment of the Canadian Nutrition Programme and the writing of Canada's Official Food Rules.

Besides providing a detailed account of what proved to be the formative period for nutrition in Canada – in terms of both its professionalization and the popularization of the "Newer Nutrition" of vitamins and minerals – this book joins a number of recent works in critical nutrition studies by focusing on the broader implications of "official" efforts to define and quantify concepts such as health, hunger, and malnutrition. As a number of historians have argued in recent years, discourses around healthy eating have long been the product not simply of objective scientific knowledge but also of a larger constellation of moral, political, and social meanings and values.[26] And in many ways, Canada's experience during the Second World War provides an important example. New methods of quantifying and evaluating the nutritional status of large populations were developed during the 1930s. Although these methods helped establish nutrition as a national priority during the war years, they had a number of unintended consequences. Nutrition experts used studies warning of a nutritional crisis that could affect upwards of 60 percent of the population to justify the launch of a national public education campaign highlighting women's wartime obligations as the gatekeepers of their families' – and therefore

the nation's – nutritional status. But these same studies also provided
powerful ammunition to critics of Canada's exiting social and political
order. By exploring the contested place of nutrition within competing
wartime discourses concerning the rights and obligations of citizenship,
this book provides a number of case studies that explore not only the ways
in which nutrition was put to increasingly political uses during the 1930s
and 1940s (the subject of excellent analyses by James Struthers and Gale
Wills in the Canadian context) but also, and more importantly, how these
debates had a direct impact on the scientific consensus within Canada's
emerging nutrition professions.[27]

The twentieth-century transformation of the science of nutrition was,
of course, simply one among many of the food revolutions that were already
well under way by the time war was declared in September 1939. The industrialization of agriculture through the use of tractors, mechanical
harvesters, and chemical fertilizers – not to mention the use of what, during
the war years, was becoming a growing arsenal of chemical pesticides and
herbicides – had already begun on some farms, albeit slowed significantly
by the Great Depression.[28] By the 1930s – as a result of developments in
transportation and industrial refrigeration – imported fruits, vegetables,
grains, meats, and other basic foodstuffs from around the globe were
becoming commonplace in many larger Canadian cities, regardless of
season.[29] Also, consolidation in industries like meatpacking and food
processing had led to the rise of domestic and multinational corporations
– Swift Canadian Co., Canada Packers, Kraft Foods, Coca-Cola, and the
Canada Starch Company, to name just a few – and these corporations
would come to dominate the postwar Canadian marketplace. Many of
these companies would oversee what American historian Harvey Levenstein
has referred to as North America's "Golden Age of Food Processing" during
the early postwar period through the development of a dizzying array of
processed convenience foods, which would soon begin to dominate grocery
store shelves. But even by 1939, the stage had been set by a whole host of
processed, instant, and frozen food products ranging from Jell-O to Kraft
Dinner to frozen peas.[30] And while the Canadian consumer landscape had
yet to become dominated by supermarkets – those massive, brightly lit
icons of consumerist culture that followed the postwar rise of the corporate
suburb – independent grocers were already being successfully challenged
by large department stores and by the rapid interwar growth of grocery
chains like Dominion, Loblaws, and Safeway.[31]

To a large degree, these twentieth-century food revolutions are all associated with the rise of a broader consumerist culture of abundance and,

more specifically, the associated transformation of North American diets (and bodies) during the postwar years.[32] In 1939, however, abundance and choice were by no means the dominant characteristics of Canadians' consumption practices. The large-scale unemployment and underemployment that characterized the 1930s meant that for many families, austerity and hunger dominated their experience of Depression-era eating.[33] Convenience foods and imported fruits and vegetables, for instance, were beyond the means of thousands of Canadian families who were struggling to afford food, shelter, and clothing at all. Added to this was the fact that a large number of Canadian kitchens still lacked even basic amenities like electricity, refrigeration, and running water. In 1941, for instance, only 40 percent of Canadian kitchens had a gas or electric stove (the remainder used wood, coal, or oil stoves) and only 61 percent had indoor running water. Refrigeration was a similar story: 21 percent of households used a mechanical refrigerator, 26 percent still used iceboxes, and as many as 49 percent of homes had no refrigerator at all.[34] These broader trends would see little movement during the war and early postwar years, as factories were increasingly turned over to war production and manufacturers and food processors alike became subject to strict quotas on raw materials and basic ingredients.[35]

In other words, it was needs rather than wants and, as Joy Parr has argued, work rather than leisure that tended to define consumption practices for most individuals and families both before and during the war.[36] It is clear that the culture of "consumerism" that we often associate with the late twentieth and early twenty-first centuries – a culture that is typically characterized by the production of desire and identity through mass-produced consumer goods and that is, for critics, linked with a kind of liberal (or neoliberal) ideology prioritizing private choice over the public good – is not really applicable to the Canadian home front during the Second World War.[37] Not only was the vast majority of a typical Canadian family's budget devoted to necessities such as food, shelter, and clothing, but, more importantly, the state's intervention and direct control over nearly every facet of the wartime consumer economy led to the emergence of a different popular vision of the consumer as a political actor. This book therefore builds on the work of Lizabeth Cohen, Magda Fahrni, Julie Guard, and others by offering an alternative account of the rise of post-war consumer culture, one that does not simply assume the inevitability of consumerism but instead highlights the efforts of ordinary Canadians – and women, in particular – to articulate and enact a range of very different visions of the rights and responsibilities of the citizen consumer.[38]

As this book will show, it is often impossible to separate the wartime politics and culture of food and nutrition from broader currents of wartime social and political change. The chapters that follow therefore offer a unique perspective on a number of the themes in the social and political history of a period that was marked by an unprecedented expansion of the powers of the federal government and that has long been considered the formative period in the history of Canada's welfare state. As a number of Canadian historians have already established, it was during the war that a new generation of university-trained mandarins in academic fields such as psychology, economics, sociology, and medicine permanently transformed the relationship between citizens and the state by applying new techniques of governance and management in fields ranging from public opinion research to psychological testing, labour relations, propaganda, and – as will be argued in the pages that follow – nutrition.[39] But this book also attempts to build on recent work by Dominique Marshall, Shirley Tillotson, and other social historians of the Canadian welfare state by exploring this larger process of state formation from the perspective of social history as well as that of public policy.[40] It therefore examines how the federal government's wartime interventions into the Canadian diet transformed both the politics and the culture of food consumption and Canadians' broader perceptions of their own social and economic rights as citizens and consumers. In doing so, it points to the ways in which historians of this period have tended to overlook the broader political effects of the wartime command economy and argues that food rationing and other controls on consumption in fact helped contribute not only to Canadians' growing faith in a more interventionist state but also to the rapidly changing political dynamics of the period.[41]

Embedded in these wartime changes in the politics and culture of food consumption were various shifting and contested gendered ideals of wartime citizenship, patriotic duty, and domesticity. As Sonya Rose has argued in the British context, wartime citizenship was never "a single, unitary status, relationship, or practice" but rather a "complex of contested rights, contradictory gendered duties, and ideals of civic virtue."[42] At no time was this truer for Canadians – and for Canadian women, in particular – than during the Second World War. Women were called upon to "keep the home fires burning" by putting Canadian households on a war footing. At the same time, they were increasingly being asked to enter the previously "male" spheres of industrial labour and military service. In other words, while men were expected to serve their country by either signing

up to fight overseas or engaging in some form of essential wartime production – with those who failed to do either of these risking both their
masculinity and their patriotism – women's wartime duties were more
fraught with contradictions. On the one hand, the social and economic
importance of women's domestic labour received unprecedented recognition during the war. Canadian women were regularly told that, to meet
wartime production goals, they would need to lead the way by transforming
their family's consumption practices and, just as importantly, by devoting
much of their leisure hours to voluntary patriotic work, work that would
– contrary to one historian's characterization of it as "busy work"[43] – provide
essential financial, material, and emotional support to allied soldiers,
civilians, and prisoners-of-war. On the other hand, the presence of women
in uniform and in war industries challenged the male breadwinner ideology that defined men's and women's "natural" gender roles in the decades
leading up to the war and, as a result, brought into question the social and
legal barriers to women's equality in both the private and public spheres.[44]

Since the publication of Ruth Roach Pierson's groundbreaking "*They're
Still Women After All": The Second World War and Canadian Womanhood*,
much of the scholarship on the changing wartime social relations of gender
has focused on the broader impact these contradictory ideals of wartime
femininity had on the lives of the thousands of women who took up the
call and enlisted either in the military or as industrial war workers.
While early work in this area tended to focus on Pierson's central question
of whether the war was emancipatory for women or was simply a temporary upheaval of the prevailing gender order, more recent work has looked
beyond this "either/or" dichotomy by instead exploring the much more
complex impact that the war had on women's experiences and identities
both inside and outside the workplace and the military.[45] But far less critical
analysis has been devoted to the impact of these contradictions on women's
lives in the domestic sphere. By looking at the war "through the kitchen
window," so to speak, the chapters that follow provide an important perspective on one of the key sites of women's labour during a period when
buying and preparing food remained one of the largest demands on
women's time and energy, whether they had entered the paid workforce
or not.[46] And although women's wartime work in the kitchen did not result
in the same kind of radical reordering of gender relations as their new
industrial and military roles, the war nonetheless transformed the moral
and symbolic worlds of buying and preparing food in a way that made
the kitchen an important site for exploring how the often contradictory

"official" visions of patriotic practice and citizenship came up against Canadian women's actual wartime expectations and experiences.

Food also provides a unique window into shifting popular perceptions of wartime masculinity.[47] Although food and nutrition were widely perceived as decidedly feminine spheres of concern, the language of wartime feeding campaigns spoke to a number of related wartime fears about Canada's ability to field strong, healthy male soldiers and maintain a productive, efficient workforce. Early in the war, nutrition experts contended that the high levels of malnutrition they were finding in their dietary surveys were in all likelihood a leading cause of the alarmingly high number of Canadian volunteers who were initially deemed unfit for military service because of poor health. They similarly warned that Canada's so-called manpower crisis was being exacerbated by malnourished – and therefore physically unfit and inefficient – industrial workers. This meant that although the blame for malnutrition tended to be placed squarely on the shoulders of the nation's wives and mothers, the country's leading nutrition professionals were nonetheless also able to successfully promote nutrition as a means to protect the kind of virile masculinity needed to win the war on the battlefield, factory floor, and farm alike. Such arguments did much to convince the federal government to allow an unprecedented degree of expert intervention in and surveillance of the diets of soldiers and war workers. Yet as a dramatic 1945 strike by thousands of western Canadian coal miners over insufficient meat rations suggests (see Chapter 2), many men, especially working-class men, also appropriated wartime fears of malnutrition-related physical degeneracy to challenge some of the government's own policies, including meat ration allotments and unemployment relief rates. Thus, wartime perceptions of the relationship between healthy eating and Canada's productive and military capacity provide another important perspective on changing notions of gender and citizenship during a time of perceived social crisis.

And, finally, by exploring the war's impact on the politics and culture of food, this book inevitably examines the social and cultural history of everyday life on the Canadian home front. As evidenced by the publication of scholarly studies like Jeffrey Keshen's *Saints, Sinners, and Soldiers: Canada's Second World War* and Serge Marc Durflinger's *Fighting from Home: The Second World War in Verdun, Quebec,* the home front has generated interest among historians over the past decade. Keshen's book, for its part, is one of the first attempts to provide a truly national synthesis of many of the broader themes in the social history of the home front, whereas Durflinger's reflects the growing prominence of scholarly and popular monographs that examine the war from the perspective of a single community, family, or individual.[48] This book shares Keshen's approach in examining the war as a national experience, not simply a local one – in large part because we cannot fully understand food rationing, price controls, the Canadian Nutrition Programme, and related endeavours without looking at the different ways they were received in communities from coast to coast to coast. The following pages therefore illuminate some areas of life on the home front that have so far gone unexamined while at the same time challenging some of the interpretations of Keshen, Durflinger, and others on the wartime experience of food rationing, the place of scientists in Canada's wartime mobilization, the impact of national conservation efforts like victory gardening, and the state's mobilization of women's unpaid and voluntary labour.

It is always difficult to write a truly national history in a country as linguistically, ethnically, culturally, and geographically fractured as Canada, and in many ways, this is doubly true of food history. Tastes, traditions, and practices differ not just among regions or ethnicities, but also within households and between individuals. This is one reason why I have chosen the federal government's efforts to transform ordinary Canadians' diets during the Second World War as the primary focus of this study. Not only does this focus make for a more manageable topic, but it also makes use of the fact that the war years, perhaps more than any period before or since, saw Canadians become subject to a profoundly centralized system of governance that touched on nearly every aspect of daily life. As one commentator noted in 1945:

> The War Measures Act converted Canada overnight from a confederation into a unitary state; the government overrode or supplanted most of the normal procedures of peace; it became the largest and most important employer of labour; it used its fiscal capacity and monetary powers to effect maximum war production, borrowing billions, raising billions by taxation, and then bringing into play a reserve power by borrowing many millions from the banking system to inflate the economy to full war capacity.[49]

So it is precisely because of this centralizing tendency of the wartime state – and the central role played by federally mandated controls on food consumption in Canadians' experience of the war – that this book is able to draw some broader conclusions about the larger national wartime experience of food and eating.

Given this focus on the changing role of the state – and the federal government, in particular – archival research for this book encompassed the records of a number of federal departments at the heart of the most important wartime changes in the governance of food and nutrition. These included, among others, the Nutrition Services Division of the Department of Pensions and National Health (later renamed the Nutrition Division of the Department of National Health and Welfare), the Consumer Section of the Department of Agriculture, the Women's Voluntary Services Division of the Department of National War Services, the WIB, and the Consumer Branch of the WPTB. However, the goal was also to look well beyond the "official" record of the war to get at Canadians' broader experiences of wartime eating. Research therefore also examined the archival records of other national organizations that played important official and unofficial roles in facilitating and overseeing these wartime efforts, including the Canadian Council on Nutrition, the Canadian Red Cross Society, the Canadian Home Economics Association, the Federated Women's Institutes of Canada, the National Council of Women, and others. This research was supplemented by examinations of popular discussions of food and nutrition in the print, radio, and film media. Cookbooks and other forms of culinary literature that have typically been overlooked by historians are an important component of this research. My research also included, among other things, an extensive review of the wartime output of popular news and lifestyle magazines such as *Canadian Home Journal, Chatelaine, Maclean's,* and *Saturday Night;* academic and trade publications such as *Food in Canada, Canadian Hotel and Restaurant,* and the *Canadian Journal of Public Health;* and the film and radio archives of the Canadian Broadcasting Corporation and the National Film Board. I have also examined the wartime women's sections of newspapers, including the *Globe and Mail, Le Devoir,* and the *Vancouver Sun.*

Although something approaching a "national" experience of food and eating did exist in wartime Canada, there were, of course, exceptions. Residents in remote northern communities, for instance, were exempt from the usual rules of coupon rationing because of their need to buy food in bulk during their long periods of isolation in the winter. And it is clear that the wartime experience of Japanese Canadian internees, to name just one prominent example, was clearly very different from that of their non-Japanese neighbours. While there are many similar exceptions that are always important to keep in mind, it is nonetheless true that the vast majority of Canadians shared a number of common experiences of state intervention in their diets. Canada's Official Food Rules were precisely that – official rules that, because they were universal, did not distinguish between regional or ethnic eating habits and were as new (and problematic) to Canadians in Cape Breton as they were on Vancouver Island. Moreover, leaving aside the expanding wartime presence of the military, the more than six hundred local Ration Boards that were created during the war often became the most visible local manifestations of the newly expanded reach of the federal government. And, for that matter, because of the thousands of regulations established by the WPTB, Canadians were bound by a common national set of rules governing their food consumption, which meant that a recipe for tealess tea or a butterless, sugarless cake would often have been as useful (and probably as unappetizing) to a home cook in Montreal as it would have been to her counterpart in Halifax or Edmonton.

The Red Cross provided a similar national touchstone for Canadians. At its wartime peak, more than one-quarter of Canadians were members of either the Red Cross or the Junior Red Cross, and there were local branches of both in nearly every region and in both French- and English-speaking areas.[50] Not only that, but the Red Cross regularly partnered with other well-established groups such as the Federated Women's Institutes, the Cercles de Fermières, and the Health League of Canada on a range of campaigns focusing on everything from wartime nutrition education to overseas food relief. This meant that the hundreds of thousands of Canadians who packed POW parcels, contributed to the national Jam for Britain campaign, or attended one of the hundreds of "War Economy Nutrition" classes held throughout the country were at least partly united by their membership in a national organization that crossed most ethnic, linguistic, and even political lines.

Of course, not all Canadians experienced the entry of these national institutions and organizations into their kitchens in the same way, and to reflect that, I have made considerable efforts to capture the ways in which different groups responded to changes in the wartime politics and culture of food and nutrition. I have reviewed multiple genres of popular food writing in both French and English during this period, ranging from community cookbooks from around the country to extensive press and media reviews. This effort has been facilitated by the fact that, perhaps more than in any other period before or since, the federal government was obsessively concerned about tracking public opinion. The widespread perception that poor morale threatened nearly every aspect of the war effort and the need to control information by resorting to massive wartime censorship and propaganda, together generated a range of novel and experimental methods of opinion gathering throughout the war on the part of the WIB, the WPTB's Information Branch, and other wartime government departments. Most of these efforts, moreover, specifically tracked changes in public opinion towards rationing and other wartime controls. These efforts included hundreds of internal public opinion polls conducted by the newly formed Canadian Institute for Public Opinion; detailed weekly press reviews of more than three hundred newspapers and magazines, which were distributed among a number of key government departments; and a mass-observation-inspired system of field reports by WIB "correspondents" in more than 140 communities. Perhaps just as importantly, these tools included the meeting minutes supplied regularly to the WPTB Consumer Branch by its dozens of Women's Regional Advisory Committees, which, in nearly every region of the country, met regularly to discuss their experiences of rationing and price controls.[51] These kinds of sources, along with interviews, memoirs, diaries, and other sources of wartime memories collected by groups ranging from the Canadian War Museum and the Defence Department to journalists, interested citizens, and volunteer groups, offer an extraordinarily diverse range of perspectives on the broader implications of the government's wartime food policies and programs.

All of this, however, is intended to support a rather basic central argument that, by the end of this book, you will hopefully find convincing, namely, that although food may not have literally won the war, it does provide us with a unique and remarkably powerful means of re-examining and reinterpreting the everyday experience of war on Canada's home front and the long-term impact of a period of profound social, political, economic, and – as it turned out – dietary change.

1

"Eat Right, Feel Right – Canada Needs You Strong"

Food Rules and the Transformation of Canada's Wartime Nutritional State

The Second World War was a high-water mark for nutrition in Canada's popular consciousness. The early years of the war saw the launch of the Canadian Nutrition Programme (CNP), Canada's first large-scale national nutrition campaign. Under the CNP, all levels of government – together with a range of private advertisers, social agencies, and volunteer organizations – promoted the importance of good nutrition on the home front and linked it to the fate of the war effort abroad. The message was often a straightforward one, speaking to wartime ideals of gender and citizenship. As a 1942 ad placed in major national magazines by the Metropolitan Life Insurance Company told Canada's mothers, "In peacetime, you owe it to yourself and your family to eat well-balanced, nourishing meals. In critical times like these, it's a patriotic duty."[1]

At the heart of this campaign were Canada's Official Food Rules. First introduced in 1942 and later revised in 1944 and 1949, this simple list of daily food requirements would constitute the central message of Canadian nutrition education for almost two decades, until the introduction of Canada's Food Guide in 1961. During the war and reconstruction periods, the Food Rules acted as a unifying force in Canadian nutrition education. They could be seen anywhere from newspaper ads to cookbooks and from posters in factory lunchrooms to flyers included with family allowance cheques. The recommendations ranged from the very specific (milk, tomatoes, potatoes, "Canada Approved Bread," liver, eggs, and cheese) to the more general (citrus fruits, leafy green or yellow vegetables, whole grain cereal, meat) and were designed to meet a scientifically determined

Figure 1.1 The 1942 version of Canada's Official Food Rules from the Swift Canadian Co. booklet *Eat Right to Work and Win* (Toronto: Swift Canadian Co., 1942).

set of nutritional requirements. With popular images of the Food Rules that portrayed anthropomorphic foodstuffs marching with rifles in hand, the overall message was clear and would form the basis of Canadian wartime nutrition advice: "Eat Right, Feel Right – Canada Needs You Strong" (see Figure 1.1).

This chapter explores the message of the Food Rules and the CNP, more generally, by examining how wartime fears about the impact of malnutrition on the health of Canadian soldiers and the productivity of Canadian war workers came to be reflected not only in popular nutrition advice but also, more importantly, in the actual science of nutrition itself. After prominent nutrition experts "discovered" a major wartime malnutrition crisis and warned that it was endangering the health of upwards of 60 percent of the population, Canada's nutrition professionals enjoyed an unprecedented expansion of their influence. This led quickly to the development of a range of state-sponsored, private, and voluntary nutrition programs in Canada. This chapter explores the ways in which the country's leading nutrition experts redefined the risks posed by malnutrition during the 1930s and '40s in order to encourage greater state intervention into the problem of malnutrition as well as to achieve a range of political and professional objectives. In their efforts to show that nutrition was a useful technology of governance and population management, Canadian nutrition experts succeeded in redefining healthy eating in a way that not only greatly expanded the number of Canadians deemed at risk of malnutrition but also prioritized the wartime and postwar labour, military, and agricultural needs of the nation at the expense of other ways of understanding the interplay between malnutrition and broader social structures.

This chapter begins by examining how ideas about "malnutrition" were constructed and deployed throughout the 1930s and '40s. It argues that the professional interests of Canada's nutrition experts came to be reflected in the content of wartime nutrition advice, which tended to frame poor nutrition as a problem of faulty education rather than income and which was ultimately less concerned about preventing serious illness than about normalizing a largely unrealized physical and cultural ideal of Canadian citizenship. The Food Rules and other educational materials are therefore examined as specific products of both this transformation in the scientific consensus as well as changing discourses about gender, class, ethnicity, and the ideal of the patriotic wartime kitchen.

The Interwar Origins of Canada's Wartime Malnutrition Crisis

Historically, hunger and malnutrition have never been constants but instead have been periodically re-evaluated in the face of shifting scientific consensus and (what is equally important) changing social values. Scientific research into the essential roles played by fats, carbohydrates, and proteins in maintaining human health and well-being during the mid- to late nineteenth century, followed by a number of primarily early-twentieth-century discoveries regarding the physiological importance of vitamins and minerals – particularly their role in preventing diseases like beriberi, pellagra, scurvy, anemia, and rickets – sparked a revolution in thinking about the importance of food and the components of an adequate diet.[2] But the application of these principles in practice always generated controversy. Disagreements over the social, cultural, and economic causes of hunger and malnutrition meant that, throughout the nineteenth and twentieth centuries, nutrition experts often found themselves at the centre of decidedly political debates concerning everything from minimum wage legislation to urban reform policies and unemployment relief rates. As much of the recent critical literature on the history of food and nutrition has shown, the concept of "health" has always been notoriously slippery, and in a science as inexact as human nutrition, attempts to define what truly constitutes "healthy eating" have often generated considerable debate and disagreement.[3]

The interwar period, in particular, witnessed a profound rethinking of the relationship between food and health. The rapid discovery, isolation, and synthesis of vitamins during this period – including vitamins A, B1, B2, B3, B6, C, D, and E – transformed the science of nutrition and facilitated the development of new and highly effective treatments for a range of serious illnesses.[4] The development of what would eventually be dubbed the "Newer Knowledge of Nutrition" by leading interwar nutrition researcher E.V. McCollum also saw the emergence of a number of new questions about the broader implications of these newly discovered nutrients. Was nutritional health, for instance, simply the absence of nutritional deficiency diseases, or was it the achievement of the full benefits of a nutritionally complete diet? Could a person be malnourished while showing no overt clinical signs of malnutrition? And, perhaps most importantly, how should human requirements for these new micronutrients be established in the absence of firm scientific consensus?[5] The need to answer these questions became even more urgent after 1929, with the onset of the Great Depression. As unemployment levels in Canada and other industrialized nations rose to unprecedented heights during the early 1930s, the question of how to prevent the very real possibility of widespread hunger and malnutrition became an increasingly important political as well as scientific issue.[6] Attempts to overcome this social and scientific uncertainty would, ultimately, lead to the discovery of Canada's wartime malnutrition crisis and would, in many ways, also lead to the emergence of nutrition as a distinct area of professional expertise during and after the Second World War. At the heart of this transformation was the Canadian Council on Nutrition (CCN) – the country's first "official" body representing the country's fledgling nutrition professions.

Founded in 1938 by the Department of Pensions and National Health, the CCN was one of Canada's first truly national nutrition organizations. Unlike other nutrition-related professional societies that formed during this period – such as the Canadian Dietetics Association (1935) and the Canadian Home Economics Association (1939) – the CCN was less concerned with setting and enforcing professional membership standards than it was with pooling the expertise of Canada's fledgling community of nutrition experts and professionals. It was composed of a broad range of groups doing work on nutrition during this period. In addition to home economists, dieticians and nutritionists, the CCN included doctors, biochemists, agricultural experts, economists, social workers, and representatives from key federal ministries, including the Department of Agriculture and the Department of Pensions and National Health. Although membership was voluntary and the organization was created to act in an advisory capacity, the CCN quickly emerged as the official voice of Canada's nutrition experts and played a key role in framing both the causes and extent of malnutrition throughout the country.[7]

Like most public health campaigns, both the CNP and its central message of healthy eating based on Canada's Official Food Rules were created in response to a perceived health crisis. In this case, that crisis was the discovery of widespread malnutrition among Canadians based on the results of five dietary surveys sponsored in part by the CCN and conducted in the cities of Edmonton, Quebec City, Halifax, and Toronto.[8] These studies, all of which were completed between 1939 and 1941, examined between seventy-six and one hundred primarily low-income families with one employed breadwinner by comparing their daily food consumption over the course of at least one week, with the nutritional requirements set out in the newly developed Canadian Dietary Standard. The most alarming discovery made by these surveys was that the vast majority of the families examined were failing to consume sufficient quantities of a range of nutrients. In the first of two Toronto surveys, for instance, widespread nutritional deficiencies were found in almost every category examined. Only 3 percent of families had sufficient caloric intake, and only 7 percent of families were consuming enough protein. Vitamin and mineral consumption was even lower, with mothers and children showing the highest rates of malnutrition.[9]

The results of the other four surveys were somewhat less bleak, but they still showed serious deficiencies in the consumption of vitamins and minerals, in particular. In the Halifax survey, for instance, the same kinds of gender inequalities were apparent and, overall, average family intakes of calcium, vitamin B1, and vitamin C were all seriously deficient.[10] In Quebec the main deficiencies were in calcium, vitamin A, and vitamin B1, with women and children faring the worst. In Edmonton, the most extreme deficiencies were in the consumption of calcium, iron, and vitamins B1 and C.[11] A second Toronto study of higher-income families found less malnutrition overall but also evidence of widespread nutritional deficiencies among women.[12] Ultimately, though, it was the authors of the Edmonton survey who provided an estimate that became a kind of shorthand for Canada's nutrition crisis as a whole: they suggested that at least 40 percent of the subjects they surveyed "get about three-quarters of what they need" while nearly 20 percent "get little more than half of what they need."[13]

Warnings of a nationwide malnutrition crisis were not new during this period, especially in the context of the widespread unemployment and economic distress that characterized the 1930s. The unemployed themselves regularly highlighted the twin problems of hunger and malnutrition in their protests and petitions to all levels of government. And their concerns were regularly echoed by social reformers, political activists, and labour leaders, all of whom frequently used malnutrition statistics to bolster their arguments against unfair wages and relief rates.[14] This was particularly true for Leonard Marsh, Harry Cassidy, and other social critics, whose own Depression-era studies made extensive use of data showing that nutritionally adequate meals were out of reach for poor families. For these social scientists, nutrition provided a powerful rhetorical tool because it represented an objective rather than a moral basis for measuring nebulous concepts such as standard of living, and it grounded social research more firmly in material realities. Marsh's landmark 1938 study, *Health and Unemployment,* for instance, utilized a range of nutrition-based measurements in its analysis of Montreal's unemployed as objective proof that relief and unemployment policies were in need of immediate reform.[15]

What differentiated the CCN's warnings of a nationwide malnutrition crisis from these earlier warnings was that they actually generated a response: for the first time, nearly all levels of government began to put real resources into addressing the problem. In part, this was because the CCN carried a kind of official legitimacy that critics and social reformers of the 1930s did not. Left-leaning social critics like Marsh and Cassidy – rather than professional nutrition experts or researchers – had largely dominated public discourse around the problem of malnutrition during the 1930s because, for most of the decade, few official statistics had been produced showing the extent of malnutrition on a national scale. No large-scale surveys had ever been conducted, and Canada's leading nutrition experts typically agreed that they knew little about what people were actually consuming or where their diets were most deficient.[16] This dearth of accurate statistics played a large part in the creation of the CCN by the Department of Pensions and National Health, which established the group to address the need for "some central authority, with special responsibility, to utilize the results of modern progress in the sciences of nutrition and agriculture in so far as they affect the health of the nation."[17]

As John Coveney and other historians of nutrition have argued, the science of nutrition is inescapably moral and political in that it has long been "part of a panoply of technologies and strategies designed to better manage populations."[18] In much the same way that Bruce Curtis has shown that the development of the Canadian census was part of a larger political process of liberal state formation, national surveys like those conducted by the CCN similarly sought to "tie individuals to places within an administrative grid and then to hold them steady so that they may become objects of knowledge and government."[19] The collection of reliable statistics about dietary practices was an important technology of governance because it enabled policy makers and social critics to objectively locate populations and to explain the probable causes (and therefore the necessary solutions) to the problem of malnutrition and ill health more generally. So it is not particularly surprising that the first few years of the CCN's existence were taken up largely with the task of conducting a series of national dietary surveys: establishing the legitimacy of the nutrition professions during the 1930s above all required the CCN to differentiate itself from other claimants to objective knowledge about Canada's nutritional state.

One way the members of the CCN achieved this larger goal of professional legitimacy was by adopting new research methodologies. The CCN's national dietary surveys were, in many ways, inspired by a series of similar studies conducted in the United States by Hazel Stiebeling, who headed the Section on Food Economics of the US Department of Agriculture, and in Britain by Sir John Boyd Orr, one of the world's leading nutrition experts. Orr and Stiebeling had gained international prominence during the 1930s after they conducted a series of large-scale dietary studies showing widespread malnutrition in their respective countries. For instance, studies conducted in 1935 and 1936 by Stiebeling found that more than 30 percent of Americans were not consuming a nutritionally adequate diet.[20] Orr's British figures were even more alarming. In his 1936 publication *Food, Health, and Income*, he presented evidence that over half of Britons were living on diets that were seriously deficient in a wide array of nutrients.[21]

Orr's and Stiebeling's dramatic survey results were, in part, the product of a shift away from strictly physiological measurements of malnutrition and towards increasingly population-based estimates. Just as Canadian social scientists like Marsh had begun using nutrition to add greater objectivity to their studies of wider social and economic issues, nutrition researchers in other countries were similarly beginning to realize that large-scale national surveys could draw attention to their own area of expertise.[22] The major innovation that made such surveys possible was Stiebeling's 1933 development of what would become one of the first widely accepted dietary standards to include calculations for human vitamin and mineral requirements. Dietary standards – which set out the daily requirements for a range of nutrients based on factors such as age, gender, and occupation – were one of the few ways of measuring the nutritional adequacy of a population's diet without resorting to expensive and time-consuming clinical examinations. By gathering information on the food consumption habits of a sample population and comparing the overall nutritional content of the food consumed against a predetermined dietary standard, nutrition researchers were able to show not only how many people were malnourished in a relatively large population sample but also which areas of their diet were in greatest need of improvement.

Stiebeling's standard also incorporated the most leading-edge international research into the importance of vitamins and minerals to human health. This interwar research tended to show that an individual could be consuming enough calories to avoid hunger and still be malnourished and that this "hidden hunger" had an impact far beyond deficiency diseases. Nutrition experts were increasingly beginning to draw explicit connections between these newly discovered nutrients and the proper functioning of a number of bodily processes including growth, the immune system, eyesight, and motor functions. But while there was at least some consensus as to the minimum requirements for avoiding starvation and deficiency diseases, it was proving to be much more difficult to measure the impacts of less overt malnutrition. This was a particular problem when it came to establishing the basic human requirements for vitamins and minerals in the form of dietary standards.[23]

Stiebeling's novel solution to this problem was to create a dietary standard
that adopted a model of health based on "optimum" as opposed to "minimum" dietary requirements. Prior to the 1930s, dietary standards had been
designed mainly to show the minimum calories and protein necessary to
prevent hunger or to enable individuals to do certain kinds of work. Studies
using these standards were directed largely at the destitute and at institutions such as schools, prisons, workhouses, and hospitals. The novelty of
Stiebeling's "optimal" standard was that it recognized the importance of
maintaining a level of consumption above what was necessary to prevent
starvation or deficiency diseases. Stiebeling therefore included a "margin
of safety" in her calculation of dietary requirements. Requirements for
vitamins, for instance, were calculated at twice what was required to prevent
the occurrence of deficiency diseases. For minerals, requirements were
based on accepted calculations of basic maintenance requirements plus a
50 percent allowance.[24] The goal was to recognize the uncertainty inherent
in any such population level measurements while also stressing the need
for individuals to consume far more than the minimal requirements in
order to achieve the full benefits of proper nutrition. Orr, a leading supporter of the new standard, described its goal as the maintenance of "a
state of well being such that no improvement could be effected by a change
in the diet." In other words, optimum nutrition would not simply guarantee the absence of disease or deficiency states but would normalize the
ideal of what Orr referred to as "perfect nutrition."[25]

Stiebeling's optimal dietary standard was enormously influential in
Canada and internationally. In 1936, the League of Nations Health Organization (LNHO) had called upon all member nations to begin studying
their own malnutrition problems and, to this end, they produced one of
the first internationally recognized dietary standards based on a set of unambiguously optimal requirements. When the CCN officially adopted
its own dietary standard in 1939, it used the LNHO and Stiebeling optimal
standards as a guide but made some adaptations so as to make them
"applicable to Canadian conditions." A principal author of the standard,
prominent University of Toronto biochemist E.W. McHenry, was concerned that the LHNO standard described a diet that, in terms of cost, was
greatly in excess of relief diets provided in Canadian cities.[26] In part, he
attributed this to the LNHO's nutritional requirements for women, which
he felt were too high because they were based on those for European
women, who "must work, of necessity, in the fields and must expend as
much energy as men."[27] The Canadian standard therefore adopted lower
energy requirements for women as a way to address both of these perceived

problems. Although these aspects of the standard reflected a more minimal vision of dietary requirements, Canadian nutrition experts generally agreed that when it came to vitamins and minerals in particular, optimal requirements such as those used by Stiebeling and the LNHO were preferable because, while somewhat arbitrary, they better captured the broader health implications associated with the underconsumption of these nutrients.[28]

When put into practice as the basis for determining the nutritional status of large populations, the new standard greatly increased estimates of the number of Canadians at risk of the "hidden hunger" of malnutrition. This was because the CCN's dietary surveys, like those of its international counterparts, judged the adequacy of an individual's diet based on its ability to meet the requirements set out in the new Canadian Dietary Standard rather than on investigations of actual clinical signs of malnutrition in individuals. In correspondence with the CCN, Orr suggested that this survey methodology was actually preferable, scientifically, because the assessment of nutrition by clinical examination was "most unsatisfactory owing to the fact that each medical man has a different standard, and the standard of the same medical man varies according to the state of the last children examined."[29] In other words, studies based on clinical examinations could only uncover the telltale signs of malnutrition such as stunted growth, low body weight, and symptoms of deficiency diseases like rickets, whereas these new standards could identify populations whose diets put them at risk of developing such nutrition-related health problems even if they were showing no physical signs of malnutrition. This is why the Stiebeling, Orr, and CCN studies were so shocking: they had uncovered a large population of individuals who likely had no idea they were even malnourished.

The CCN studies were even more ambitious than their international counterparts because they actually examined the diet of each individual family member separately, whereas studies in Britain and the United States typically examined the consumption habits of entire families. In the first Toronto survey, for instance, researchers required that the food used by each individual in a family over the course of one week be weighed and recorded by dieticians from the staff of the Red Cross Visiting Homemakers Association.[30] The other surveys adopted similarly expensive and time-consuming methodologies, and the result was five of the most comprehensive and specific nutrition surveys undertaken up to that point – particularly insofar as they generated nutrition statistics that were comparable both between and within families. This approach led to some notable and disturbing findings, including the fact that adult women and children were at greater risk of malnutrition because of a tendency within most families to favour the male breadwinner at the expense of other family members. This finding corresponds to those of more recent studies by historians, sociologists, and anthropologists examining the unequal distribution of food within families in patriarchal societies (like Canada during the 1930s and 1940s), but the sheer scale of this inequality across the lines of geography, ethnicity, and class seems to have taken the Canadian researchers by surprise and reflects one of the major strengths of these early Canadian studies.[31]

The studies were granted significant legitimacy by the fact that the CCN's findings and methods corresponded with and, in some cases, were more detailed than more well-known estimates of malnutrition in the United States and Britain. Equally important was *how* the CCN framed the problem of malnutrition in its public pronouncements. These studies suggested that malnutrition was not solely a problem of the unemployed but that, in fact, upwards of 60 percent of Canadians were suffering from inadequate nutrition. Especially after Canada began actively mobilizing for total war in September 1939, CCN representatives rarely neglected to mention the serious impacts that malnutrition could have on Canadian soldiers. Perhaps just as important, however, was that the scientists responsible for the CCN studies were able to frame the causes of malnutrition and the solutions to it in ways that facilitated changes in government nutrition policy. E.W. McHenry – who, besides being a prominent figure on the CCN's Scientific Advisory Committee, was the lead author of the two Toronto studies – rejected the idea that insufficient income was the primary cause of malnutrition. McHenry argued that the data did not provide "a clear-cut conclusion regarding the effect of income."[32] Even though his own 1941 study of higher-income families showed significantly less malnutrition than did his earlier low-income study, he went so far as to suggest that the improved results in the second survey suggested that higher-income families "obtained better food value for their money than the families in the low income group."[33]

For McHenry, the results pointed mainly to a failing of mothers. Adult women were by far the most malnourished group among those surveyed because of their tendency to sacrifice their own dietary needs to those of their husbands. Nonetheless, he argued, "if the woman had been less unselfish, the families as a whole would have been better off."[34] But for McHenry, the most pressing threat was women's seeming inability to shop economically. To demonstrate this, his report on the first Toronto study included an examination of two families with the same per person weekly income but with significantly different nutritional outcomes. He attributed this to the purchase by the undernourished family of luxuries such as tea and sugar as well as to less economical meat purchasing habits. The lesson of the surveys, McHenry argued, was clear: mothers needed to be better educated in the "principles of nutrition and in economical purchasing."[35]

While McHenry played a prominent role in crafting the CCN's interpretation of the survey results, there was by no means a consensus within the Canadian nutrition professions regarding the relationship between nutrition and income. McHenry's conclusions regarding the 1939 Toronto survey, for instance, were at odds with those of others involved in it. Through a series of non-CCN publications, Marjorie Bell, a prominent Canadian dietician and a lead researcher on the 1939 study, would challenge McHenry's conclusions about the relationship between malnutrition and poverty (see Chapter 5). But in the first three years of the CCN, it would be McHenry and a small group of mostly male scientists and doctors who controlled the direction of the CCN and its research through its Scientific Advisory Committee. While Bell was a member of the CCN, she and most female dieticians and home economists were excluded from the work of that key committee. Thus, over considerable protest from Bell and others, scientists like McHenry were able to control the CCN and its message during its formative years while excluding voices of female nutrition professionals and others critical of their approach to Canada's nutrition problems.[36]

Perhaps unsurprisingly, then, the findings of the other four CCN surveys largely reflected those of McHenry concerning the relationship between income and nutritional status. For instance, while the authors of the Edmonton study acknowledged that their findings indicated that "diet tends to improve automatically with increase in income," they suggested that this was "a slow process" and that "the only means left to try to maintain the health of the population ... is to teach people to make the most of their available money."[37] The Quebec study similarly acknowledged that multiple factors influenced nutritional status, but, in the end, it focused on the need for better education to solve the problem of malnutrition. This report noted that "the high infant mortality rate in Quebec has been lowered through educational effort ... The authors feel that education along nutritional lines would have a similarly beneficial effect."[38]

These surveys were interpreted widely within and outside Canada's nutrition professions as proof that the country was facing a wartime malnutrition crisis. McHenry and others in the leadership of the CCN therefore wielded significant power in framing the nature of and possible solutions to this crisis. As a result, they would end up playing central roles in establishing the long-term direction and the philosophical core of what would eventually be Canada's first national nutrition program. When word began to spread in early 1941 that the federal government was looking to establish a nutrition division, for instance, many of the nutrition professionals who had been left out of the CCN's decision making articulated their own vision for a national nutrition program. Canadian home economists and dieticians, in particular, hoped that the division would not simply mirror the research-focused, male-dominated, and non-inclusive CCN. Petitions submitted by Bell and others within the Canadian Home Economics Association and the Canadian Dietetics Association to the Minister of Pensions and National Health and to the National Council of Women emphasized that many Canadian women had been trained to carry out the job and that women like Stiebeling had been in charge of the American nutrition program for years.[39] McHenry, for his part, made his preferences quite clear in a letter to the deputy minister: "For the sake of getting things done sensibly, I hope the senior appointment goes to a man and not to a dietician."[40]

In the end, the structure of the Nutrition Services Division tended to mirror the nutritional philosophy and the hierarchy that had already been established within the CCN. The newly appointed director, Lionel Bradley Pett, had received an MD and a PhD in organic chemistry and had been a lead researcher on the Edmonton dietary survey. The five female staff hired by Nutrition Services in its first year were trained dieticians and nutritionists, but even so, Pett's appointment reflected a clear tendency towards what Ruby Heap has identified as the "professionalization and masculinization of the nutritional sciences" in the postwar period, wherein men were placed in higher-level, policy-making positions while women did much of the front-line educational work.[41] Just as importantly, Pett's appointment meant that the CCN's survey methods and findings and its focus on the need for scientifically educated and thrifty mothers would have an enormous influence on the CNP and its first public announcement, Canada's Official Food Rules.

Normalizing the Ideal of Perfect Nutrition

The findings of the CCN nutrition studies were taken very seriously by Canadians, and this quickly led to a shift in the ways that the problem of malnutrition was perceived at nearly every level of government. Before

the war, nutrition tended to be seen as simply one aspect of broader public
health campaigns directed primarily at pregnant and nursing women or
of education programs directed at girls and new mothers. Few governments
employed full-time nutritionists or dieticians; instead, most Canadians
relied on a haphazard array of nutrition services that differed from community to community.[42] After 1941, however, nutrition experts saw their
influence and job opportunities expand dramatically. Especially at the
federal level, they began to benefit from a large expansion and professionalization of Canada's wartime civil service.[43] Besides being hired by
the new Nutrition Services Division, nutrition experts saw their influence
growing within departments as varied as Defence, Agriculture, and External Affairs. They even found themselves doing everything from designing
new military ration scales to setting larger agricultural and nutritional
policies as Canada's representatives on international bodies like the Combined Food Board and the UN Food and Agriculture Organization.

A similar expansion became apparent at the provincial and municipal
levels. Quebec had led the way by hiring a provincial nutritionist even
before the perceived national malnutrition crisis, but having started early,
its program expanded considerably during the war. In 1942, for instance,
the Quebec government formed its first nutrition committee, made up
of thirty-eight of the province's leading nutrition experts. By 1943, municipal programs were under way in municipalities such as Quebec,
Montreal, Magog, St-Hyacinthe, Sorel, Granby, Waterloo, Trois-Rivières,
and Grand-Mere.[44] These developments began to be duplicated in nearly
every province. At the municipal level, Vancouver, Montreal, Kingston,
Hamilton, Toronto, Saskatoon, Regina, and Winnipeg all launched major
wartime nutrition campaigns with the financial support of local and
provincial health departments as well as charitable organizations like the
Red Cross, Société Saint-Jean-Baptiste, Women's Institutes, the National
Council of Women, and the Health League of Canada. The overall result
was that more than eighty community nutrition campaigns were operating
by 1943, where there had been only seven in 1941.[45] By 1950, all the provinces but one had a fully functioning nutrition program.[46]

The scale of these changes suggests just how important these new ways
of measuring the nutritional status of large populations had been for
Canada's nutrition professionals. The use of the Canadian Dietary Standard in the CCN studies reframed both the scale and the meaning of the
term malnutrition and, in the process, identified a new threat to the war
effort and to the nation's health more generally. While these changes were

clearly taken seriously by policy makers and ordinary Canadians alike during the war, they have nonetheless fared less well in terms of Canadians' historical memory. In part, this is because the 1940s are typically associated with an improved standard of living, increased average lifespan, and an overall decrease in mortality from infectious diseases – not with widespread malnutrition affecting most of the population. Nutrition historian Aleck Ostry has attempted to account for these contradictions by reassessing the CCN surveys using "modern standards." He concludes that the CCN likely overstated the incidence of malnutrition, given that contemporary standards are "based on more accurate methods of vitamin chemistry and a better understanding of the role of vitamins in human physiology." He then, problematically, uses mortality statistics from the 1930s to conclude that "under- and mal-nutrition was not widespread among vulnerable sub-populations in Canada during the 1930s."[47]

As Cynthia Comacchio and others have suggested, there are many problems with relying solely on the inconsistently collected vital statistics from the 1930s when making broader claims about the nutritional status of Canadians.[48] But perhaps just as importantly, Ostry's analysis does little to explain either why nutrition experts genuinely did believe there was a malnutrition crisis or why the changing scientific definition of malnutrition had such a profound impact on Canada's nutrition professions. For one thing, the use of "modern standards" to judge the accuracy of historical nutrition research ignores the fact that, to this day, debates about what truly constitutes an adequate daily requirement for vitamins and other nutrients continue unabated. In 2010, for instance, the US Institute of Medicine and the Canadian Cancer Society recommended daily requirements for vitamin D between 300 and 500 percent higher than Health Canada's official guidelines, with some doctors and scientists arguing that even this did not go far enough.[49] As both historical and contemporary scientific controversies about human nutritional requirements suggest, at stake in these debates is the ability to define what, precisely, constitutes the ambiguous and often politically charged concept of "health." Is it the simple absence of disease, or is it the ability to meet one's maximum physical and intellectual potential? Because these are moral as well as scientific questions, dietary standards necessarily straddle a tenuous and often contentious line between the medical and social meanings of concepts like "health" and "malnutrition." As a result, they provide an important point of entry into the transformations that nutrition underwent during this period and its connections with larger currents of social change.

Science and technology studies theorists have long argued that historians need to start their examinations of scientific knowledge production by looking at the actual process, as opposed to the end result, of scientific discovery if they hope to understand *how* and *why* certain ideas become facts.[50] As Bruno Latour has suggested, the status of a fact is not due to some intrinsic quality but rather to the strength of its network of support among both human and non-human allies both in and outside the laboratory.[51] The international scientific consensus on optimal dietary standards in the late 1930s and early 1940s, for instance, was not due to a collective ignorance of the facts on the part of scientists but rather to a number of conscious decisions to prioritize a certain vision of "health" over other competing possibilities. At the heart of this was the choice to define malnutrition, not simply as the absence of specific clinical manifestations of disease or illness, but as the achievement of a certain level of "optimal health" defined much more broadly.

Most scientists within and outside the CCN freely admitted there was a great deal of uncertainty regarding how to measure human requirements for most nutrients. In fact, their decision to adopt large margins of safety in setting nutrient requirements was a deliberate one based on broad agreement that it was important to consume more than minimum nutritional requirements for vitamins and minerals and – given that the kinds of studies capable of ascertaining how much more than the minimum was enough were a long way off – that it was important to err on the side of safety. In the second edition of his landmark 1936 study, *Food, Health, and Income*, Orr directly addressed criticisms that his optimal standard – which he suggested reflected "the minimum for maximum health" or "what is needed to enable people to attain their maximum inherited capacity for health and physical fitness" – was too high and that "perfect nutrition" reflected a "utopian" goal.[52] Orr responded that "in animal husbandry, an optimum standard, far from being utopian, is regarded as good practice." "If children of [lower income] groups were reared for profit like young farm stock," he added, "giving them a diet below the requirements would be financially unsound."[53]

Of course, the goal of "perfect nutrition" also matched Orr's social and political vision, which was to raise the food intake of the poorest Britons to the level of the wealthiest and, in the process, use increased food consumption to spur an economic recovery driven largely by increased agricultural production.[54] For Orr, this was a wholly realistic goal, as proven by the fact that his survey showed that nearly 50 percent of Britons were able to achieve an optimal diet even in the midst of a severe economic depression. By normalizing the diet of the wealthiest as the nutritional ideal for the entire population, Orr therefore sought to place nutrition at the centre of a broader political consensus on redistributing wealth to achieve the population's maximum physical and intellectual potential.

While many Canadian nutrition experts did not share Orr's utopian social and political vision, they did agree that a dietary standard should measure more than simply the absence of disease and that it, instead, should capture the broader health and social impacts of malnutrition. Addressing malnutrition was no longer simply about preventing nutritional deficiencies but about allowing individuals to meet their maximum physical and intellectual potential. Malnutrition was therefore a public health threat that spoke to much larger concerns about the nation's military, industrial, and intellectual fitness. At the same time, the threat of malnutrition had the effect of increasing the number of social and health problems that could be addressed by expert nutritional intervention and supervision. This became quite apparent in public discussions of the problems posed by malnutrition in the aftermath of the CCN surveys. Nutrition experts still spoke of the relationship between the levels of malnutrition discovered and certain physical maladies, particularly among those found to have consumed below 75 percent of the standard for various nutrients. The Edmonton survey report, for its part, predicted that in a more comprehensive survey of the same individuals, "it is almost certain that clinical evidence of faulty bone, anaemia, and vitamin deficiency would be found."[55] But much more common than these specific predictions was a more generalized discussion of the broader health and social implications of malnutrition. The published findings of the second Toronto survey, for instance, made no specific predictions as to the clinical effects of its findings. Instead, it quoted a rather utopian prediction made by the president of the American Medical Association: "In the future, it promises those races who will take advantage of the newer knowledge of nutrition, a larger stature, greater vigor, increased longevity and a higher level of cultural attainment."[56]

As John Coveney has argued, nutrition has long tended to both help define and "to some extent create, the social problems it sought to solve."[57] And in fact, it was this new language of suboptimal nutrition as both a health problem and a social one that helps explain its wartime appeal. Although there was little in the way of nutrition-related mortality statistics that experts could point to in support of the warnings by Pett and others that, according to the CCN surveys, "only about 40 percent of the people studied could be considered adequately nourished," those same experts did succeed in connecting malnutrition to a number of Canada's most

serious wartime crises.[58] Perhaps the most pressing of these was the perceived crisis among military recruits. According to figures released by the
federal government in 1942, upwards of 43 percent of Canada's first 50,000
army volunteers had initially been rejected for medical reasons. Although
the reasons for these rejections ranged from stomach and foot trouble to
bronchitis and rheumatism, the CCN surveys offered a ready explanation
for their alarming scale. The impact of suboptimal nutrition, it was argued,
was wide ranging: it could be a predisposing cause of infectious diseases
such as tuberculosis; it had a profound impact on growth and structural
development; and it could have serious effects on an individual's overall
capacity for physical activity.[59] These claims were further supported by
British studies showing that recruits who had initially been rejected on
medical grounds were able to pass their second medical exam after only a
few weeks on a nutritionally supervised diet.[60]

Suboptimal nutrition was also often connected to Canada's growing
wartime "manpower" crisis. As early as 1941, key industries faced significant
labour shortages caused by the exit of tens of thousands of military-aged
men from the labour market. As the need to maintain production of goods
essential to the Allied war effort increased, the need for government intervention to deal with these labour shortages therefore became more urgent.
Part of this intervention involved a campaign to encourage both married
and single women to take jobs in essential war industries, even if it meant
filling traditionally "male" industrial jobs. The manpower crisis also saw
the creation of a National Selective Service bureaucracy to channel workers
towards "essential" industries and to prevent those already working in
these industries from seeking other, higher-paying jobs.[61] But as Jennifer
Stephen argues, Canada's perceived wartime "manpower" crisis also brought
increased attention to problems of industrial efficiency and productivity.
As Canadian industries were forced to make do with fewer employees,
workers themselves were called upon to work longer and more difficult
shifts. Maintaining the productivity of these remaining workers therefore
emerged as a major concern, especially among industrial producers.[62]

Stephen focuses on ways in which psychologists and management experts singled out women as biologically less efficient and reliable than their
male counterparts. But it is clear that nutrition offered another approach
by linking malnutrition with military rejections and with Canada's "manpower" problem. L.B. Pett was quick to draw such parallels, warning at
one point that "there is a nutrition problem in Canada which is delaying
production for our war effort, and which is sapping the strength of our
whole population."[63] Suboptimal nutrition was also frequently connected

to common medical conditions affecting an individual's ability to work. According to a 1942 article by Pett, the impact of malnutrition on productivity was far reaching. Malnutrition, he suggested, "means increased sickness and fatigue. It means backaches and sore eyes, and sore muscles, and tired eyes, and apathy, and accidents, and stomach troubles, and worry, and more colds, and many other common causes of absenteeism or decreased production."[64] According to other nutrition experts, malnutrition also meant reduced "health," "mental alertness," "pep," "vitality," and "working efficiency."[65]

Like the term "manpower crisis" itself, the language used to describe the effects of malnutrition on Canada's war effort was decidedly gendered and spoke to fears of a broader wartime "crisis of masculinity." For many, the perceived inefficiency of the men who were staying behind to work in the factories and fields on the home front, combined with the high rates of military rejections in the early years of the war, clearly suggested that a significant number of Canadian men were failing to achieve their masculine physical and productive potential. To address this problem, nutrition experts increasingly began promoting science-based dietary reform as a means to produce (and reproduce) strong, virile young men of the kind who would be needed to win the war on the battlefield, the factory floor, and the farm. In doing so, they were borrowing from long-held perceptions of Canadian masculinity, especially working-class masculinity. As Craig Heron notes, the body had long been central to the construction of working-class masculinities in Canada, particularly in the first half of the twentieth century. Heron suggests that throughout this period, men's bodies acted as "the clear measure of achievement (successful laborer, athlete, lover, or happy drunk) and the visible sign of failure (weakness, malnutrition, dismemberment, disease, degenerate drunkenness, death)."[66] The wartime rhetoric of the properly nourished, productive soldier and worker built on these already widely held masculine ideals but reframed them as more than just physical markers of the successful, respectable worker. These were now also the defining characteristics of the patriotic (male) citizen who was ready to do his essential (manly) duty on the home front or in battle. Women continued to be cast as the gatekeepers of their family's nutritional status. Now, however, through posters in factory lunchrooms and educational flyers slipped into their pay packets, men were also being reminded of their duty to maintain a healthy diet (see Figure 1.2).

Increasingly, in other words, Canada's leading nutrition experts were presenting malnutrition as primarily a threat to the nation's virility and strength. Both the language used to describe the results of the CCN studies

Figure 1.2 This poster promoting the newly formed Nutrition Division shows the intimate connection between nutrition and the goal of promoting maximum working efficiency. *National Film Board of Canada, NFB–1E [1939-45].*

and the philosophy underlying the optimal dietary standard they were based on suggested that malnutrition rates said more about "productivity," "efficiency," and "optimal performance" than they did about physical manifestations of "illness" or "disease." As the war progressed, it became more common for public statements by nutrition experts like Pett to describe malnutrition in terms of lost "man-hours" or even the number of bombers not produced rather than in terms of mortality or deficiency diseases.[67] Moreover, by framing malnutrition as "an essential part of the war effort to make men available for the armed services, to accelerate industrial production and to prevent the loss of time through illness," nutrition experts inserted themselves into important social debates and positions of authority in ways that they had not prior to the war.[68] By defining optimal nutrition as the achievement of a physical ideal rather than simply the prevention of disease, these experts were equating good nutrition with patriotic citizenship in that it promised maximum physical, economic, and even cultural returns.[69]

In 1942, the CCN executive reaffirmed its commitment to the ideal of optimal nutrition by unanimously adopting a new dietary standard that was even more unambiguously grounded in the notion of "perfect health." In 1941, the US National Research Council (NRC) developed the most comprehensive dietary standard produced up to that point. These "Recommended Dietary Allowances" (or RDAs) contained recommendations for a variety of nutrients not included in the 1939 Canadian Dietary Standard. Nutrition experts widely acknowledged that the RDAs contained a number of recommendations that had "no experimental basis."[70] Even so, the CCN adopted them as the new Canadian Dietary Standard – partly in order to ensure international uniformity but also because a number of organizations, such as the Canadian Dietetics Association, had already begun using the more comprehensive American standard.[71] The most interesting feature of the RDAs, though, was the rationale used to justify the optimum recommendations they represented. From the start, the NRC stated that the RDAs were intended specifically for the purpose of "building up [the American] people to a level of health and vigor never before attained or dreamed of." To achieve this goal, they were designed to be "sufficient for maximum health and vigor of any individual under any normal circumstances."[72]

The "margin of safety" used to define "optimal" vitamin and mineral requirements was therefore set intentionally at the theoretical needs of the largest and most active individuals, even though most people would actually require far less – often only half the recommended allowances. Thus, when Canada adopted the ambitious and utopian RDAs as the basis for the Canadian Dietary Standard in 1942, it was also adopting a definition of malnutrition that had become unambiguously tied to notions of productivity, efficiency, and perfect health in a way that no previous standard had done. This would have wide-ranging effects on the implementation of Canada's wartime nutrition efforts.

Making Canada's Official Food Rules

The popular education campaign developed in response to Canada's malnutrition crisis reflected both the wartime nutritional priorities of the CCN's leaders and their tendency to privilege faulty education over lack of income as the leading cause of malnutrition. When the Nutrition Services Division was created in 1941, for instance, two areas of intervention were given priority: a large-scale popular education program targeted primarily at mothers and the inspection of food service facilities in key war industries. But even the latter function was aimed primarily at education rather than the structural causes of poor nutrition. This was because, although Nutrition Services staff inspected and rated the food facilities for 723 war production plants over the course of the war, they had limited power to make meaningful changes. Legal sanctions such as fines were never used. Instead, Nutrition Services relied on persuasion through education and promises of increased production to convince the management of these facilities to improve their food services.[73]

The Canadian Nutrition Programme (CNP) was the public face of the work being done by Nutrition Services and was meant to serve a function similar to that of the war industry inspections. Both approaches defined malnutrition primarily as a problem of faulty education, and both strongly emphasized the threat that malnutrition posed to production and the war effort. This was clear in one of the CNP's early slogans: "Eat Right, Feel Right – Canada Needs You Strong." The same priority was reflected in Canada's Official Food Rules, whose release in July 1942 marked the CNP's first major public announcement. The Food Rules had been designed to act as the central message of a much broader educational campaign, one that would, by the end of the war, see Nutrition Services produce dozens of educational pamphlets, brochures, monographs, film strips, displays, and posters in both English and French. The idea was that these materials, unified around the basic message of the Food Rules, would not simply form the basis of nutrition education at the federal level but would also be used extensively by provincial, municipal, and charitable organizations as part of their own educational campaigns.

As dietary advice, Canada's Official Food Rules and their 1944 and 1949 revisions were a product of the malnutrition crisis that the CNP had been created to solve. To this end, they were designed to act as a simple, meal-based guide to nutritional planning based on the concept of "health protective" foods – such as milk, tomatoes, potatoes, bread, and eggs – that "supply minerals, vitamins and good quality protein, or any one of these, in suitable amounts according to reasonable daily intakes."[74] They were therefore organized into six food groups that, when consumed, would provide optimal intakes of vitamins, minerals, and protein as set out in the 1942 Canadian Dietary Standard.[75] But the Food Rules were not intended to represent a total diet and, to that end, they did not actually reflect an individual's complete caloric requirements. Rather, based on the assumption that individuals would easily make up the remainder of their energy needs with non-protective foods, Canadians were advised to "eat these foods first, then add these and other foods you wish."[76]

The 1942 Food Rules did, however, make some minor concessions to wartime supply concerns. For example, because milk shortages were believed to be a possibility, the Food Rules recommended only minimal rather than optimal requirements for the nutrient riboflavin. Largely, though, the ambitious ideals of optimum nutrition were treated as the norm against which individuals should judge their diets. Even the minor concession to the Department of Agriculture represented by the 1942 milk recommendations was ultimately rejected by the CCN, which – with support from the dairy industry – passed a motion in 1943 that it could not "take any part in food lists based on 'existing supply' nor 'expediency'" and that the Food Rules needed to be "based on optimal nutrition requirements."[77] Thus, in 1944, faced with formal protests from the Department of Agriculture and the Wartime Prices and Trade Board, the CCN revised the Food Rules to fully reflect optimal dietary requirements through increases in the recommendations for milk, cheese, and butter:

I. CANADA'S FOOD RULES
Approved by the Canadian Council on Nutrition

THESE ARE THE FOODS FOR HEALTH.
EAT THEM EVERY DAY. DRINK PLENTY OF WATER.

1. *Milk* – Adults, ½ to 1 pint. Children, 1½ pints to 1 quart.
2. *Fruit* – One serving of citrus fruit or tomatoes or their juices; *and* one serving of other fruit.
3. *Vegetables* – At least *one* serving of potatoes; at least *two* servings of other vegetables, preferably leafy, green or yellow, and frequently raw.
4. *Cereals and Bread* – One serving of a whole-grain cereal *and* at least four slices of Canada Approved Vitamin B bread (whole wheat, brown or white) with *butter.*

5. *Meat and Fish* – One serving of meat, fish, poultry, or meat alternates
such as beans, peas, nuts, eggs or cheese. Also use eggs and cheese at
least three times a week each, and liver frequently.

*A fish liver oil, as a source of vitamin D, should be given to children and
expectant women, and may be advisable for other adults.*

Iodized salt is recommended.

While other, more cosmetic changes were also made – including the removal
of the word "official" from the Food Rules' title, the reduction of the number
of rules from six to five, the addition of recommendations regarding water
and iodized salt, and the omission of kidney and heart "because of the very
limited supplies available and the uncertainty of their necessity in addition
to meat" – the nutritional message remained constant: good nutrition was
optimal nutrition.[78]

By basing the Food Rules on the somewhat utopian ideal of optimum
nutrition, the CCN and Nutrition Services were setting an ambitious goal
for Canadians. This was reflected in the hyperbole of the editors of *Saturday
Night,* who suggested in a January 1943 editorial that Canada's national
nutrition efforts were "going to effect what is probably the most radical
change in the living habits of a nation that has ever been brought about
by the conscious effort of its rulers and its scientific and intellectual
leaders" – the goal of which was ultimately to create "a race of super-
Canadians."[79] Although Pett himself did not resort to the language of
race, his vision was similarly utopian – for him, nutrition would lead to
"a wonderful new social order in which abundance of the right foods,
adequately used by everyone, would bring a degree of health and vigour
never before considered possible."[80]

Besides expressing a physical and aesthetic ideal, the Food Rules also
represented an ambitious set of culinary assumptions and goals. The staff
of Nutrition Services, for their part, claimed they had designed the Food
Rules to "conform to the average food pattern of Canadians as nearly as
known," but it would probably be more accurate to say that they reflected
a specific Anglo-European cultural ideal rather than the reality of many
Canadians' diets.[81] In the United States, by way of contrast, the federal
Food and Nutrition Board created a Committee on Food Habits whose
task was to translate the new RDAs into non-technical language that
would be understandable to the ordinary American when they read educational materials such as the "Basic Seven" (the American equivalent of
the Food Rules). Under the direction of anthropologist Margaret Mead,

the committee was sensitive to the need to appreciate ethnic differences and, to this end, it sought to promote the democratic development of a unified national identity that would reflect America's multiple cultures.[82] No such efforts were made in the Canadian context: the dominant attitude within Nutrition Services and the CCN was that culture was something that Canadians needed to *overcome* in order to achieve the rationalizing goals of scientific nutrition.[83] A 1947 article written by Nutrition Services staff titled "Food Fads and Fallacies" made this philosophy quite clear:

> Food habits, like other cultural patterns, have developed more from chance occurrences and personal ideas than from systematic observations and logical conclusions … The difference between this and many other customs, is that food can be approached with a relatively objective yardstick. The science of nutrition, young though it is, can be used to show how stupid, wise, how ludicrous, or how unlikely are many of the fond beliefs about food that people may have.[84]

Of course, the Food Rules were themselves an extremely culturally specific text that, more than anything, tended to mirror the interests of Canada's main domestic agricultural producers. In this regard, the Food Rules' core recommendations had a clear agricultural purpose in mind. Although an exception was made for citrus fruits, the Food Rules recommended the daily consumption of *Canadian* agricultural staples in quantities "definitely in excess of those actually consumed in order to provide a clear goal for improvement." The staff at Nutrition Services estimated that if all Canadians based their food intake on the Food Rules, consumption of products such as milk and tomatoes would increase by between 25 and 35 percent, with similar increases in domestic consumption of fruits, vegetables, and whole grains.[85] In the 1942 and 1944 revisions of the Food Rules, moreover, the inclusion of "Canada Approved Bread" (a product that, instead of being fortified with B vitamins, used an alternative milling technique to boost its vitamin content) and the long-maintained opposition of Canadian nutrition experts to the fortification of foods more generally, similarly reflected this support for Canadian agricultural producers. While officials in the United States and Britain encouraged the fortification of certain foods – such as bread and margarine – as a low-cost response to specific deficiencies shown in dietary surveys, Nutrition Services and the CCN actively opposed these practices. They argued, instead, that Canada produced more than enough nutritious food to meet every person's dietary needs and that by approving fortification of common foods like bread, they would be implying that existing foodstuffs were nutritionally inadequate.[86]

The promotion of agriculture had always been an important goal of optimal nutrition. Proponents like Stiebeling and Orr suggested that nutritionally planned agriculture offered a solution to – and might even have prevented – the economic collapse that had devastated agricultural producers during the 1930s.[87] During the war, these ideas found a growing number of adherents internationally, and many Canadians saw nutrition as the key to a peaceful postwar recovery. In a 1943 speech, for instance, the WPTB Oils and Fats Administrator Phyllis Turner told a Montreal audience she was "convinced that the establishment of an international economic set up, having as one of its chief objectives a system of controlled agricultural production based on nutritional needs, would provide one of the surest methods of safeguarding the future peace of the world."[88] Nutritional planning of the sort advocated by Turner dominated the agendas of many of the food experts and diplomats who gathered to found the UN Food and Agriculture Organization in 1945 and helped spur the election of Orr as its first director.[89] Many within the CCN were similarly enamoured with the possibilities of nutritionally planned agriculture. They envisioned the Food Rules playing an important role in Canada's postwar reconstruction and, at one point, they passed a resolution calling for the Canadian government to plan agricultural production on the basis of the nutrition requirements laid out by the Food Rules.[90]

Although the Food Rules could be used in multiple ways to market Canadian products and for long-range economic planning, they were, at their most basic level, an educational tool. By the end of the war, Nutrition Services had incorporated the simple message of the Food Rules into a wide-ranging media campaign that included dozens of flyers, pamphlets, posters, cookbooks, and films. Some of these, like the widely distributed booklet *Healthful Eating*, provided detailed instructions to nurses and teachers regarding how to use the Food Rules in their work, with the ultimate goal of "bridging the gap between text books and actual practice."[91] Most, however, sought to promote the message of the Food Rules to the general public and included pamphlets aimed primarily at mothers such as *Let's Talk Food Mother* and *The Lunch Box Is on the March*. The National Film Board also produced a number of filmstrips for Nutrition Services aimed at children. The films – which included titles such as *Johnny Eats His Vegetables* and *Peppo* – used anthropomorphic animals and foods to promote the benefits of different food groups. Nutrition Services even promoted the Food Rules to industrial workers through "Pay Envelope

Flyers," which, by end of the war, had been stuffed into more than four million pay envelopes.[92]

Besides familiarizing Canadians with the Food Rules, many of these educational materials served a kind of diagnostic function. This was particularly true of the popular – but overly complicated – booklet titled "Check Your Food by the Colour Test" and of the much simpler, one-page "Score Sheet for Each Day's Meals." The latter, especially, was widely distributed and saw multiple printings. In it, each group from the Food Rules was represented by quantities of foods, and each food was assigned a point value. At the end of the day, the points were tallied and, based on the scores, the groups were given a rank of "very good," "good," "fair – try to improve" or "poor – make every effort to improve." One common way that Red Cross nutritionists used the score sheet during the war and early postwar years, for instance, was to have students bring the score sheet home from school and, with the help of their mother, calculate the nutritional value of one day's meals. Afterwards, the child brought the completed sheet back to school, where it was used as part of a lesson on good nutrition.[93] Because the sheet itself clearly outlined the relationship between the points earned and a child's nutritional status, it quickly became apparent to mothers whether they were feeding their children "properly." In this way, both the child and the mother were supposedly being educated in good nutrition while, at the same time, the mother's cooking habits were also being brought to the attention of the teacher.

For most Canadians who used the Food Rules or the score sheet as diagnostic tools to assess their nutritional status, the results confirmed what the experts had already been telling them: they were not eating enough of the right foods. This was the message of a January 1943 national Gallup Poll sponsored by Nutrition Services that, among other things, found that the vast majority of Canadians were deficient in at least one of the six food groups laid out in the Food Rules. Upwards of 25 percent were not consuming enough milk and cheese, 40 percent were failing to consume enough breads and cereals, and as many as 83 percent of those polled were not eating enough fruit. While the food groups for vegetables, meat, and eggs seemed to fare better, the overall picture was of a population that, as a whole, was not eating enough of the right foods.[94] These kinds of results were consistently reconfirmed during the war and early postwar years, particularly after nutrition experts began to use the Food Rules and/or the score sheet in their own scientific studies. One large-scale 1946 study conducted by Pett found that, out of a sample group of 1,500 British Columbia schoolchildren, 68 percent were deficient in up to three of the eight foods recommended in the Food Rules, while an additional 25 percent were deficient in as many as six. According to Pett, only 6.5 percent had what could be classified as a "good" diet.[95]

These findings of supposedly widespread undernutrition or malnutrition reflected the reality that most Canadians were simply unable to meet the requirements set out in the Food Rules due to a combination of economic, social, and cultural factors. For many Canadians, an insurmountable barrier was income. The war had led a general increase in Canadians' disposable incomes, but this was by no means universally true, and according to the staff at Nutrition Services, the Food Rules were "commonly criticized because they are too expensive."[96] This fact was well recognized by social workers, dieticians, and others working directly with low-income families. Calculations of the cost of a diet based on optimal nutrition requirements consistently showed that insufficient income was preventing many families from achieving the kind of diet represented by the Food Rules.[97] As will be discussed at greater length in later chapters, moreover, Canadian nutrition policy during this period involved little in the way of relief for families who could not afford nutritious foods. While Britain made efforts to redistribute protective foods to the poorest through a system of milk depots, communal canteens, and nutritionally determined ration allotments – and the United States offered Food Stamps to more than four million low-income Americans – Canada's national nutrition program included little in the way of comparable wealth redistribution efforts.[98] The national director of nutrition services for the Canadian Red Cross Society summarized the contradictions faced by nutrition educators in the absence of protective social legislation: "When we say to Mrs. Jones whose Husband's salary is $4,000 or over, 'Follow the Canada Official Food Rules,' the problem is capable of solution, but say this same thing to Mrs. Smith with an income of $1,000, and we have presented her with a problem incapable of solution."[99]

Even for families who *could* afford to make the basic purchases required to follow the Food Rules, there were additional social and cultural barriers. One was the sheer quantity of food being recommended. The reality was that the Food Rules were based on ambitious optimal dietary requirements that more closely reflected the dietary needs of the largest and most active (male) individuals – that is, not the average Canadian. Front-line nutrition workers often reported that both they and their clients had a hard time simply consuming the rather large quantities of milk, potatoes, cereals, and bread outlined in the Food Rules.[100] For most Canadians, moreover, the Food Rules did not simply "conform to average food patterns" but rather required a significant change in food culture and day-to-day eating habits. This was perhaps most true for Canadians whose diets deviated from the Anglo-European norm that formed the basis of the Food Rules. Not only did the combination of foods laid out in the Food Rules have little application to a number of Canadian regions – particularly the North – but they also pathologized the culinary traditions of ethnic groups with cuisines less centred on dairy products such as milk, cheese, and butter. This was obvious in an advertisement approved by Nutrition Services for publication in *Liberty Magazine*. Titled "Men without Milk," the ad showed a bowlegged Japanese soldier walking towards a ruined "oriental" city. "The short stature of the Japanese," the ad reads, "their bowed legs, their frequent poor eyesight are all blamed on inadequate diet – particularly lack of milk!" The inevitable victory of the Allies, on the other hand, is attributed to milk: "Canada drinks *lots* of milk. Canada *likes* the rich flavor and tempting taste which milk and its products give to our food."[101]

The designation of certain foods as simultaneously essential *and* Canadian did not simply pathologize the diets of Canada's enemies. Significantly, the authors of the 1946 study of BC schoolchildren discussed above found that a group of 157 Chinese students attending the Strathcona School in Vancouver presented a "more serious nutrition problem" than other children. According to the study, almost three times more Chinese students had "poor" diets and none of them had "good" diets. These results were attributed largely to the fact that many of the Chinese children consumed few or no dairy products and, instead, relied heavily on products such as white rice, tea, and sugary desserts. The study's authors conceded that some aspects of the typical Chinese diet in Vancouver were more nutritious than that of their non-Chinese neighbours – for example, Chinese Canadian families typically ate more vegetables, cooked their foods for less time, and regularly consumed organ meats. Moreover, when the Chinese Canadian children were given physical exams, the main difference from other children was that they were thinner – something that is associated with the underconsumption of calories and, at the time, was generally recognized as being a consequence of poverty rather than of poor food choices. In the end, however, the study's authors stood by the Food Rules and concluded that although Chinese culinary practices might be nutritionally adequate in China, that was not the case in Canada. In discussing the reasons for the rates of malnutrition found among Chinese children, they saw the inability of Chinese immigrants to find substitutes for native foods as the main problem, noting that "Canada's Food Rules may be complied with by many types of national and racial food patterns, but it is a difficult thing for people to change the actual foods eaten, even when they no longer have access to those with which they are familiar."[102]

By the late 1940s it had become increasingly clear that, even during a period of growing acceptance of some "ethnic" cuisines by the Canadian mainstream, the Food Rules and nutrition advice more generally had come to define the "official" limits of culinary accommodation. This was particularly the case when it came to Canada's nutrition policies directed at Aboriginal peoples. The kind of diet represented by the Food Rules had little application to many First Nations, Metis, and Inuit peoples, particularly those living in remote northern areas and relying on traditional livelihoods such as hunting, trapping, fishing, and gathering. Yet when researchers from the Department of Indian Affairs, the RCAF, and the New York–based Milbank Memorial Fund discovered widespread malnutrition in a number of Cree First Nations in northern Manitoba – which in many cases amounted to outright hunger and near-starvation – they interpreted these conditions not simply as arising from poverty exacerbated by a collapse in fur prices and a recent decline of local fish and game populations, but also as the result of a hybrid diet of wild "country" and imported "store" foods.[103] As one 1948 press release from Indian Affairs promoting its own nutrition efforts among "bush Indians" made clear, there was no room for hybrid cuisines among indigenous peoples. "Canada's northern Indians," it argued, "have lost the art of eating":

> They have abandoned the native eating habits of their forefathers and adopted a semi-civilized, semi native diet which lacks essential food values, brings them to malnutrition and leaves them prey to tuberculosis and other disease. The white man, who unintentionally is responsible for the Indians' changed eating habits, now is trying to salvage the red man by directing him towards proper food channels.[104]

This kind of "direction" took a range of both coercive and non-coercive forms. These forms ranged from the total denial of indigenous culinary traditions in Indian residential schools to the use of family allowances as a means to direct the food purchases of Inuit peoples and northern First Nations. For instance, whereas all other Canadians received cash payments, so-called bush Indians received their family allowances as an in-kind payment limited to certain "essential" foods and clothing items, and the foods chosen were often justified by their fit within the nutritional ideal of the Food Rules.[105] In the end, the Food Rules did little to define an identifiable Canadian culinary tradition. They were, instead, far more successful in defining which dietary practices were not sufficiently "Canadian" and therefore were in need of reform.

Nutrition at War

To a certain extent, the Food Rules truly did create a unified message concerning the basic components of a healthy diet during the war and early postwar years, appearing as they did in everything from community cookbooks to popular magazines to flyers placed alongside family allowance cheques. But it was a message filtered through a number of different organizations and interests that were ultimately as responsible as Nutrition Services (if not more so) for disseminating educational messages and materials. Especially in its early years, Nutrition Services was constrained by a small staff and limited financial resources. It was given sufficient funds to produce a range of educational materials, but it had little in the way of infrastructure to distribute or properly promote them.[106] While Nutrition Services would eventually come to rely on provincial and municipal programs to promote its healthy eating message and distribute its educational materials, many of these organizations were only in their infancy during the war. Nutrition Services therefore regularly turned to the print and broadcast media as well as major commercial, charitable, and women's organizations – many of which were already heavily involved in nutrition publicity and education – in order to get its message out to the public.

To facilitate the launch of the Food Rules, for instance, L.B. Pett reached out to a number of corporate partners, who agreed to provide significant levels of free advertising for the CNP, the Food Rules, and nutrition more generally. After being approached by Pett, for instance, the Association of Canadian Advertisers prepared a complete advertising and promotion package that was made available for sponsorship by individual companies. These promotional materials included copy, illustrations, layouts, "drop-ins" for use in regular ads, posters, copies of slogans, and proofs of the Food Rules.[107] Individual advertisers, moreover, developed their own materials. The Swift Canadian Company, for instance, produced a sixteen-page, full-colour nutrition booklet titled the *Eat Right to Work and Win,* which – besides being illustrated with characters from popular King Features comics such as Blondie, Flash Gordon, and Popeye – included one of the first illustrated versions of the Food Rules in the form of anthropomorphized food groups marching off to war (see Figure 1.1). It even included a glowing foreword by Pett lauding the booklet for being "of real value in showing the way to better eating habits."[108] The booklet was quite popular, and Nutrition Services began to distribute it – along with a number of full-colour posters advertising the Food Rules produced by the Toronto Milk Foundation – with its own educational materials.[109]

Some non-food companies also devoted ad space to the message of the Food Rules and the CNP. But, unsurprisingly, it was the food industry that showed the most enthusiasm towards the campaign. Various brands had been advertising the nutritional value of their particular products for years, and the CNP granted a certain "official" legitimacy to these efforts.[110] For most companies, the Food Rules were an easy sell because the message to "eat more" food for health was essentially open-ended. Any food could be sold as part of a diet based on the Food Rules. Many food advertisers therefore chose simply to highlight the rule that applied to their particular product. An ad for a Toronto bakery, for instance, printed only the rule regarding bread, placing the words "USE MORE IF YOU CAN" at the centre of the ad in large bold letters. Food companies selling products that were not even mentioned in the Food Rules, moreover, often ran ads referring to the rules. One ad, for instance, advised readers to "follow Canada's Food Rules and flavour with Windsor Salt."[111] Nutrition Services and the CCN created a "Canadian Crest" to be used on "certain approved advertising" in order to prevent such abuses but quickly realized that they lacked the resources to devote to such a scheme and that it would be difficult to meet the quick turnaround times that advertisers required.[112] They did occasionally make exceptions to this rule and – as was the case with the aforementioned "Men without Milk" ad and Swift's *Eat Right to Work and Win* – would allow the printing of ads and other materials explicitly "approved by Nutrition Services."

Newspapers and magazines were similarly attracted to the message of the Food Rules. *Canadian Home Journal* sold itself to advertisers as the best place to "interpret the nutrition question" and produced a booklet titled *Canada's Nutrition Program and the Food Advertiser*.[113] But nutrition was also a source of easy copy because Nutrition Services, the CCN, and other organizations regularly provided the media with free articles, interviews, and recipes – many of which were then published verbatim. Just as Nutrition Services was struggling with a small staff and limited resources, newspapers and magazines faced the same kinds of personnel shortages as most other Canadian industries and therefore welcomed any ready-to-publish copy. By November 1942, Nutrition Services was preparing as many as six articles a month for publication in newspapers and magazines.

It was making roughly the same number of speeches on the radio and before business associations, women's groups, and social clubs. Perhaps more importantly, it was making extensive use of the News Feature Service of the Wartime Information Board to send weekly releases to the women's pages of magazines and newspapers.[114]

Whether or not the information being provided through the mass media followed the officially sanctioned line of Nutrition Services or the CCN, a number of common themes ran through much of the Canadian wartime writing about nutrition. At the most basic level was a strong connection between good nutrition and patriotic citizenship. The war effort, Canadians were regularly told, depended on healthy workers and soldiers. Canadians who refused healthy food were "fifth columnists" and were committing acts of "wartime sabotage." Or, as the title of one *Saturday Night* article put it: "Canada's Faulty Diet is Adolf Hitler's Ally."[115] At the heart of these patriotic messages were the fears associated with both the high medical rejection rate of Canadian soldiers and Canada's ongoing "manpower" crisis. The concern, as illustrated in a White Spot restaurant placemat, was that Canada was becoming a country of "Straw Men." Showing three scarecrows representing an industrial worker, a farmer, and a soldier, the placemat warned that without good nutrition, "Canada could never have an efficient army – in the field – on the farm – or in the factory."[116] Canada's manpower and military crises, in other words, required a change in Canadians' diets.

Messages reminding Canadians of their duty to empire and nation were invoked frequently in nutrition-related materials aimed at children. Some articles on nutrition in popular children's magazines such as *Canadian Red Cross Junior* attempted to appeal to children's vanity through titles such as "Do You Want to Be Good-Looking?" or "Do You Want to Be Captain of Your Team?" But the primary message of these materials aimed at children was that they needed strong bodies and minds in order to be ready for the sacrifices that would be asked of them.[117] In one article, Dr. Ernest Couture, Ottawa's Director of the Division of Child and Maternal Hygiene, reminded children of their duty to "suivez les conseils et les recommandations des hygiénistes en alimentation. Sinon, vous ne pourrez accomplir ce qu'on attend de vous!"[118] A radio program developed by the Kingston Community Nutrition Council similarly alluded to these unnamed future sacrifices: "You boys and girls are so important to your country, that we want to tell you how you can keep yourselves healthy – so that, whatever you may be called upon to do for Canada, you will be strong and fit and eager to do it."[119]

Patriotic messages aimed at adults on the home front also linked good nutrition to the obligations of wartime citizenship. "Manpower" and working capacity played the most prominent role in this regard. To promote the RCAF's efforts to improve the nutritional content of its rations and to educate Canadian airmen and airwomen, for instance, the military produced a big-budget motion picture titled *Training Table,* which according to one account "was of such interest that Famous Players of Canada reproduced it in Technicolor, and it was distributed as a regular showing in practically all motion picture houses in Canada."[120] The Air Force, in conjunction with the Canadian Medical Association (CMA) and the Life Insurance Companies of Canada, also distributed over 1.5 million copies of a full-colour, glossy pamphlet titled *What They Eat to Be Fit Is Good for the Health of All Canadians* (see Figure 1.3). It reminded "industrial workers, housewives, everybody in Canada today" that they owed it to themselves and to their country to "keep fit": "That is why it is vitally important for every Canadian to know what foods are essential to maintain good health – and never fail to eat them. Good health means better work – more work – and the spirit that wins. Eat to keep fit, and work to win."[121]

While such patriotic messages were commonplace, it is important to note that the vast majority of nutrition-related materials produced during the war were directed at mothers. McHenry and others within the CCN had consistently laid the blame for Canada's poor nutrition at the feet of mothers before the war; wartime messages simply added a patriotic twist to this familiar theme. The message was typically an unambiguous one that reinforced a gendered ideal of citizenship that emphasized women's domestic responsibilities for their family's health. As Edith Adams, the *Vancouver Sun*'s fictional home economics expert, told her readers: "The Canadian woman, armed with a knowledge of home nutrition and domestic economy, wields a powerful weapon in defense of her country and democracy. She has been quick to recognize her sacred responsibility."[122] These messages of wartime "sacred responsibility" and "patriotic duty" for the family's health were regularly addressed to "the housewives of Canada," "homemakers," or, as the Canada Starch Company referred to them, "Canada's Housoldiers." The CMA booklet *Food for Health in Peace and War* perhaps put it most simply: "We have a war to win. We must be fit for whatever task is required of us. Every housewife can do her bit – and help others do theirs – by keeping her family's health at a high level."[123]

The message of wartime nutrition advice was, in other words, by no means new and tended to draw extensively from pre-war discourses on women's domestic responsibilities to their family and the state.[124] In part,

Figure 1.3 Cover of *What They Eat To Be Fit Is Good for the Health of all Canadians* (Life Insurance Companies of Canada/Canadian Medical Association, 1943).

this reflected the entrenched nature of such discourses, but it also reflected the fact that – on the ground at least – Canada's wartime nutrition education programs continued to be carried out by the same public health departments and charitable organizations that had been involved in public health campaigns during the 1920s and '30s. While the long-term focus of Nutrition Services was on schoolchildren through a major expansion of nutrition education at the elementary and secondary levels, the reality was that most schools were not well equipped for this. A study by the Canadian Education Association found that as late as 1949, only 36 percent of schools

gave any nutrition instruction at all. Most schools lacked the kitchen facilities for practical nutrition lessons, and most teachers had no training
in scientific nutrition.[125] At least in the short term, Nutrition Services had
little choice but to use existing channels of adult education to get its
wartime message out to Canadians. This meant that, besides securing the
cooperation of local and provincial governments, Pett spent a great deal
of his first year as Nutrition Services Division director soliciting the support of women's and voluntary organizations such as the Red Cross, the
National Council of Women, the Société Saint-Jean-Baptiste, and the
Health League of Canada, as well as rural organizations such as the Federated Women's Institutes and the Cercles de Fermières.

Spurred by wartime patriotic enthusiasm, a number of the groups approached by Nutrition Services launched local nutrition campaigns. I
examine these efforts by volunteers at a local level in more detail in later
chapters, but it is quite clear that tens of thousands of Canadian women
received some form of direct nutrition instruction during the war through
the work of these groups. The Red Cross played perhaps the most active
role in offering direct nutrition education to Canadian women during the
war. In the 1930s, the Red Cross had taken the national lead in nutrition-
related matters. These efforts were pioneered by the Ontario Red Cross
(ORC), which hired its first full-time nutrition supervisor in 1929. By
1940, the ORC had three full-time nutritionists on staff and four of its
regional branches had hired their own nutritionists. Then, in response to
the CCN's national nutrition surveys, the Red Cross founded its own
National Committee on Nutrition, which included some of the country's
leading nutrition experts. By the end of the war, the BC, Manitoba,
Ontario, and New Brunswick divisions all employed full-time nutritionists. Many of the wartime efforts of Red Cross nutritionists focused on
public education through lectures, courses, and home visits through their
Visiting Homemaker service. Over the course of the war, it held 590 nutrition classes across the country with a total enrolment of 22,828.[126]

The educational content of most of these campaigns bore the ideological imprint of their middle-class reformist organizers and volunteers.
While many Canadians from a variety of social backgrounds were attracted
to these courses after hearing dire public warnings about malnutrition, it
is clear that the message was often intended primarily for low-income
households. This was true, for instance, of the Red Cross's highly successful
national War Economy Nutrition program.[127] The lessons themselves were
generally non-technical in nature and relied primarily on the basic message

about protective foods. To this end, they typically hinged on a comparison between two fictional homemakers: Mrs. Economy and Mrs. Extravagance. While Mrs. Economy was a portrait of the educated, scientific homemaker who was always able to stretch a dollar by avoiding processed foods, expensive cuts of meat or foods that were out of season, her counterpart consistently put her family at risk because of her preference for unnecessary luxuries (roast beef), packaged cereals (Corn Flakes), and out-of-season produce (fresh tomatoes). In the lesson on "the Market Basket," for instance, students were shown a detailed nutritional breakdown of the two women's shopping habits, and it was suggested that, through smart budgeting and proper planning, Mrs. Economy would be able to obtain nine times more minerals, four times more protein, ten times more vitamins, and four times more food energy than Mrs. Extravagance. This basic message was repeated throughout the lessons, each of which included general guidelines for shopping and cooking as well as four or five "economical" recipes such as Macaroni and Tomato ("to save cheese for Britain"), Liver Loaf, Parsnip Fritters, Baked Bean Salad, and Braised Beef Hearts.[128]

The kinds of lessons outlined by the War Economy Nutrition course were repeated by other wartime nutrition campaigns. The Vancouver Council of Social Agencies produced its own educational pamphlet, *Practical Nutrition for Wartime Living*, which was used for classes in nutrition and household economy held by the Greater Vancouver Health League and the Family Section of the Coordinating Council for War Work and Civilian Services. As with *War Economy Nutrition*, its primary focus was on family budgets. Generally, the lessons provided little in the way of actual nutrition instruction beyond the message to consume more protective foods. Instead, they typically consisted of low-cost weekly menus, "economical" recipes, cooking tips, and suggested alternatives to scarce and expensive foods. The general recommendations, which best capture the booklet's tone, included tips such as these: "Day-old bread is better than fresh bread and is usually less expensive"; and "Save all vegetable water for soups, stews, baking beans, gravies, etc., vegetable water is excellent to drink."[129]

As usual, the ultimate blame for malnutrition in most wartime nutrition courses, pamphlets, and advertisements fell on the shoulders of the individual mother. Good nutrition therefore typically meant emulating the budgeting and planning practices of Mrs. Economy and not falling into the familiar traps of Mrs. Extravagance. In other words, what was being taught in most wartime nutrition classes and in wartime educational materials was not so much the science of nutrition but rather a particular idealized middle-class vision of domestic life and the progressive ideal of educated, scientific motherhood. As with most popular nutrition education manuals, *Food and the Family Income* – which was given out in 1942 to the thousands of participants in Montreal nutrition classes – did not limit itself to advice related to shopping and cooking but was also deeply concerned with the moral conduct and individual character of Montreal housewives. In its chapter on food preparation, for instance, it made it abundantly clear that good nutrition did not depend simply on more healthy foods. Food, it told readers, "should always be served on clean plates at a clean table, because this makes it more attractive and acts as an aid to digestion." Also, mealtime should be "a happy time" because "quarrelling interferes with digestion, and the meal time is neither the time nor the place to settle family troubles."[130] For its part, *Practical Nutrition for Wartime Living* advised mothers to shrug off the often seemingly impossible demands of their domestic work: "we must be enthusiastic to make budgeting a success. Enthusiasm makes fun of work and drudgery a pleasure."[131] In the same way that the Food Rules created a rather specific cultural ideal that pathologized many non-Anglo-European food traditions, nutrition education established a gendered ideal of citizenship that represented, for many women – but for low-income and working-class women especially – an unrealistic and often simply impossible ideal.

Conclusion

The war's end in 1945 also marked the end of the militarized and "patriotic" dietary advice that had dominated the early years of the CNP. Even so, the nutritional message of the war years lived on and would serve as the basis of much postwar nutrition advice. Educational materials produced during the 1940s would continue to be revised and reprinted throughout the 1950s. Even in the new materials, however, the broader message remained similar. When the final revision of Canada's Food Rules was introduced in 1949, it in many ways continued to reflect the priorities of the malnutrition crisis that had originally sparked the creation of the CNP. Some small alterations were made to reflect changes in the postwar food supply. Recommendations for Canada Approved Vitamin B Bread, which had long been opposed by the baking industry, were removed from the rules after they failed to make any headway in the market. Lobbying from consumers looking for a cheaper alternative to butter also caused the CCN to abandon its opposition to fortified margarine, whose sale had just recently been made legal. For the first time, synthetic vitamin supplements were also included in the recommendations.

Overall, however, the five rules looked remarkably similar to their 1942 and 1944 counterparts. They included daily recommended servings of milk, citrus fruit or tomatoes, leafy green or yellow vegetables, potatoes, whole grain cereal, bread, and meat, in addition to occasional servings of liver, cheese, and eggs. Optimal nutrition also continued to form the nutritional basis of the Food Rules, even though – as will be discussed later – its scientific and ideological justification faced significant challenges from within Canada's fledgling community of nutrition experts.[132] But the Food Rules would nonetheless remain the central message of Canadian nutrition advice until 1961, when they were replaced by the remarkably similar Canada's Food Guide.

To some extent, the continuity between the 1942 and 1949 Food Rules suggests how wartime notions of gender, citizenship, and health continued to resonate among Canada's nutrition authorities and policy makers long after the war had ended. This was partly because these educational materials supported their professional and political aspirations. Not only did the sizable and very specific recommendations of the Food Rules suggest to most Canadians that they were in need of at least some expert guidance if they hoped to meet the nutritional requirements of their families, but the Food Rules also continued to represent both a nutritional and cultural model of social stability that stressed the role of individuals in the maintenance of their own well-being. Moreover, they reflected a larger set of national goals that sought to produce a well-fed, productive (male) workforce; educated mothers whose work would be confined primarily to the home; growing children who could meet the military and productive needs of the new international order; a thriving market for domestically produced agricultural goods; and a cuisine that represented a national food culture defined not by region, ethnicity, or language but by a similarly scientific outlook towards food. To this end, malnutrition continued to be framed within a larger gendered vision of what constituted good citizenship in the early postwar period. As I discuss in later chapters, although many within and outside Canada's community of nutrition experts offered an alternative social and political role for nutrition in the postwar period, they had largely rejected the progressive vision that had driven many of the early proponents of optimal nutrition – a vision of nutrition experts and governments

working together to create a scientifically regulated welfare state – by the
late 1940s. Instead, the consensus that the Food Rules and the Canadian
Nutrition Programme represented was a far more conservative one, one
that framed malnutrition as an individual rather than a social problem
and yet also sought to normalize the utopian goal of perfect health as the
basis of state-sponsored nutrition advice well into the postwar period.

2

The Kitchen and the State

Food Rationing, Price Control, and the Gender Politics of Consumption

In a December 1944 article in *Chatelaine*, outspoken social work pioneer and conservative feminist Charlotte Whitton had a warning for Canadian women about the expanding reach of the state, particularly in light of their general exclusion from the levers of political decision making:

> More and more, as the state enters the home, even governs the conditions under which it is set up at all, directly or by implication, it dictates the ways of all our life ... In other words, the walls of the home have been knocked down: all its members roam in and out of a community into which it has merged, and the public authority ranges at will through all its traditional intimacies and sanctities.[1]

For Whitton, the solution was clear: "If the state enters the home and home life merges in the expanding economic and social network of the state, woman must recapture within that broadened scene her traditional place and direct influence on the life and character of the home and family." Women, in other words, "must again directly influence the household of the nation, must participate directly in its ordering."[2]

Although many would likely have read Whitton's call to arms in the context of her vocal opposition to the growth of the welfare state through new programs such as Family Allowances, her imagery would nonetheless have had a familiar ring. The war had indeed seen the state enter Canadians' households – and their kitchens in particular – in profound ways following the implementation of an unprecedented set of wartime controls on both the price and distribution of consumer goods. Each meal consumed on the home front was governed by increasingly complex state interventions at nearly every link in the food chain, as well as in the production and distribution of basic kitchen appliances. Coupon rationing – which remains one of the dominant symbols of Canada's wartime mobilization on the home front – was directed primarily at foodstuffs, and the effects of price controls were felt most acutely during Canadians' regular trips to the grocer, baker, and butcher. In other words, the profound impact of the wartime command economy was brought home on a daily basis in the kitchen and at the dinner table, and it was mainly women, who did most of the buying and preparing of food, whose daily routines were most strongly altered.

This chapter examines Canadians' shared experience with price controls and food rationing in order to better understand the scale of state intervention in the wartime economy and shifting perceptions of the relationship between citizens and the state during the 1940s. In particular, it expands on existing historical accounts of wartime controls on consumption, which tend to focus on those who broke the rules by engaging in black market transactions or which (more commonly) portray them as small wartime sacrifices that Canadians made out of patriotic duty but that had few long-term social or political effects.[3] This chapter, by contrast, examines price controls and food rationing for what they really were: not only an unprecedented instance of state intervention in the Canadian economy but also a surprisingly popular aspect of the government's wartime mobilization on the home front. In examining both the strongest supporters and the most vocal critics of wartime controls, it argues that Canadians did not support wartime economic controls solely out of patriotic duty but in fact came to see the wartime command economy as a possible alternative to an economic status quo that had brought only depression, unemployment, and poverty during the 1930s. Building on recent Canadian and international scholarship on the history of consumption and consumer activism, this chapter also examines the growing number of women who used their support for food rationing and price controls as a means to articulate and enact an alternative – and surprisingly expansive – vision of social and economic citizenship that stressed their rights as consumers to fair prices and equitable food distribution.[4] By tracing women's support for wartime economic controls through their wartime work with the Consumer Branch of the Wartime Prices and Trade Board (WPTB) to the postwar boycotts, buyers' strikes, and petitions of the Housewives Consumer Association (HCA), this chapter suggests that many women indeed took up Whitton's

THE KITCHEN AND THE STATE

call for them to assert their political rights as wives and homemakers – albeit as a means of calling for more, not less, intervention by the state into the affairs of the kitchen. As a 1945 Co-operative Commonwealth Federation (CCF) pamphlet reminded voters: "Good homemakers today must take political action. For politics is the key to the kitchen cupboard."[5]

Controlling Wartime Food Consumption

Throughout the war, Canadians were bombarded with messages linking their personal food consumption practices to the overall success of the war effort. Slogans like "Food Is a Weapon of War" and "Food Will Win the War" appeared frequently in film, radio, and print as part of a broader wartime call for Canadians to divert surplus foods to the war effort either by limiting their consumption to only what was necessary or by taking part in conservation efforts aimed at converting household waste products like fat and bones into bombs and other war materials.[6] While many of these household conservation efforts would contribute only a small fraction to Canada's war production, as will be discussed in the next chapter, it was nonetheless very much true that food remained one of Canada's primary contributions to the war effort. Britain depended on Canadian imports for its survival, and Canadians were regularly made aware of their role in supplying the British with essential foodstuffs like wheat, meat, cheese, and butter. As it turned out, this diversion of food to Canada's allies largely relied on subsidies, price guarantees, and other state controls over agriculture.[7] Even so, Canadian civilian consumption had to be transformed to meet Canada's wartime food commitments.

The sheer scale of Canada's food commitments meant that the government could not rely solely on propaganda and appeals to patriotic duty to bring about the necessary changes to Canadians' food consumption habits. Instead, Ottawa was forced to implement a regime of wartime economic controls that would ultimately govern nearly all transactions among consumers, retailers, distributors, and producers. Perhaps the most important of these controls – symbolically at least – was the coupon rationing of daily necessities, including meat, sugar, butter, preserves, tea, and coffee. Because Canadians had managed to avoid mandatory coupon rationing during the previous war, the need to carry a ration book to buy groceries was unprecedented. Ration books therefore became a powerful symbol of the effect of the war on ordinary Canadians and of the much larger scale of state intervention into their everyday lives. But the state's reach into food consumption practices went much further than this. Regulations passed by the WPTB not only governed the maximum price of nearly every type of food but also mandated meatless days; set limits on the packaging of consumer goods; regulated the size of cuffs on pants; prohibited the sale of sliced bread, hot dog buns, and iced cakes; and determined the production and sale of nearly every kind of kitchen appliance, automobile, or consumer durable.

The public servant who came to represent the face of these wartime controls over Canadians' eating habits was Donald Gordon. Between 1941 and 1947, Gordon was the director of the WPTB, or, as he was sometimes called by his critics, the "Price Czar" – a title that was, in some ways, not far from the truth. Gordon wielded enormous power over a government agency that was responsible for regulating the sale and distribution of nearly all consumer goods, setting basic domestic production quotas, maintaining maximum price ceilings, paying subsidies to primary producers, and enforcing what would eventually amount to thousands of individual regulations. The WPTB was established on 3 September 1939 and, from the beginning, had an unprecedented mandate to prevent the kind of inflationary spiral that had led the country into an economic depression and widespread social unrest after the First World War. It would do so by establishing "safeguards under war conditions against any undue enhancement in the prices of food, fuel, and other necessaries of life, and [ensuring] an adequate supply and equitable distribution of such commodities."[8]

Despite this broad mandate, the WPTB played only a peripheral role in the lives of most Canadians before Gordon's appointment in the fall of 1941. Controls were limited mainly to the production and distribution of commodities and were not always readily apparent to the average Canadian. This changed rather dramatically when, on 8 October 1941, Prime Minister William Lyon Mackenzie King announced that comprehensive price, rent, and wage controls would be introduced starting on 1 December based on prices set during the basic period between 15 September and 11 October. This unprecedented state intervention into the consumer economy was spurred by an inflationary spike between August 1939 and October 1941 that saw food prices alone rise by more than 24 percent.[9] Much of this inflationary pressure was driven by the kind of rising consumption usually associated with periods of rapid economic growth. As a result of rising wages and nearly full employment, per capita civilian consumption soared between 1939 and 1943: milk products, by 18 percent; meat, by 12 percent; eggs, by 24 percent; and tomatoes and citrus fruits, by 20 percent. Canada's export commitments and the need to feed a rapidly growing military meant that food producers struggled to keep up with demand, and the result was both rising prices and shortages. Early in the war, the most serious shortages were of imported foods like tea, coffee, sugar, and rice. But by 1942 regional shortages of nearly every kind of commodity had begun to appear.[10]

While price controls promised to stem the inflationary tide before it destabilized the economy, it was clear that shortages and other supply problems necessitated additional state intervention. The WPTB's initial response was to establish regulations enforcing the equitable distribution of goods by wholesalers and manufacturers. But it quickly became apparent that regulation alone was not going to be sufficient, and the board was ultimately forced to take direct control over the distribution and purchase of commodities in short supply – including tea, coffee, sugar, and rice – by creating individual commodity administrations or larger bodies like the Wartime Food Corporation.[11] But even with WPTB intervention at the wholesale level, it soon became apparent that these controls were not enough to ensure fair distribution at the retail level. Throughout 1941 and 1942, consumers had to endure lineups, scour multiple stores for scarce goods, and navigate the kinds of informal and unfair rationing systems set up by shopkeepers. The WPTB initially responded to widespread sugar shortages by introducing laws against hoarding and by launching a national propaganda campaign. These laws were followed, however, by the introduction of a system of voluntary rationing in January 1942. The system made it illegal for any person to purchase sugar at the rate of more than three-quarters of a pound per person per week. This amount was reduced to half a pound in May. Over the next year, similar orders were established governing purchases of tea, coffee, and butter (see Figure 2.1). Unlike formal rationing, these orders were based on the "honour system," which meant in essence that consumers and retailers were being asked to police themselves. While this system was cheaper and less labour intensive than coupon rationing, many in the WPTB admitted that it had the drawback of "causing bitterness on the part of those who believe that their neighbors are less law-abiding than themselves."[12]

From the start, the public was skeptical of voluntary rationing, particularly because it was ultimately left up to retailers to ensure that all customers received a fair share. A February 1942 poll on voluntary sugar rationing suggested that 65 percent of Canadians felt that ration cards were necessary while only 29 percent felt that the honour system would work.[13] As it turned out, the public was largely right: shortages continued unabated, and informal rationing by retailers proved to be anything but fair. As a

Figure 2.1 Voluntary rationing was introduced for a number of products starting in early 1942 but was quickly replaced with coupon rationing. *Library and Archives Canada, PA108300.*

result, coupon rationing for sugar came into effect in July 1942, followed soon after by tea and coffee in August, butter in December, and meat in March of the following year (see Table 2.1). Consumer rationing by permit was introduced for a range of other items such as household appliances, alcohol, electrical supplies, phones, and farm machinery – things that were purchased infrequently or only by certain groups. But most household consumer durables became increasingly difficult to find as factories were converted to war production.[14] The result was that, except in remote communities and much of the North – where distribution was controlled by something approximating a permit system – coupon rationing of food and gasoline became the face of Canada's wartime command economy.

Table 2.1

Canadian per-person weekly ration, December 1942 to December 1946

Year	Sugar[a]	Butter	Meat	Tea[b]	Coffee[b]
1942	8 oz	8 oz.	–	1 oz	4 oz
1943	8 oz	8 oz.	1 to 2.5 lbs	1⅓ oz	5⅓ oz
1944	8 oz	7 oz.	–[c]	–[d]	–[d]
1945	6 oz	7 oz.	1 to 2.5 lbs	–	–
1946	7 oz	6 oz.	1 to 2.5 lbs	–	–

[a] Does not include preserves or canning rations, which varied between product and often by region.
[b] Limited to those over twelve years of age.
[c] Temporarily suspended starting in March 1944, resumed in September 1945.
[d] Suspended starting in September 1944.

"Three Million Price Cops"

Given the WPTB's broad mandate to control the prices and distribution of nearly all consumer goods, it became clear from the start that the success or failure of its economic controls would depend, in large part, on the voluntary cooperation of Canadians and that actual enforcement of these rules would prove to be a daunting and complex task. Price controls alone proved to be a massive regulatory headache. Because price ceilings were based on the maximum price that any given good was sold for during the basic period, this meant that ceilings varied, not only between communities or regions but from store to store. Occasional national rulings set maximum prices that superseded local ones, but this was not the case for the vast majority of consumer goods.[15]

An enforcement branch was created within the WPTB shortly after the imposition of price controls, but Gordon and other board officials decided from early on that they had neither the personnel nor the public support to hire the army of enforcement officers necessary to police thousands of regulations passed by the board. They instead decided to focus on achieving voluntary compliance. According to Gordon, not only did limiting the number of enforcement officers free up necessary "manpower" for the military and for essential war work, but it also went to the heart of Canada's fight against fascism because it would "prove to the world that *cooperation, not compulsion*, is the strength of *democracy*."[16] But even if the board had wanted to go the opposite route, Canada's so-called manpower shortage made it impossible. The Enforcement

Administration was, from the very outset, provided with only a limited staff.[17] Prince Edward Island, for instance, was initially assigned only one investigator and one enforcement counsel for the entire province. And, by 1943, the Enforcement Administration as a whole consisted of a national staff of only five hundred officers and fewer than fifty solicitors.[18] The WPTB therefore tended to ration its investigators' time, with the focus on specific, often symbolic prosecutions that boosted public confidence in wartime controls. In the early years, for instance, there was a clear tendency to concentrate mainly on infractions at the retail level and, even then, to undertake prosecutions "only in flagrant cases" so as to "avoid prosecutions of those who through mere ignorance and without gross negligence are guilty of an infraction."[19]

The WPTB relied on persuasion rather than coercion to encourage public compliance. It directed much of its attention to enlisting "Mrs. Consumer" – the WPTB's term for the typical housewife who, in the average family, was responsible for upwards of 85 percent of all retail purchases – to join in the fight against inflation and black marketeering. In his first public address after being appointed WPTB director, Gordon explicitly linked women's role as "the household buyers of the nation" to their patriotic duty to follow and indeed *enforce* the Board's regulations:

> Every woman must be a guardian of the price law. If you find some bootleg dealer, who wants you to conspire with him to break the law, you must not only refuse; you must also let him know, in unmistakable terms, that he is an enemy of his country ... The housewife must be the real guardian of the law. Her job, for her country, will be to watch prices every day. She is the soldier in the battle line.[20]

In a later speech to the Toronto Women's Canadian Club, Gordon was even more explicit about women's wartime responsibilities for the moral regulation of the marketplace. "In every walk of life," he told his audience, "the real arbiters of social conduct are the women":

> It is women who determine what kind of conduct is an offence to decent-living people. Women set our moral standards and nothing is more really devastating than an organized boycott by women ... It would be a very healthy and beneficial thing if women were to take a hand in disciplining some of those annoying people who are constantly belittling, disparaging and complaining.[21]

Figure 2.2 This WPTB poster perhaps best represents the board's vision of "Mrs. Consumer" as a specifically middle-class ideal. *Library and Archives Canada / Wartime Prices and Trade Board Collection / e010944100.*

Patriotic citizenship, in other words, carried with it important gendered ideals of national service. But implicit in the well-worn middle-class ideal of Mrs. Consumer the patriotic mother and responsible household manager was her much more important wartime role as first line of defence against illegal and unpatriotic behaviour in the marketplace (see Figure 2.2).[22] The WPTB therefore went to great lengths to gain women's support and direct participation in its efforts to regulate the consumer economy.

At the heart of these efforts to mobilize Canadian women was the Consumer Branch, which was created by the WPTB shortly after the introduction of price controls, and which, unlike much of the civil service, was run largely by women. Initially, the Consumer Branch was established with the stated goal of providing consumers with "a two-way representation; a channel through which they might convey their views to the Board, and through which Board rules and regulations might be simplified and passed on to organized groups."[23] Although Charlotte Whitton had played a key early role in the organization of the Consumer Branch, her resignation within only a few weeks of its creation led to the appointment of well-known *Chatelaine* editor Byrne Hope Sanders as the branch's first director. By June 1943, 75 women were employed by the Consumer Branch, including prominent Québécois journalist Corrine de la Durantaye as the Assistant Director and Head of Operations in Quebec, and well-known radio and newspaper personalities Kate Aitken and Irene Gougeon as senior representatives of the branch.[24] Early on, the Consumer Branch hoped to build women's trust by differentiating itself from other government departments. In particular, it tried to "approach consumers on problems concerning them, from their own viewpoint as consumers." Not only did most materials appear primarily in the women's sections of newspapers and in women's magazines, but they were also directed at a largely female audience in other ways. Strategies included the WPTB-produced radio soap opera *The Soldier's Wife* – or *La Métairie Rancourt* – which, in addition to its melodramatic story line, included an introduction by the "Household Counselor" or "L'Ami du Consommateur," who gave advice and updates on recent Board regulations.[25]

Although persuasion was an important aspect of the Consumer Branch's strategy, its efforts to garner more direct and durable links with individual women and women's organizations proved to be far more effective.[26] One of the Consumer Branch's earliest efforts was the introduction in 1942 of what became known as the "Blue Books" (because of their distinctive blue covers). These were essentially personal "Purchase Books" and were small enough to be carried in a woman's handbag. The idea was that shoppers would use these books to record the size, price, and other information about commonly purchased articles so that they could develop their own figures for each store's maximum ceiling prices.

Retailers were almost immediately wary of the Blue Book strategy and expressed concern that the WPTB would turn women into "three million price cops" whose goal was "to make their lives miserable."[27] For that reason, the WPTB was careful to remind women to avoid taking their task too far. The Blue Books themselves warned that the board did not want the shopper to be a "police woman" and that her job was just to "observe." Also, Gordon and Sanders publicly combatted the notion that women were serving as "informers," "snoopers," or "stool pigeons" by stressing the patriotic intentions of Consumer Branch volunteers as well as the fact that their presence limited the need for a more expensive and invasive enforcement apparatus.[28] In any case, most within the WPTB viewed the Blue Books less as an effective tool for securing convictions than as a symbolic resource upon which women could draw. One postwar analysis concluded that the books were important partly because "they served a definite purpose in lieu of a badge or price watching insignia, helping to identify women with the price control program [and] they were a constant reminder that women had been asked to do a job."[29]

In terms of enlisting ordinary women to participate in the WPTB's work, perhaps the most effective tool of the Consumer Branch was its national network of Women's Regional Advisory Committees (WRACs). By the end of the war, there were more than four hundred local WRACs, whose nearly 17,000 volunteers were committed to maintaining price ceilings and combatting local black markets. The typical WRAC consisted of a central administrative committee located in a major regional centre along with a network of subcommittees in each city or region. The goal was to establish some form of Consumer Branch representation in most Canadian cities or regions. To this end, the board initially called upon Canada's national women's organizations to elect liaison officers who would represent their local branches on these committees and subcommittees. By the end of the war, hundreds of English- and French-language committees were operating throughout the country, ranging in size from twenty-five to five hundred women. The overall membership was often quite diverse and included representatives from the more prominent middle-class women's organizations as well as women's labour union auxiliaries. Most importantly, more than one-third of Consumer Branch volunteers were francophones.[30]

At first, the Consumer Branch sought to use this network of volunteers as a kind of front-line force in their efforts to educate the public about the WPTB's regulations and how they would benefit consumers. Thus, WRACs became a key distribution channel for all kinds of educational and propaganda materials. The WPTB estimated that, because there were Consumer Branch liaison officers in nearly every women's organization in the country, this network had the capacity to reach as many as one-third of all Canadian women.[31] Materials distributed using these channels therefore included pamphlets with titles such as "Is the Cost of Living Index Phoney"; posters depicting "Mrs. Consumer's Nightmare of Inflation"; and even one-act plays, pre-written public speeches, and displays designed for fall fairs. Perhaps the most important use of this network as a distribution channel, however, was for the monthly publication *Consumers' News,* which contained information on all kinds of supply, price, and rationing regulations. By the fall of 1945, the circulation was 206,500 for the English edition and 107,000 for the French *Le Bulletin des Consommateurs,* both of which were distributed primarily through the WRAC network.[32]

Relatively quickly, volunteers began to exert more control over their local committees. Local WRAC meetings regularly discussed new regulations and rulings, but as often as not they also discussed consumer complaints about both local retailers and the WPTB itself. The September 1943 meeting of the Victoria WRAC was, in many ways, typical of the hundreds of meetings that were held around the country throughout the war. It began with a reading of new meat regulations, followed by a number of practical questions from attendees seeking clarification on matters such as the price of eggs and what constituted a dressed fowl. Most of the meeting, however, was devoted to suggestions for improvements to WPTB regulations. Resolutions were passed on to Ottawa regarding underwear supplies, the need to ration all "essential commodities" in short supply, and the need for more meat, fish, and fowl sandwich pastes. Other suggestions passed along included complaints about the size of jam containers, the distribution of faulty canning rings, the wastage of food in restaurants, and the need for meat coupons that could be divided into smaller purchases. The members even found the time to criticize the WPTB radio drama *Soldier's Wife* because "the information was valuable but the story itself was very mediocre."[33]

The Consumer Branch quickly began to use these kinds of WRAC reports and meeting minutes as an important means of gauging the public response to specific WPTB policies. With thousands of individuals sending letters to the board either lodging complaints about regulations or reporting infractions of the board's rules, WRAC reports became an essential means for judging the reliability of this correspondence. By the end of the war, the branch was operating on the assumption that "any complaint or expression of opinion which appeared over and over again in these reports from different parts of the country, could reasonably be taken as representative of the general public feeling on the matter."[34]

By 1943, the Consumer Branch was also asking volunteers to participate in more comprehensive, statistical studies of the effectiveness of consumer controls. This effort included Consumer Questionnaire Panels that involved between 2,500 and 3,000 women filling out detailed questionnaires about anything from home canning practices to sugar usage and the rationing of preserves.[35] WRACs were also used to establish what, at its wartime peak, would be 116 individual Price Study Panels located in a number of urban and rural communities across the country. Essentially, these panels were groups of Consumer Branch volunteers who provided monthly reports on the prices paid at local stores for a selected list of items as well as occasional reports on topics such as the use of ration coupons, shortages of certain goods, and the quality of foods like Canada Approved Flours.[36]

One of the key reasons why the WRAC network proved to be such an important resource – not only providing information on changing local conditions and public opinion but also supplying volunteers to sit on at least 70 percent of the more than six hundred local ration boards that were established after 1942[37] – was that many women began to strongly identify with the WPTB's stated goals of maintaining equitable distribution and curbing inflation. Patriotism no doubt played an important part in this, but for many, the experience of the pre-rationing and pre-price control period was an important motivating factor. Coupon rationing, for its part, proved to be a respite from dealing with shortages and subjecting oneself to the whims of individual shopkeepers. Historians have often assumed that rationing was only a burden on shoppers, yet WRAC meetings often included resolutions requesting that *additional* items be rationed. Prior to the coupon rationing of butter, for instance, many women complained to the board that voluntary rationing was insufficient. Working women in Montreal expressed resentment that "butter stocks in some stores were sold out before they got home from work" and "felt they had been penalized for the faults of others."[38] In 1942, prior to the introduction of meat rationing, a recently married soldier's wife told the CBC:

> In Halifax, the large meat stores have it, but they keep it for their regular customers. Since we've just been married a short while, we are out of luck. The other day I went into a store and saw some Hamburg Steak on the counter: now that is a poor substitute for the beef I wanted, but it would have done. So I said to the butcher, "Will you give me a pound and a half of hamburger?" But he refused. And that was that.[39]

Even when this kind of informal rationing had a more honest motive, it was, as one Dartmouth, Nova Scotia, resident told the WIB, no substitute for coupon rationing. "Our stores very often have goods marked 'one to a customer.' One housewife, who has a family of five to provide for and so has to go [to] a store five times, remarked that rationing is so much fairer."[40]

The success of the WRACs and their subcommittees can therefore also be attributed partly to the fact that they enabled women to take some direct action to defend their interests as consumers and as citizens. Although the official propaganda narrative of the Consumer Branch stressed the *obligations* of wartime consumer citizenship, many women also began to articulate a parallel discourse, one that stressed their *rights* as consumers. Many groups even sought to take an active role in the enforcement of WPTB regulations. In January 1944, the Montreal WRAC – perhaps one of the more militant in the country – went so far as to create and widely publicize a telephone number that the public could use to lodge anonymous complaints about retailers. Soon after, they were receiving seven hundred calls per month.[41] In October 1944, the same WRAC conducted a sweep of fruit and vegetable prices in 454 stores that uncovered a total of 279 infractions. Although not all WRACs went as far as the Montreal group, many regularly reported price and supply violations to the WPTB, and to that end enforcement officials around the country even began to use the WRACs to screen public complaints before investigators were sent to examine the alleged infraction in person.[42] Clearly, due to a combination of patriotic enthusiasm and a growing sense of their rights as consumers, Consumer Branch volunteers had become a vital component of the WPTB's efforts to ensure the success of its unprecedented economic stabilization program.

Equality of Sacrifice

Consumer Branch volunteers undoubtedly represented a segment of the population who were most committed to wartime controls. There were many indications, however, that controls had also garnered broad support among the public as a whole. Both within and outside the WPTB, many expressed surprise when a poll taken shortly after the December 1941 introduction of comprehensive wage and price controls showed 76 percent of respondents expressing their support for both sets of controls. This was partly confirmed by other polls from the same period, which found that most Canadians felt they were not being asked to make *enough* sacrifices for the war effort. Throughout the early years of the war, in other words, many saw rationing and other controls as not only inevitable but also necessary to support Canadian allies and soldiers overseas.[43]

In part, this support for food rationing and other WPTB programs reflected the fact that controls on consumption were not nearly as onerous as those in Europe. In Britain, meat rations were half the size of their Canadian equivalents, all fats (and not just butter) were rationed, and there were limits placed on cheese consumption. German-occupied France was getting by on even less: its weekly ration for meat was one-seventh of Canada's, its butter ration a little more than half, its sugar ration one-quarter, and bread and milk were also rationed.[44] Besides which, most Canadians had at least some access to unrationed sources of nearly all rationed foods. Farm families that produced their own meat or butter faced few legal checks on their consumption, only the request that they try to "live within the spirit of the ration."[45] In cities, Canadians had regular access to additional rationed commodities in restaurants, hotels, bakeries, corner stores, and a range of other establishments selling pre-prepared foods. This kind of off-ration consumption was limited, to a certain degree, by legal restrictions on portion sizes, the introduction of meatless days on Tuesdays (and later Fridays), and the fact that such establishments were subject to industrial rationing based on a quota system. Even so, many Canadians were able to supplement their sugar, meat, butter, tea, and coffee consumption without the use of coupons.

But the WPTB quickly realized that even its generous ration allotments and the multiple outlets for off-ration foods did not guarantee long-term public support for its policies. By 1943, complaints about various aspects of the board's economic controls had begun to mount, and after a series of internal polls conducted throughout the year, many board members began to fear they were losing public support. For instance, a national poll completed in September 1943 found that support for price and wage ceilings had fallen from 80 percent at the beginning of the year to a low of 69 percent nationally, with even weaker support in Quebec.[46] Another poll, conducted earlier in the year, had found that only 45 percent of respondents supported the implementation of more restrictions even though plans for meat rationing had yet to be officially announced.[47] These polls still suggested that the vast majority of Canadians supported the continuation of most existing controls. Even so, the WPTB began to worry that the public was growing "war weary" and correspondingly more likely to attempt to bypass legal supply channels. Others interpreted these polling data as proof, not just that war weariness was taking root, but that official propaganda and public education efforts had thus far been insufficient.

Under the leadership of John Grierson and a new group of civil service mandarins trained in the social sciences, the government's new propaganda arm – the Wartime Information Board (WIB) – launched a campaign that went beyond simple appeals to patriotism and instead stressed the self-interest of consumers in avoiding the inflationary spiral of the previous war. As William Young has noted, the WIB crafted a message "that took into account their research on the attitudes of the individual citizen as consumer" by emphasizing the concept of "participant citizenship and the responsibilities of the individual."[48] At the same time, it emphasized that economic controls were grounded in the principle of "equality of sacrifice" and therefore promised a net benefit to all Canadians.[49]

Clearly, this kind of shift in persuasive techniques was doomed to fail if Canadians could not see evidence that controls were actually working and were – perhaps more importantly – truly fair. The problem in 1943 was that many Canadians had begun to see compelling evidence that they *were* being unfairly penalized by certain wartime controls. During the first round of meat rationing, for instance, the WPTB received complaints from Catholics that they were being asked to make a greater dietary sacrifice than non-Catholics, given that they already abided by meatless Fridays for religious reasons.[50] But it was not until a national protest over the rationing of canning sugar in 1943 that the WPTB realized that, when confronted with blatant unfairness, even its strongest supporters might turn against its rules and regulations.

At the heart of the canning sugar controversy was a growing popular perception that some regions were being treated unfairly following a change in the way canning sugar was allotted to households. When sugar rationing was first introduced in July 1942, the WPTB decided against setting an upper limit on how much sugar could be purchased for canning or jam making. Instead, consumers were asked to fill out purchase vouchers signed by the storekeeper that limited sugar purchases to one half-pound of sugar for each pound of fruit being preserved. The following year, the increased popularity of home canning combined with limited sugar supplies led to the adoption of a stricter rationing system. Each ration district was given an overall per capita canning sugar allotment based on an average consumption of 10 pounds for urban and 11 pounds for rural households, but the actual size of these rations was left up to local ration boards. The result was nationwide divergences in ration allotments, which now ranged from 8 to 15 pounds. In the twin cities of Kitchener and Waterloo, Ontario, for instance, the Kitchener ration board allotted 11.5 pounds for urban and 13.5 pounds for rural residents, while in Waterloo it was 11 and 12 pounds.

In Penticton, BC, in one of Canada's leading fruit-growing regions, residents wondered why they were receiving 10 pounds while Vancouver residents were getting 11 pounds.[51]

The WPTB was unprepared for the scale of protest against the 1943 canning sugar allotments. Almost immediately after the announcement, the board was flooded with petitions and angry letters from a range of individuals and organizations around the country. In Victoria, a Sugar Protest Committee was formed by local women's, farmers', and labour organizations. Other protests came from groups – ranging from local ration boards, WRACs, and newspaper editorial boards – that had otherwise been the board's strongest supporters. This outcry was driven in large part by the unfairness and seeming randomness of the ration allotments. The *Halifax Herald* was "indignant" that its residents were only allowed eight pounds while parts of Quebec got fifteen pounds, calling it "one of the most unjust and unreasonable impositions of a long series of discriminations."[52] Many rural women wondered why areas with the highest domestic production of fresh fruit were being asked to cut down on their preserving in order to provide sugar to urban women who had never canned before and who thus would likely either spoil good fruit through inexperience or simply put the sugar to other uses. And as members of the Hillmond, Saskatchewan, WRAC argued, canning was essential to the rural household economy in a way that was not true for most urban families. Rural residents of the Prairies had little access to items available in cities like maple syrup, molasses, and raisins, not to mention store-bought off-ration desserts and sweets. The result, they argued, was that most rural women "depend[ed] entirely on the fruits of their gardens and wild fruits for stocking their cupboards the year round."[53]

These protests highlighted the importance of maintaining a sense of equality of sacrifice when it came to distributing scarce goods. Most women recognized that they would not be able to preserve as many foods as they had in the past and that the world sugar situation demanded they make sacrifices. But they also needed to be convinced that they were making the same sacrifice as every other Canadian family. In particular, the rural protests highlighted how difficult it was to maintain this sense of equality in a country divided between starkly different urban and rural economies. Sugar had a very different meaning for rural women than for urban residents because the latter had far greater access to consumer goods like store-bought jam, preserves, and baked sweets. The situation was therefore only defused after the WPTB adopted a new rationing system that was more consistent and that responded to this rural/urban divide: a universal national ration of ten pounds per household was adopted, but rural women were given the option of converting their preserves coupons for up to thirteen additional pounds of canning sugar over the course of the year.[54] The latter change, in particular, did not simply reflect an improved sugar supply but also recognized that the home production of preserves was as economically important as the industrial production of these goods.

To a certain extent, the 1943 canning sugar protests highlighted some of the inequalities inherent in the WPTB's system of controls. The board contended that rationing was fair and demanded an equal sacrifice from all Canadians, yet it was apparent that many groups, regions, and occupations felt they were being treated unequally. Quebecers were always high on the WPTB's list of "danger groups" whose support for controls was perceived as being soft.[55] Of course, it is important not to overstate opposition to wartime controls in Quebec, given that polls rarely showed support dropping below 50 percent in the province. That said, WPTB officials nonetheless did have cause for concern.[56] Anti-federalist sentiment in Quebec had been rising during the war, partly because of the prolonged controversy over conscription and partly because Ottawa was extending its reach into what were believed to be provincial affairs. Maurice Duplessis, leader of the Union Nationale, for his part attacked controls as "restrictions, vexatoires, stupides, inopportunes, intempestives," and warned that "la BUREAUCRATIE remplace la démocratie."[57]

Wartime polls may have reflected the fact that many French Canadian nationalists harboured a strong mistrust of the federal government's wartime economic policies. But in addition to this, Gordon and other WPTB officials tended to overlook their own role in facilitating anti-WPTB sentiment in Quebec. With the notable exception of the Consumer Branch, the WPTB bureaucracy was overwhelmingly anglophone and, as many have noted, the WPTB director had a poor relationship with his personnel from Quebec. This led to difficulties retaining trained staff and, ultimately, to communication problems between the board and French Canadians more generally. Translations of WPTB orders, for instance, were often of very poor quality and often arrived days after their English versions.[58] As Christopher Waddell has suggested: "Without a strong French presence in the controls programme, French Canadians had no trouble in seeing the WPTB and its activities as an exercise that applied only to the English."[59]

Gordon, for his part, argued that the WPTB's approval ratings in Quebec were low because "the temperament of French Quebec differs from that of the English speaking elements in its attitude towards the law." He added that many simply didn't understand the regulations and, therefore, that "prosecutions have been instituted by a feeling on the part of the trade that 'we can't help it; if we are caught we will pay the fine. It's part of the cost of living business in wartime.'"[60] Yet there is considerable evidence that this attitude – especially among retailers – had much more to do with the policies of WPTB enforcement officials than with the "temperament" of French Canadians. As discussed earlier, most provincial enforcement officials chose to gain public support for controls by being relatively lenient in their treatment of violations in the early months of price control and rationing. Investigators around the country tended to let individual retailers or consumers off with a warning if there was evidence that WPTB rules had been broken by accident or without malicious intent. The Nova Scotia office, for instance, reported that it had decided in the early years to "pursue a policy of education and persuasion with the merchants, rather than prosecution and coercion."[61] In Quebec, however, the office chose to take what it described as "the reverse attitude": "the first step to be taken in educating the public was to strike vigorously at the offenders which [fell] into the hands of our investigational staff." According to leading provincial enforcement officials, new investigators were "enlisted in a crusade against the war's profiteers" and were "scandalized when they de[t]ected the slightest infraction."[62] And although Quebec's investigators were willing to use highly effective but controversial strategies such as "test purchasing" – in which used plainclothes enforcement investigators attempt to buy goods illegally – such strategies were avoided in other parts of the country such as northern Ontario and the Maritimes because test purchasing was "deemed not publicly acceptable."[63]

One immediate effect of such policies was that they created a perception that Quebecers were more likely to bypass regulations. The larger number of convictions, coupled with the tendency of Quebec courts to come down harder on violators of WPTB regulations, buttressed the already widespread opinion among English Canadians that Quebec led the country in black market transactions.[64] Historians to the present day accept as "fact" that Montreal was the worst offender in wartime black market transactions. The persistence of this myth is strong evidence that the WPTB's policies in Quebec were something of a self-fulfilling prophecy: assumptions about Quebec drove stricter enforcement policy there, which reinforced the assumptions on which that policy was based. All of this strengthened public resentment against the WPTB in Quebec.[65]

In addition to such variable enforcement regimes, there are a number of ways in which anti-WPTB sentiment was closely tied to perceptions – and often the reality – that certain regions or groups were being discriminated against. Organized labour often complained that the official cost-of-living index was being manipulated in order to prevent workers from gaining the cost-of-living bonuses to which they were entitled. When wage controls were introduced in late 1941, wage increases were tied directly to changes in the cost-of-living index, and this led many workers to wonder whether the board's policies were keeping down the prices of items on the index while letting prices for other, no-less-essential goods rise. Food, which accounted for 31 percent of the index, was singled out for criticism because the prices of foods *not* included in the official grocery basket of 47 items tracked by the index – such as fresh fruits and vegetables – rose much more quickly than the items that *were* on the list. By 1943, for instance, in many Ontario communities, the prices of products like cabbage and lettuce had increased by 100 to 300 percent over 1942 levels.[66]

Although some WPTB officials suggested that these perceptions were due to both a misunderstanding of how the index worked and women's "natural tendancy [sic] to exaggerate," the reality was that such criticisms were not so far-fetched.[67] Indeed, many of the WPTB's consumer and producer subsidies were disproportionately skewed towards foods specific-ally included in the index, such as milk, oranges, tea, coffee, and sugar, to the point that Christopher Waddell has argued that the board used subsidies to "manipulate the official cost of living index, creating the impression of controlling inflation while preventing the payment of cost of living bonuses to the nation's workers."[68] In other words, claims of unfairness were often grounded in instances when there was a genuine gap between the WPTB's rhetoric and the reality of its policies.

Perhaps the most dramatic protest against the class and regional biases of WPTB policies began in September 1945, when more than nine thousand coal miners in Alberta and British Columbia walked off the job for nearly three weeks to protest the reintroduction of meat rationing following its temporary suspension in March 1944. According to the miners, the strike began as a protest against the size of the meat rations, which they argued were insufficient for men doing "heavy work." Their demands were for "double rations" of red meat and the "removal of restrictions on certain cooked specialties" from the new ration order, which – unlike its less restrictive predecessor – required the use of ration coupons for a wide range of cooked, smoked, and preserved meats.[69] In some ways, the miners' complaint was not a new one. The WPTB had dealt with calls for "dif-ferential rationing" from workers in heavy industries like logging, steel production, and coal mining since rationing was first introduced in 1942. Generally, the issue was framed in terms of the "common sense" idea that male workers in heavy industries required more food than women, children, or "white collar" urban workers. A resolution passed in support of the miners by a group of farmers and lumber workers in Clearwater, BC, for instance, argued: "If 2 lbs of meat a week are sufficient for M.P. Ministers and M.L.A. it is not enough for the real workers."[70] Another attacked the "various Women's Society's [sic] who are in favor of Meat Rationing" by pointing out that "these ladies don't have to work at 8.00 in the morning in a factory or do any manual work so they can live on Plum Pudding or Ice Cream and Cake."[71]

Such arguments built upon widely held assumptions about the embodied requirements of working-class masculinity that, in all likelihood, had also contributed to the higher rates of malnutrition observed by Canadian nutrition experts among women and children *within families* during the 1930s and 1940s. Men, it was widely assumed, simply needed more food – and more meat in particular – in order to do the kinds of manual labour associated with working-class occupations, even if it came at the expense of other family members' nutritional needs. And in fact, such notions seemed to be supported by the rhetoric of Canada's leading nutrition experts, who – especially in the early years of the war – offered their expertise as a possible solution to both Canada's manpower shortages and the alarmingly high rates of military rejections.

These popular views about working-class masculinity and men's nutritional needs were widely held during this period, to the degree that even Donald Gordon worried that the extra needs of industrial workers were threatening to derail Canada's meat rationing program because "the logic underlying such a demand [was] almost unanswerable."[72] At the same time, WPTB staff recognized that operating such a system would be a logistical nightmare and that the general public would not accept a system that was too complicated or that was perceived as unequal. Fortunately for Gordon, the WPTB's Advisory Committee on Nutrition came out in support of the board's 1943 meat ration allotment by arguing that the weekly ration of approximately two pounds of edible meat plus other non-rationed sources actually provided "more protein from animal sources to satisfy nutritional requirements than is required for a person of any occupation."[73] While few workers in heavy industries truly accepted this, the reality during the first round of meat rationing in 1943 and 1944 was that few workers were limited to two pounds per week. In part this was because all family members were provided with equal ration allotments, regardless of age. A family of five, for instance, received a ration allotment of at least ten pounds, even though most children required a fraction of their parents' consumption. Also, many workers had access to unrationed meats in canteens and restaurants as well as through the purchase of non-rationed cooked or smoked meats, canned meats, and sandwich spreads. In addition, industrial canteens were exempt from the rules governing meatless days and were given more generous meat quotas than restaurants. As a whole, this meant that most workers were able to consume as much meat as their pre-war norm and in some cases more.

This was not equally true for all workers, however. Workers in smaller cities and rural areas had decidedly less access to off-ration foods than their urban counterparts, and this was particularly true for coal-mining areas in western Canada and the Maritimes. This led to a number of labour actions, culminating in the 1945 meat strike. Most of these originated in complaints over the size of ration allotments, which miners argued were too small to account for their heavy underground work. Face-to-face negotiations with WPTB officials sometimes did lead to important compromises. During the 1943 negotiations over the size of the butter ration between WPTB representatives and miners in Glace Bay, Nova Scotia, for instance, the board was able to convince the miners to stay on the job, but only after agreeing to investigate miners' complaints about prices and supplies and to provide them with extra supplies of substitute sandwich spreads in short supply, including canned meat, preserves, and peanut butter. Later protests similarly saw agreements wherein the WPTB agreed to deal immediately with local shortages in butter, potatoes, children's clothing, and alarm clocks.[74]

The threat of labour action by miners and other workers in heavy industries sometimes succeeded in gaining exemptions to the rationing rules. In 1943, for example, the threat of a work slowdown enabled underground soft coal miners to reach an agreement with the WPTB wherein they could gain double rations of tea and coffee based on the quasi-medical reason that "the nature of their work requires a substantial extra intake of fluids while at work."[75] The reality, however, was that these extra rations amounted to a recognition by the board that most industrial workers in urban areas had access to off-ration sources of tea and coffee during their breaks and that miners were in need of some special consideration. This was true for other occupational groups as well. During harvest and threshing season, the ration allotments for farmhands were increased by two-thirds to allow for two extra meals per day, and unionized railway employees whose work kept them from home for periods of more than thirty-six hours were given extra allotments of most rationed items. The most dramatic concession, however, was when the board provided loggers eating in work camps with a quota that allowed for nearly four times the civilian meat ration – nearly seven pounds per person per week – and nearly three times the civilian sugar ration. The board justified this unequal treatment in part because loggers had no access to sources of off-ration foods but also because they worried that it was simply "not feasible" to reduce these rations much more than the pre-war consumption of twelve pounds of meat per week in most logging camps without risking work stoppages and manpower shortages.[76]

It was perhaps no surprise, then, that the western coal miners were able to gain important concessions from the board following their twenty-day strike. While they did not receive the double meat rations they had initially demanded, a system was established wherein miners with fewer than two children under the age of twelve and no local access to restaurants or canteens were provided with an additional two ration coupons per month from their local ration board – a roughly 40 percent increase over normal civilian meat rations. In other words, the agreement recognized that miners with young children were at a distinct advantage over those without and that miners in remote areas had less access to off-ration foods than workers in cities under the new, more restrictive ration regime.[77] Although, to a certain extent, this and other instances of differential rationing are examples of how essential workers applying pressure on the WPTB could occasionally receive special treatment, they are perhaps even more important as examples of how the success of the ration system depended on the belief that it was fair and equitable to all.

"Thank God for Price Control"

In spite of the government's worries about "war weariness" – and despite a handful of high-profile protests against WPTB policies – public support for price controls and rationing showed signs of strengthening from its 1943 lows. Rationing, in particular, managed to regain surprisingly high levels of public support. In separate polls conducted in March and July 1945, more than 90 percent of Canadians agreed that rationing had done a good or fair job in achieving equitable distribution. Even in Quebec, where there was supposedly the most public opposition, only 16 percent reported dissatisfaction with rationing.[78] As one postwar WPTB analyst summed up Canadians' attitudes, "rationing has consistently given evidence of being the most popular among Canada's wartime controls, a fact that is especially significant when one remembers that it has been more a part and parcel of every day living than any of the other controls have been."[79] Moreover, the fact that women were consistently the strongest supporters of rationing was not lost on WIB analysts, who remarked that this support was "all the more striking because of the more direct impact of rationing on [women]: they do the shopping, handle the ration books, and eat fewer meals in restaurants."[80]

The broad base of this support was also indicated by polls conducted regarding the possibility of rationing being continued after the war. In a January 1944 poll, 70 percent of the respondents agreed that rationing would be necessary well into the postwar period, with only 18 percent disapproving of such plans. Even a predicted public backlash against the reintroduction of meat rationing in September 1945 largely failed to materialize, despite polls suggesting weak support for the plan.[81] In part, this was because opposition to rationing had been significantly weakened by an unpopular national butchers' strike that, in Montreal, degenerated into violence, intimidation, and looting after clashes between police and protesters led to more than seventy-five arrests and one police officer being hospitalized with a fractured skull.[82] Canadians had at first been sympathetic to the butchers' position that voluntary rationing would be sufficient to reduce meat consumption. Many, however, came to feel alienated by a strike that hit consumers the hardest. Indeed, national polls indicated that few outside of heavy industry considered the new meat ration to be a hardship, with 77 percent agreeing that the newly reduced meat ration was sufficient.[83] The same was largely true in terms of public support for other economic controls. In separate WIB and WPTB polls conducted during the spring and summer of 1945, more than 85 percent of the public expressed approval of price and wage controls – a considerable improvement over their 1943 lows.[84]

Part of this improvement can be attributed to the fact that many of the issues that had weakened support for wartime food rationing and price controls had been at least partly addressed. Whether it was through individual negotiations with unions or through the modification of unpopular regulations such as the 1943 canning sugar ration allotments, the board was generally able to respond quickly to sources of major discontent. In part, this was because it had developed a remarkable range of opinion-gathering tools, which included regular public opinion polls, field reports by WIB "correspondents" in more than 140 communities, WRAC meeting minutes, and a weekly national press review of more than three hundred newspapers and magazines.[85] By the war's end, the Consumer Branch had even developed a network of nearly 1,700 "labour liaisons," who regularly reported on problems with price controls and rationing among workers in a range of different industries.[86] For organized labour, the program brought greater attentiveness to their local issues – and often timely solutions to problems related to prices and supplies. In addition, the reports of the labour liaisons gave the board a sense of where "pressure" and "resentment" among organized labour was rising.[87] Although most male labour liaisons balked at Consumer Branch activities such as price checking – which, according to the chief labour liaison Christine White, "they consider to be a woman's job" – they nonetheless showed appreciation for even this token representation within the WPTB. Through their regular communications with the Consumer Branch, moreover, they even enabled White to help avert a number of threatened strikes.[88]

But perhaps the most important reason for these high approval ratings for food rationing and price controls was that – for most Canadians, at least – they had succeeded in keeping down inflation and distributing goods equitably. Both wartime observers like the US Brookings Institute and later historians have generally agreed that despite the sheer enormity of the task and the WPTB's limited ability to enforce compliance with its own directives, Canada's economic controls were "unquestionably the most successful of that of any of belligerents."[89] This verdict is partly borne out in Canada's wartime inflation statistics. The official cost-of-living index had risen by 17.8 percent prior to the introduction of price controls but by only 4.7 percent between the universal price and wage freeze in December 1941 and the end of the war in August 1945. And even the prices of foods *not* included in the index began to stabilize or decrease in the final years of the war due to improved supplies and the establishment of firmer price ceilings on fresh fruits and vegetables. The success of rationing and other controls on supplies was similarly borne out by the fact that Canada continued to meet and often exceed its export commitments to Britain and other allies throughout the war even while maintaining domestic levels of consumption in rationed and non-rationed goods that were comparable to and often in excess of pre-war norms.[90]

The successes of food rationing and price controls have largely been overlooked in recent social histories of Canada's Second World War, which have more often focused on the "less inspiring" story of those who engaged in black market transactions. Jeffrey Keshen in particular has written extensively on the operation of wartime black markets and has shown that, throughout the war, thousands of Canadians skirted the rules regarding rationing, price controls, and other WPTB regulations.[91] It is difficult to measure the scale of the wartime black markets with any accuracy, given

86   CHAPTER 2

the WPTB's limited enforcement capacity and the difficulty in quantifying illegal activities, but the evidence that does exist suggests that only a small minority of Canadians were knowingly involved in sustained black market activity. For instance, while WPTB enforcement officials investigated nearly 35,000 possible infractions every month, the number of convictions never exceeded 5,000 per year – a surprisingly small number, especially given that there were literally thousands of separate prices and supply regulations in place.[92] In part, these low figures reflect the limits placed on the Enforcement Administration, which tended to treat smaller infractions leniently. Even so, there is little compelling evidence that more than a small minority of Canadians regularly broke the rules. At the time, regional enforcement officials typically reported widespread compliance with major board regulations, and public support would likely have been significantly lower had Canadians felt that their neighbours were regularly getting more than their fair share.[93]

Perhaps far more interesting than the fact that some Canadians broke WPTB rules was that a significant majority of Canadians actually chose to follow these increasingly complex regulations in the context of an unprecedented level of state control over nearly every economic transaction, or that they even expressed support for continuing such controls well into the postwar period. To a certain extent, this latter trend could be viewed as part of the much broader growth in support for increased government intervention in the economy during peacetime, not just to prevent inflation and ensure equitable distribution, but also to ensure that all Canadians had access to food and other necessities. In one 1943 poll, 44 percent of respondents actually agreed with the seemingly radical proposal that "it would be a good idea for the government to run all industries that handle and distribute certain necessities of life – like milk, bread, meat and fuel – and sell them to the public without profit."[94] This was followed by a December 1943 poll which found that by more than a two-to-one margin, Canadians preferred public over private ownership of utilities like water, gas, and electricity.[95]

This desire for significant changes to the economic status quo was also reflected in growing national support for the social democratic message of the CCF and in the significant leftward lurch of the Liberal and (newly Progressive) Conservative parties in the face of a growing public consensus that state intervention in the postwar economy was both necessary and desirable.[96] Historians have paid considerable attention to this latter trend, yet their analyses are typically disconnected from discussions about Canadians' experience with the wartime command economy. There is, however, evidence that the success of controls on food prices and supplies played no small role in changing public attitudes. In part the wartime controls seemed to promise a marketplace governed by a kind of "moral economy" in which consumers' rights to fair prices and to a fair share of scarce necessities were guaranteed by the state.[97] Many consumers found this a great improvement over an unregulated capitalist marketplace that, particularly in the early years of the war, saw retailers unilaterally oversee massive price increases and impose "unofficial" rationing for the benefit of preferred customers. In the aftermath of the Montreal butchers' strike, for instance, one Montrealer who favoured the reimposition of meat rationing wrote to the WPTB, "If the merchants want fair treatment let them in turn give fair treatment to the consumer. The trouble appears to be that they will not be able to fool the public as they have been doing in the past."[98]

Perhaps the most consistently enthusiastic supporters of the WPTB's price control and rationing efforts were the women who volunteered their time to their local WRAC. In a series of more than one thousand questionnaire surveys filled out by Consumer Branch volunteers in December 1945, the respondents tended to indicate enthusiastic support for continuing controls. Rationing was generally popular, with some, like Mrs. Wm. Taylor of Toronto, suggesting that extending rationing to items like shortening and soap chips "would be a grand solution, and a wonderful saving of time and nervous energy." Price controls seemed to be even more popular, with Mrs. Bazil Darling of Victoria writing that she "hoped that Price Control will be kept in effect for a long time yet" and Mrs. J. Purdie simply declaring, "Thank God for Price Control!"[99]

These questionnaire responses seemed to indicate that Consumer Branch volunteers did not support price controls and food rationing simply out of a sense of patriotic duty, although that was indeed an important motivation. These women's voluntary participation as Consumer Branch liaisons or on local ration boards was also rooted in the belief that the WPTB's economic controls were helping them defend their economic rights to fair treatment as consumers and as citizens. One Consumer Branch official would reflect after the war that the WPTB's efforts succeeded in large part because consumers "felt that price control was their programme."[100] Indeed, many WRACs felt comfortable enough in their authority as representatives of the broader interests of consumers that they were often highly critical of the WPTB. At the March 1944 meeting of the Northern Ontario WRAC, for instance, there were some "very spirited and hot discussions" on the topic of "political economy." As a result, the members passed an astute motion criticizing the statistical methods used to calculate cost-of-living increases and requesting that "a more revealing table of living prices be compiled."[101] The same WRAC, however, did not see this criticism as undermining its members' overall support for the WPTB's program. At one point, they went so far as to pass a resolution affirming that they "will cooperate cheerfully in this effort for our country's welfare."[102]

Clearly, many Consumer Branch volunteers did not see themselves simply as passive defenders of WPTB directives. Volunteers in many of the more active WRACs felt emboldened, empowered, and politicized through their work for the Consumer Branch. The Toronto Price Study Panel described its regular meetings as resembling "a university seminar or forum studying Price Control." Their meetings, however, were not used to simply learn and interpret WPTB regulations. Instead, the members were united by their common goal of keeping down the cost of living and, to that end, described the fight against inflation as "not only a government undertaking but a political undertaking."[103] For these women, in other words, participating in a forum designed to ensure fair prices and equitable distribution of consumer goods was a way for them to articulate and defend their rights as both consumers and citizens. As Alice Kessler Harris has argued, gender "constitutes a central piece of the social imaginary around which social organization and ideas of fairness are constructed and on which social policies are built."[104] In other words, as they embraced their wartime role as "Mrs. Consumer," thousands of ordinary women in Canada turned to the Consumer Branch and their local WRAC to make their voices heard and to challenge their exclusion from the governance of the marketplace.

One of the unintended consequences of their Consumer Branch work was that many women began to feel that not *enough* was being done to protect their economic rights. For instance, following a discussion of the deteriorating quality of goods during a June 1944 meeting of the Montreal WRAC, one member suggested that women resort to more radical measures if the board was unwilling to respond to their complaints:

> Why do the women not get together and boycott these organizations selling inferior goods? We should all get together and do something. We should do something through our Women's organizations. Resolutions going to the government are not attended to, unless we have concerted action ... In our organization [Women's Volunteer Services Bureau] we have 34 Branches

across Canada; when we want anything we all go after Ottawa together, and we always get what we want. They don't like us, but we get what we want.[105]

Although this particular passage was deleted from the minutes later sent out to members, the same WRAC made it clear at a later meeting that its members were not averse to applying the same techniques to the WPTB itself after WRAC members threatened to stop reporting offences to the board unless they saw better responsiveness to their complaints.[106] Indeed, although the Consumer Branch had generally managed to channel this kind of frustration into officially sanctioned activities, it became increasingly clear following the end of the war that many Canadian women were far more committed to the continuation of economic controls than to the WPTB itself.

Organized Consumers and the Postwar Politics of Consumption

Early in the war, the editors of the trade magazine *Food in Canada* half-jokingly warned that women's participation in the work of the Consumer Branch could lead them to "acquire a better technique in the use of the boycott" and suggested that they "hate to think what three million housewives could do to a product's market if they decided it wasn't worth the price asked!"[107] But after the war, when housewives across the country launched a series of protests against an October 1946 increase of between 17 and 33 percent in the ceiling price for milk, it became clear to government officials and retailers that Canadian women were indeed willing to take direct action in the face of rising prices.[108] These early protests ranged from a petition signed by nearly three thousand Moose Jaw residents calling for a return of the milk subsidy to an actual boycott during which hundreds of Ottawa housewives cut their milk purchases by 50 percent in an effort to reverse the three-cent-per-quart increase in milk prices.[109] All of this was soon followed by an unprecedented wave of organized consumer activism in opposition to the government's postwar decontrol policies and the rapidly rising cost of food after 1946.

At the heart of this rise in consumer activism was a growing tension between women who had grown to value the government's regulation of the consumer economy during the war and WPTB officials who were eager to see a rapid return to the pre-war market economy. The business community had been lobbying vigorously for a rapid return to the "normalcy" of the pre-war status quo, and it found allies within the WPTB commodity administrations, which were largely led by industry representatives.[110] Government officials such as Gordon, while publicly maintaining a hard line about continuing wartime economic controls well into the postwar period, moved quickly to wind down operations in a number of key areas as early as 1944. By January 1946, the WPTB had reduced its own staff by 20 percent and had removed price ceilings from a large number of "non-essential" consumer goods like drugs, cosmetics, tobacco, and books. More important from the perspective of consumers, the WPTB had also begun to make significant upward adjustments to the ceiling prices for a variety of essential goods like milk and meat.[111] By January 1947, the price ceilings had been removed from most non-essential consumer goods. Soon afterwards, the WPTB announced that it would be proceeding with the decontrol of prices on food and most other consumer goods.[112]

The government and the business community were eager to speed up the decontrol process. Consumers, for their part, were far less enthusiastic. A poll taken in early 1947 found that a surprising 66 percent of Canadians objected to the removal of price controls. In part, this seemed to reflect the public's growing unease with the significant increases they had already seen in the prices of milk, meat, and other consumer goods under the WPTB's "orderly decontrol" policy.[113] Even the cost-of-living index – which tended to exclude most of the "non-essential" goods that had been subject to decontrol – rose by an alarming seven points between December 1945 and December 1946, with food alone seeing a twelve-point increase (see Table 2.2 for annual averages). The fact that most of these increases had occurred within the existing price ceilings caused many to worry about what would happen when the ceiling was removed completely. And Canadians only had to look to their neighbours south of the border to see the dangers of rapid decontrol. After the US Congress abruptly removed price ceilings on all consumer goods in June 1946, inflation skyrocketed. Within a month, food prices jumped 14 percent and meat prices doubled. By November, food prices in the United States had jumped 32 percent over August 1945, wiping out a significant portion of the gains in wages and benefits that American workers had seen during the war.[114]

After the 1947 removal of price ceilings on most foods, the scale of consumer protest in Canada increased substantially. Protests included meat boycotts in Regina and Toronto, consumer picketing by housewives outside Vancouver stores, the distribution of various anti-decontrol petitions

Table 2.2

Cost of living index, 1939-49

Year	Total	Food	Fuel/light	Rent	Clothing	Furniture	Miscellaneous
1949	162	211	138	133	182	169	132
1948	156	196	125	121	174	163	127
1947	136	160	116	117	144	142	120
1946	125	140	107	113	126	125	117
1945	120	133	107	112	122	119	114
1944	120	131	111	112	122	118	113
1943	119	131	113	112	121	118	112
1942	117	127	113	111	120	117	108
1941	112	116	110	109	116	114	105
1940	106	106	107	106	109	107	102
1939	102	101	101	104	101	101	101

Note: 1935-39 = 100

Source: Statistics Canada, *Historical Statistics of Canada, Section K: Price Indexes,* http://www.statcan.gc.ca/pub/11-516-x/pdf/5500100-eng.pdf, accessed 8 December 2010.

in a number of major cities, and the arrival of two high-profile delegations of housewives in Ottawa calling for government intervention to curb rapid postwar inflation.[115] One of the more colourful and widely reported protests was the 1947 children's chocolate bar boycott that took place across the country in response to an overnight 60 percent increase in the price of this popular children's treat. In Victoria, nearly two hundred children protested outside the BC legislature, calling for a rollback of prices. In Ottawa, more than three hundred students from Lisgar Collegiate marched on Parliament Hill carrying signs reading "We'll eat worms before the eight-cent bar." They were joined by students in Ladysmith, Edmonton, Regina, Toronto, Montreal, Fredericton, and other cities and towns[116] (see Figure 2.3).

At the centre of these and many of the highest-profile postwar protests against decontrol was the Housewives Consumer Association (HCA).[117] Having been founded in Toronto in 1937, the HCA gained a national presence after it organized popular protests against increases in milk and beef prices in 1946 and, later on, through a "Roll-Back-Prices" campaign that saw newly formed branches across the country organize rallies, petitions, and buyers' strikes. As Julie Guard has shown, the HCA grew initially

Figure 2.3 Children's chocolate bar boycott rally in Ladysmith, BC, 27 April 1947.
© *Vancouver Sun.*

during the late 1930s by attracting a broad, cross-class, multi-ethnic membership of mostly progressive and radical women.[118] Before 1939, though, the HCA branches had been limited mostly to Ontario, with footholds in British Columbia and Manitoba. During the war, however, the organization's members had focused their efforts on working with the Consumer Branch. In that regard, the HCA expressed strong support for government interventions in the economy, including price controls and rationing.[119]

In the postwar period, the HCA emerged as a truly national organization. Expanding through existing women's organizations, union auxiliaries, and WRACs, by April 1947 the HCA claimed a national membership of 100,000 women in one hundred branches across the country.[120] Much of this growth was a result of its persuasive and colourful campaigns as well as its popular calls for government intervention to stabilize the cost of living, for the curtailment of production on luxury goods, and for the introduction of standardized labelling. The organization's influence peaked in 1947, when two separate delegations brought these demands directly to Parliament Hill.[121] The June delegation drove home the "Roll-Back-Prices" message by wearing tiny, handmade rolling pins to their meeting with federal politicians. In a similar vein, newspaper photographs of the delegation showed HCA members brandishing full-sized rolling pins in front of the Parliament Buildings.[122]

Contributing strongly to the HCA's rapid rise as a national political force was the fact that the war had done much to legitimate a critique of Canada's political economy that had, during the organization's formative years in the late 1930s, been viewed as far more radical. By 1947, many Canadian women had come to see price controls and even rationing as essential means to protect their rights as consumers to affordable and accessible food. Having done their part to hold the line on prices throughout the war, many women had become sensitized to the dangers that inflation posed to their families and communities. They therefore increasingly came to see the WPTB's decontrol policies as a betrayal. So, it is no surprise, then, that the HCA adopted the Consumer Branch's wartime language regarding the dangers posed by runaway inflation. One way they did this was to adapt the wartime ideal of Mrs. Consumer to the HCA's own ends by invoking similarly gendered notions of consumer citizenship as a means to call for greater input from women into the governance of the peacetime economy. The HCA therefore rarely missed an opportunity to highlight its members' wartime cooperation with the WPTB, and it often framed its more radical actions – such as boycotts and buyers' strikes – in the same terms that the WPTB had resorted to when encouraging Canadians to report violations of price controls and rationing regulations during the war. Women now were simply being asked to refuse to buy products that did not reflect prices they considered fair or reasonable.

The federal government, for its part, attempted to undermine the organization's authority and credibility. It threw its support behind the newly created Canadian Association of Consumers (CAC), contending that *it* was the true representative of consumers' interests. The CAC had been formed in 1947, and its leaders had been drawn mainly from the ranks of middle-class organizations such as the National Council of Women. As Joy Parr notes, the CAC was "liberal in political philosophy, and loyal to the governing Liberal Party."[123] The Liberals even provided CAC with a $15,000 grant to cover its start-up costs. The organization – which was typically more concerned about issues such as consumer education and product standards than the cost of living – would continue to receive federal funding throughout its lifetime.[124]

The CAC never captured anything like the popular support the HCA enjoyed in its early campaigns, but it did outlive its competitor, in part because of a highly cynical yet effective campaign to discredit the HCA by accusing it of being a communist front. The first accusations of this nature came following revelations that some of the leaders of the first HCA delegation to Ottawa had been members of the Labour Progressive Party or, at the very least, were affiliated with other communist organizations. In early 1948, Liberal Finance Minister Douglass Abbott rebuffed the HCA when it attempted to present the government with a petition of more than 700,000 signatures from Canadians calling for a return of price controls on food following a 14 percent increase in prices over the previous year. Abbott claimed that he would not meet with them because he "believed the delegation was being used for communistic propaganda purposes."[125] This kind of red-baiting was a convenient – and effective – means to paint the entire anti-decontrol cause as misguided and as not representing the popular will. Yet in fact, the petition was a powerful testament to the popular support the HCA had generated. In a December 1947 poll, for instance, 76 percent of Canadians agreed that the government should reinstate price controls. This broad public support would continue, particularly after food prices soared by 23 percent in 1948 – a nearly 50 percent total increase in food prices since the end of the war. Even in 1950, 59 percent of Canadians agreed that the government "should control prices of food stuffs in the stores, like eggs, butter, meat, and so on."[126]

Despite apparent widespread support for the HCA's actual policies, however, the organization was crushed by ongoing accusations that it was a communist front. These accusations alienated many of its more moderate supporters who, like many Canadians, were caught up in the growing anti-communist Cold War hysteria that followed the Gouzenko Affair. (Igor Gouzenko was a cipher clerk in the Soviet Embassy in Ottawa, who defected, warning after he did that the Soviets had infiltrated the Canadian and US governments. His defection helped escalate what were already growing tensions between Canada and the Soviet Union.)[127] Even the CCF, whose members formed an important part of the early leadership of the HCA, began to discourage participation in the organization. In 1948, the party went so far as to force former Ontario CCF MPP Rae Luckock to choose between the HCA and the CCF. These efforts, combined with the discouragement many women felt after the federal government ignored their efforts to preserve the WPTB, helped bring about the dissolution of the HCA by 1950.[128]

Conclusion

During the war, Canadians had been subject to the most extensive state intervention in the economy in the country's history. And, as Christine White, chief labour liaison of the Consumer Branch, reflected in a 1947 *Saturday Night* article, they had been changed by this experience:

> For over five years the "moving finger" of history has been writing a new and exciting chapter in our Canadian story entitled "Economic Controls." Somewhat to our own surprise we rather enjoyed this chapter, and, now that the time has come to turn the page, we are finding that it will be somewhat difficult to wipe out the deep impressions that our adventure into the realm of a controlled economy has made on our national consciousness.

For White, the war had provided Canadians with an "unapprehended challenge" to a free enterprise system whose performance would now be "measured against the measuring stick of the compulsion of government regulation." Even the "regimentation of rationing," White argued, "did not bear too heavily on people who had always been rationed by price anyway." Indeed, rationing proved to be quite popular because of "the feeling of 'equality' produced by the fact that all ration books were alike."[129]

For Canadian women in particular, this "feeling of equality" was the most appealing aspect of Canada's wartime command economy. Lizabeth Cohen has argued that in the United States, the war helped redefine the consumer as not just a purchaser of goods, but also a *citizen consumer* who was able to "put the marked power of the consumer to work politically ... to safeguard the rights of individual consumers and the larger 'general good.'"[130] To a great extent, the same appears to have been true in Canada. While buying only within price ceilings and voluntarily limiting one's consumption of goods in short supply were patriotic acts expected of all consumers, they were also accompanied by legal guarantees of a fair price and equitable distribution of goods within the marketplace. Many consumers came to believe that these guarantees amounted to an acknowledgment of their economic rights as consumers and citizens to a fair share of affordable necessities. And when they felt that they were being treated unfairly, Canadians were clearly willing to make their voices heard to seek redress, be it through their local WRAC or one of the many postwar boycotts, petitions, and consumer protests launched by the HCA. In the process, ordinary women succeeded in bringing their domestic concerns to the forefront of both wartime and postwar political discourse. As Magda Fahrni has argued, the "household politics" of the reconstruction period "involved both the renegotiation of roles within the household in the wake of the war, and, more particularly, the placing of household issues in the public sphere and on the formal political agenda."[131] Both the Consumer Branch and the HCA offered the possibility that if women asserted these rights, they would have a say in political decisions that were having a real impact on the conditions of their domestic labour and their family's quality of life.

Ultimately, however, Canada's postwar social and political consensus turned out to be a much more conservative one than many had predicted. The pre-war market economy had returned largely intact, and the rights of consumers were being framed not in terms of access to a reasonable standard of living and nutritious foods but rather in terms of their ability to choose freely from the myriad products of postwar consumer capitalism. By 1950, moreover, it was becoming clear that the political possibilities of consumer citizenship espoused by the HCA and others had been eclipsed by a growing consensus around the rights of the male breadwinner and the returned soldier. And, as discussed at greater length in later chapters, while family allowances appeared to offer some recognition of women's economic contributions to the national economy, the fact that this program was not tied to changes in the cost of living meant that its impact on family budgets would decline as the postwar inflation that the HCA and other groups fought against rapidly chipped away at its value. Perhaps the most lasting legacy of this period was the lesson that members of the HCA were forced to learn the hard way: even with widespread popular support for their cause, it was ultimately impossible for them to have their voices heard on an equal footing in the context of a political system that still largely excluded women from the levers of real political decision making.

3

Mobilizing Canada's "Housoldiers" and "Kitchen Commandos" for War

Food, Volunteers, and the Making of Canada's Home Front

In hundreds of thousands of Canadian households, the popular slogan "Food Is a Weapon of War" was made tangible through the wartime transformation of a number of everyday acts of household food preparation, production, and consumption into both material and symbolic contributions to the war effort. This was the central message of an especially memorable propaganda campaign sponsored by the Department of National War Services to promote the salvaging of fats and bones. Most often, the advertisements for this campaign published in newspapers and magazines featured the image of a giant cast-iron frying pan pouring drops of hot fat that, as they fell, were transformed into bombs aimed at either enemy U-boats or caricatures of the hated leaders of Germany, Italy, and Japan (see Figure 3.1). Fats and bones, these ads reminded Canadians, were an essential component of munitions production and therefore needed to be conserved in order to give Canada's soldiers and allies a fighting chance. As the copy to one ad suggested, "The next time you are frying or roasting something, just imagine the satisfaction it would give you to pour that hot fat right down the back of Adolph, Tojo or Benito."[1]

This chapter examines the multiple ways that Canadians rallied around patriotic food production, conservation, and service. It does so in order to explore the changing symbolic and material role that food played on the home front and, more importantly, in order to analyze the shifting wartime politics and culture of gender, domesticity, and citizenship in the context of Canada's broader mobilization for total war. In particular, it focuses on the ways in which, through wartime propaganda and other

Figure 3.1 A Department of National War Services advertisement, encouraging Canadians to fight the Axis in their kitchens. *Cariboo Observer*, 27 March 1943.

means, food became central to the very idea of the "home front" – a concept that itself depended on the notion that what was once private and domestic needed to be mobilized in order to serve a larger public good. This symbolic shift was necessary in order to "bring the war home" in a very literal sense but also to boost morale and encourage ordinary Canadians to believe that they each had a key role to play in meeting essential national production goals – not only through their cooperation with the legal requirements of wartime economic controls, but also through conservation, thrift, and other wartime domestic virtues. In particular, this chapter argues that whether or not conservation campaigns like victory gardening or the collection of fat and bone actually contributed to Canada's war production goals ultimately proved to be less important than the role those campaigns played in fostering a broader feeling of solidarity and individual participation in the nation's mobilization for total war.

Private acts of food conservation and thrift were important components of the war effort, but these contributions ultimately proved to be relatively small compared to the impressive mobilization of the voluntary labour of millions of Canadians in support of wartime patriotic campaigns directed at fundraising, home defence, providing comforts to soldiers, and producing food and other essential goods for Canada's overseas allies. While different in scope, however, these two types of wartime contributions did share important similarities. In the same way that wartime food conservation campaigns brought the war into the home, many of the more prominent patriotic voluntary campaigns often publicly extended women's assumed domestic and maternal skills in order to provide comfort, nourishment, and other forms of material and emotional support to Allied soldiers and civilians both at home and overseas. This chapter therefore also seeks to examine a number of food-related patriotic voluntary activities as a way of interrogating the role played by food production, consumption, and service in determining the boundaries of gendered ideals of wartime citizenship. In particular, it argues that, although many women rallied the private sphere and feminine domestic virtues in ways that seemed to mirror pervasive and gendered propaganda images stressing their obligations to the nation and empire as wives and mothers, they also simultaneously challenged the distinction between public and private spheres that typically defined popular ideas about gender, citizenship, and the value of women's unpaid labour.

Private Virtues, Public Service – Creating a "Home Front"

As soon as war was declared in September 1939, Canadians – and Canadian women, in particular – were called upon to bring the battle into their homes. The "home front," as it was often called, was envisioned by government officials and wartime propagandists as precisely that: a mobilization of the private lives and domestic spaces of ordinary Canadians in order to meet the changing needs of a nation at war. Almost immediately, many familiar slogans from the previous war were resurrected.[2] *Chatelaine* reminded its readers in November 1939 that home defence "begins in the kitchen, and Canada expects every housekeeper to do her duty there."[3] *Canadian Home Journal* similarly called upon its readers to "Man the Food

Front" and stressed that the average woman must regard her work in the kitchen as "definitely important, indeed vital, to that final outcome for which she prays."[4] Women were confronted with a range of idealized images of patriotic service on the home front. These included the "Housoldier," who in a prominent ad from the Canada Starch Company was shown standing at attention, wearing an apron, with a wooden spoon in place of a rifle, while in the background men filed towards a distant factory. The company's wartime cookbook, for its part, reminded readers that "the housewives of Canada are the 'Housoldiers,' serving the nation truly and well by providing appetizing and nourishing meals that protect and preserve the health of their families"[5] (see Figure 3.2).

The popular imagery of the home front played heavily on familiar gender tropes regarding women's perceived domestic roles and responsibilities as mothers, household managers, and cooks. As Lara Campbell has pointed out, cooking during this period was never viewed merely as a domestic skill. It was also "a way to demonstrate a woman's concern for her family and therefore an important component of proper womanhood."[6] Wartime propaganda therefore often relied on appeals to the middle-class values of thrift, patience, and scientific motherhood that had long been the staple of advice columns and household management textbooks.[7] *Chatelaine, Canadian Home Journal*, and countless local newspapers' women's pages reminded readers that women's place in the war effort always started in the home. For government propagandists and for private boosters of the war effort alike, the kitchen proved to be an essential symbolic resource because it spoke to a biological imperative that was central to the "Housoldier" ideal: as wives and mothers, women were expected to keep the nation's future soldiers and current war workers healthy, fit, and in peak productive and fighting condition. In this way, women's work in the kitchen and the marketplace became symbolically and physically linked to women's responsibilities for household production as well as reproduction.

This valorization of women's household duties did more than promote the material goals of the state. As discussed earlier, both price controls and food rationing depended heavily on women's cooperation, which meant that "Mrs. Consumer" was quickly enlisted to do her part by buying only what she needed, conserving and salvaging scarce goods, and putting up with the various strictures that the war had placed on her family's dinner table. And this kind of wartime propaganda served another role that was just as important: it was intimately linked to the maintenance of morale both at home and abroad. At home, this wartime celebration of domesticity spoke to the lived experiences of women who, throughout the war, were

Figure 3.2 The cover to the Canada Starch Co. cookbook, *Economy Recipes for Canada's "Housoldiers"* (Montreal/Toronto: Canada Starch Co., 1943).

often asked to make significant sacrifices. They were being forced to take on the duties of childrearing alone – often for years at a time – while their husbands were overseas, and in addition to that, their already full burden of domestic labour was being extended on a number of fronts, particularly in the kitchen. Most women were used to scraping by on goods in short supply and generally "making do" after years of Depression-era living.[8] Now, however, the war was bringing additional challenges. As a number of historians have noted, the disappearance of both major and minor consumer durables from stores often imposed a significant burden on women's labour in the kitchen.[9] Most households had been forced to put off purchases of modern appliances like gas or electric stoves and mechanical refrigerators during the hard years of the Depression, and the war offered little respite from this, given that it was often impossible to replace or even repair aging iceboxes, coal or wood stoves, and basic kitchen appliances due to restricted supplies and shortages of skilled repairmen. Cooking with the aging appliances used in most Canadian homes was not easy at the best of times and was now even more difficult in the face of these problems as well as the periodic food and fuel shortages that had become the wartime reality for most Canadians. Government propagandists therefore hoped that if they connected these everyday domestic tasks to other kinds of war work, Canadians would be more willing to face these sacrifices and inconveniences with few complaints for the sake of the soldiers overseas.

These celebrations of domesticity also helped reinforce an image of social stability during a period of rapid social, economic, and cultural change.[10] It seems that in a time of uncertainty, changing gender roles in the workplace, and emotional hardship as families were broken up in order to send soldiers overseas, the utopian goal of a normative heterosexual, male-breadwinner-centred domestic sphere was a source of comfort for many soldiers and government officials. This meant that even while married and unmarried women were increasingly called upon to enter the previously "male" domains of the industrial workplace and the military during the war, government policy tended to underscore that such changes were only temporary. Wartime propaganda typically played upon this contradiction by suggesting that women take on the patriotic double duty of being both "Rosie the Riveter" and the "Housoldier" for the duration of the war.[11]

The net result of this particular wartime cult of patriotic domesticity was that the kitchen became imbued with new symbolic, material, and political meanings. Shopping, cooking, and eating came to be closely linked to the state's production goals and to the material needs of Canada's soldiers and overseas allies in part because of a gendered vision of social stability that stressed women's role in both social and biological reproduction. This broader mobilization of the home front also meant an increased recognition of the importance of the home itself as a site of both production and consumption. The result was that Canadians were provided with a number of important tools for enacting and performing a range of competing gendered visions of wartime patriotism, citizenship, and domesticity, whether this was through making and sharing the kinds of "patriotic" and

Figure 3.3 One of the many posters created to encourage women to save fats, bones, and other materials. *Library and Archives Canada, C-087533.*

"war" recipes discussed in later chapters or – as discussed below – by placing their homes on a war footing through their participation in patriotic conservation and salvage activities such as victory gardening and the salvaging of fats and bones (see Figure 3.3).

Victory Gardening

Victory gardening remains an enduring symbol of the Canadian home front. During the war, the vacant lots, front lawns, and flower gardens

that had been conscripted into wartime food production served as a powerful image of a nation whose every resource was being devoted to total war
and that could ill afford to waste any of its abundant land or its citizens'
leisure hours. In the First World War, victory gardening – or "war gardening," as it was also commonly called – had been widely touted by the
Canadian government and the media as a patriotic form of wholesome
leisure. By the spring of 1940, the practice was again being embraced by
ordinary Canadians and, by 1944, upwards of 209,200 victory gardens had
been planted across the nation, producing an estimated total of 57,000
tons of vegetables.[12]

For promoters of victory gardening, the rationale was rather simple: the
more produce Canadians could grow in their front yards and on vacant
lots, the more food, soldiers, and munitions could be shipped to Canada's
allies overseas. Victory gardening helped meet existing export commitments by freeing up much-needed space on Canada's overburdened rail-
ways, thereby reducing what by 1941 were widespread shortages of a range
of foods and other essential consumer goods. Victory gardens, then, offered
many Canadians what seemed to be a direct role in meeting the nation's
ambitious agricultural production goals. At the same time, it also promised
tangible material, moral, and even spiritual benefits. There was something
about Canadians rolling up their sleeves, digging in the dirt, and harvesting
the fruits of their own hard work and perseverance that made starting a
new garden the ideal symbol of renewal and abundance during a time of
profound austerity and destruction around the world. Just as importantly,
it was a wholesome activity that the whole family could take part in. As a
number of historians have observed, it harkened back to a pre-industrial
past, to popular ideals of family and community solidarity, and to notions
of respectable, middle-class citizenship.[13] These associations became even
stronger in the context of the war, particularly given that victory gardens
promised real material benefits: they helped individual families overcome
local shortages of fresh produce and enabled them to increase their consumption of the vitamin- and mineral-rich "protective foods" outlined
in Canada's Official Food Rules. Planting a victory garden thus quickly
emerged as a form of wholesome, patriotic leisure that would (it was
argued) strengthen families and awaken their dormant productivity.

From the outset, victory gardening was a decidedly urban phenomenon.
Home food production was already a common practice in rural Canada,
where the transformation of pre-war kitchen gardens into victory gardens
involved mainly a semantic change. Because the goal was to increase the
acreage of land devoted to food production, the ideal victory garden was

therefore one that transformed previously unproductive urban land into agricultural space. Victory gardens could be planted anywhere: front lawns, vacant lots, school playgrounds, or municipal parks. Across the country, municipalities and private owners offered vacant land to gardeners, usually for a small annual fee. In many cities, these endeavours were coordinated by existing organizations like the Nova Scotia Women's Institute – which launched a wartime campaign to "enlist soldiers of the soil" into "gardening brigades" – as well as by new, grassroots organizations like Victoria's Victory Garden Brigade. By 1942, for instance, the Community Garden League of Greater Montreal had filled some 1,400 allotments in sixteen districts. The Ottawa Horticultural Society, which for years had managed gardens for the city's relief recipients, helped to establish a more modest sixty-seven garden plots.[14]

Despite these efforts to create public spaces for gardening that were open to everyone – but especially to lower-income families with no access to their own private yards – victory gardening appears to have been more common among middle-class homeowners. Wartime advertisements, for their part, were dominated by images of middle-class domesticity. Ads for Coca-Cola, Metropolitan Life Insurance, and other corporations often employed images of well-dressed neighbours working in their own private gardens, often chatting with each other across a low picket fence.[15] Indeed, the most extensive wartime survey of victory gardens conducted during the war suggests that this image was not far from the truth: 82 percent of victory gardens were being cultivated at the home of the householder, 15 percent were in a nearby vacant lot, and only 3 percent were in a community garden area.[16] In part this was because the congestion caused by wartime population movements meant that in many cities, there was often little public or vacant space available for victory gardens. In Saint John, authorities reported that "housing accommodation is such that many people living in rooms within the one house are fortunate to find quarters to sleep and eat let alone expect to find space within the house to store vegetables." In even more crowded Halifax, local authorities suggested that "Victory Gardens in this locality exist mainly in name only."[17]

Available space was not the only factor limiting victory gardening. In Quebec City and Toronto it was estimated that the acreage tilled by victory gardeners on public lands in 1943 was only 25 and 50 percent, respectively, of the land that had been under cultivation by relief gardeners during the Great Depression. The practice of relief gardening has been largely overlooked by Canadian historians of the Depression era, even though at the time, it was common for municipalities to allow families on relief to use or rent vacant lands for supplementary food production.[18] At the peak of the Depression, in Quebec City, families on relief were actively gardening between eight hundred and one thousand plots totalling fifty to sixty acres. After the war began and the unemployment rate fell, though, working-class gardeners tended to abandon these relief gardens. When Quebec City tried to revive the custom for the purposes of victory gardens, moreover, it was able to attract only half the number of gardeners. It also found that such gardens were started by "a different kind of worker" who was motivated "mostly from a patriotic attitude." The same was true in Toronto, where, by one estimate, only half the land worked by families on relief during 1937 and 1938 was being used by victory gardeners in 1943. According to one report, the message was clear: "the appeal to patriotism together with individual fears of possible food shortages were not as potent as absolute necessity in promoting home gardening."[19]

The typical victory garden, then, was planted on private property and often tended by inexperienced gardeners. Children, for instance, were encouraged to take part in their family's garden or to participate in victory gardens through their school or church group. In 1942 in Sydney, Nova Scotia, the Canadian Junior Red Cross and the provincial Department of Agriculture worked with a class of grade four boys at the Holy Redeemer School to plant a garden and reported that it had been a "triumphant success" that helped the children gain valuable experience and the "satisfaction of helping to produce wholesome Canadian food and the joy of contributing to Canada's war effort."[20] Similar efforts were made by school and Junior Red Cross organizations across the country. In many cases, children either donated their produce to local military bases or held vegetable sales in order to raise money for causes such as providing food relief for "undernourished children" in Greece, Poland, Yugoslavia, Belgium, France, and China.[21]

The most important new gardeners, however – and the ones who dominated wartime imagery of victory gardening – were men. While popular images of household gardening prior to the war often portrayed it as a women's sphere of non-productive and largely ornamental labour, many wartime promotional materials and advertisements promoted it as a new kind of respectable (and decidedly middle-class) masculine domesticity.[22] These ads focused on encouraging men to take up their patriotic hoes and spades. This was the message of the 1943 NFB animated short *He Plants for Victory*, for instance, in which a husband shows up his wife's pathetic-looking kitchen garden after "leading a garden squad down to a vacant lot" and getting to work (see Figure 3.4).[23] The Nova Scotia

Figure 3.4 Stills from the NFB film *He Plants for Victory* (Ottawa: National Film Board of Canada, 1943).

Department of Agriculture's 1943 booklet *Gardening for Vim and Vitamins* was similarly directed at men. This text was full of cartoons that resorted to military metaphors about the struggle between the gardener and nature, showing men carrying out a variety of duties in the garden. At one point, it even cautioned against buying certain kinds of seeds because of the "glamour girls" on seed catalogues.[24] Newspapers and magazines regularly played on the supposed novelty of male gardeners. One 1945 ad, for example, portrayed a wife marvelling at how her husband was now in the garden "without having to be coaxed, pushed or bribed."[25]

For many proponents of victory gardening, the movement of amateurs into gardening was one of the campaign's benefits: it was teaching Canadians a new set of domestic skills, increasing their self-sufficiency, and boosting their respect for farmers and other food producers. Yet from the perspective of the Federal Department of Agriculture and the Wartime Prices and Trade Board (WPTB), the mostly inexperienced new gardeners were, in all likelihood, getting a poor return on their investment of time, money, and energy in their first few seasons. For that reason, little was done at an official level to promote victory gardening in the first three years of the war, despite regular calls from the media, local gardening clubs, and the general public for a national campaign to encourage the practice. Indeed, during the 1942 gardening season, the WPTB angered many when it went even further than ambivalence by publishing a pamphlet titled "Home Vegetable Gardening and Home Canning of Vegetables in Wartime" that actively discouraged "city-folk" from planting food gardens. This pamphlet "urged" unskilled gardeners to refrain from gardening because "they would create the demand for equipment such as garden tools, fertilizers and sprays, which are made from materials needed by Canada's war industries and because Canada's vegetable seed supply can best be employed by experienced gardeners with equipment on hand."[26]

When the federal government reversed its position and began to promote victory gardens during the 1943 growing season, this was less a change in attitude regarding their contribution to Canada's food supplies than a recognition that the benefits of victory gardens extended well beyond their contribution to the national food supply. Canadians had already shown that they were willing to start their own victory gardens, with or without government approval, so it made sense for the government to try to harness this patriotic enthusiasm. Many officials in the Department of Agriculture remained convinced that an expansion of urban gardening would lead to considerable waste of both effort and materials. But in light of an improved seed situation, they had concluded that inexperienced gardeners probably would not threaten the country's larger agricultural goals.[27] Similarly, the BC government had concluded that victory gardens were not a particularly efficient means of supplementing a non-farming family's income but nonetheless promoted them as "a wholesome form of recreation" that would make use of "the skill and energy that in times of peace are frequently utilized on the tennis courts and on golf courses."[28]

This image of victory gardening as a form of patriotic leisure in many ways captures its essential importance as a symbolic rather than purely productive activity. From a morale standpoint, victory gardens linked a wholesome and familiar form of domestic labour to the larger war effort in a way that involved the entire family and that was highly visible to friends and neighbours. For urban middle-class husbands (whose private outlets for manly patriotic enthusiasm were limited) and for children (who could learn important lessons about food production through gardening), the victory garden was a powerful domestic venue for home front participation in the larger war effort. For many, moreover, it was also an enjoyable diversion from the less pleasant realities of total war.

Fats and Bones Salvage

Fats and bones salvage played a symbolic role similar to that of victory gardening in the mobilization of the home front. While victory gardening connected domestic spaces to Canada's larger wartime agricultural production goals, fats and bones salvage connected Canada's kitchens to the work being done in munitions factories and other war production facilities. As the illustrated advertisements published in newspapers and magazines by the Department of National War Services (NWS) regularly reminded Canadians, fats and bones were essential to munitions production. Bones provided essential materials for industrial glues, and, as one ad evocatively informed readers, "Fat Is Ammunition" – one pound of fat supplied "enough glycerine to fire 150 bullets from a Bren gun," and two pounds would "fire a burst of 20 cannon shells from a Spitfire or 10 anti-aircraft shells." One NWS advertisement promised, "You can be a munition maker right in your own kitchen."[29]

Like victory gardening, household salvage initially gained official sanction primarily as a response to patriotic enthusiasm rather than to the supply needs of Canadian industry. When the NWS launched its first national salvage drive for metal items in April 1941, for instance, Minister J.T. Thorson admitted that it had been inaugurated "to satisfy the patriotic desire of many of our people who had written … suggesting that they be permitted to organize voluntary salvage corps as was being done in Great Britain."[30] In response, the NWS created the National Salvage Division to coordinate the collection of items such as aluminum pots, rags, glass, and paper. Communities were encouraged to form salvage collection committees, and basic prices were set for salvage materials. Soon afterwards, however, Canada began to face real shortages of a range of metals and other raw materials. In the case of edible oils and fats, for instance, Canada imported as much as 50 percent of its annual requirements.[31] With the country having been cut off from many of its principal sources of oil and fats since the beginning of the war in the Pacific, government officials began to worry that shortages could threaten Canada's war production. A vigorous oils and fats collection campaign was therefore launched that included extensive print, radio, and film ads. At the same time, meat processors and retailers were compelled to pay consumers and salvage committees between 4 and 4.5 cents per pound for rendered and strained fat.

Canadians responded enthusiastically to these calls to salvage and recycle potential war materials. By 1944, 1,836 voluntary salvage committees were operating across the country, and between May 1941 (when the campaign began) and October 1943, Canadians collected nearly 430 million pounds of salvage materials.[32] Some of these committees were formed by local municipalities. Others, however, were fundraising arms of local and national war charities, or they were independent, stand-alone organizations. In Quesnel, BC, for instance, a local salvage committee was formed as part of the local Red Cross, while in Hamilton, Ontario, salvage pickup was incorporated into the regular municipal garbage services.[33] In Winnipeg, the Patriotic Salvage Corps had been formed independently a year prior to the creation of the National Salvage Division. Over its five years of wartime operations, it would collect 690,554 pounds of bones and 323,001 pounds of fat.[34]

At the heart of all these local campaigns was a mobilization of individual householders to collect kitchen scraps and other household waste materials. Wartime appeals for household fats and bones collection typically played on gendered ideas about women's domestic responsibilities. Such messages were often directed specifically at housewives, who according to a number of *Toronto Star* editorials were enlisting as Canada's "Kitchen Commandos" and "salvage collection corps" through their salvage and conservation work.[35] Perhaps even more than victory gardening and other household activities, household salvage of fats and bones spoke to the gendered ideals of thrift and good household management. They therefore became an important symbol of the mobilization of the kitchen in support of the war effort. In reality, however, these salvage activities were more of a small inconvenience than a major sacrifice. While they did require some additional time and effort to ensure that bones were cleaned and that fats were strained and stored in a cool place, such jobs were relatedly minor ones that in many households were given to children.

As Hamilton School Inspector J.W. Van Loon reported, salvage had a number of educational advantages suited to the patriotic mobilization of children: "There is no age limit in this patriotic effort. Through these collections children realize they are sharing in a great cause, that they are providing material to carry on the active war and, as well, they are being taught valuable lessons in thrift."[36] Across the country, children were encouraged to participate in salvage collection in their classrooms and through organizations like the Boy Scouts, Girl Guides, and Junior Red Cross. In a number of cities, movie theatres rewarded such activities by holding salvage drives that enabled children to see a matinee in exchange for between one and two pounds of fat. As one government official suggested to the *Globe and Mail*, it was the "psychological effect" of such events, rather than the actual return in fats, that was the most important part of such promotions, for they boosted morale and, more importantly, encouraged future participation in other patriotic activities.[37]

Ultimately, fats and bones collection proved to be far more effective as a symbolic resource for Canadians than as a significant material contribution to the war effort. In the case of fats, in particular, national supplies were improved mainly through controls at the producer rather than the consumer end. Mostly this was achieved through government subsidies and other incentives designed to encourage a massive expansion of oilseed and livestock production. Flaxseed production, for instance, increased from a prewar figure of 1.5 million bushels to 18.4 million in 1943, transforming Canada into an exporting rather than an importing nation. The massive increase in livestock production during the war, combined with the requirement placed on slaughterhouses that they salvage internal fats before selling a carcass, similarly played a much more important role than consumer salvage in capturing waste fats.[38] Even so, the salvage campaign – like victory gardening – was essential to maintaining morale. Besides promoting thrift and careful household management and underscoring the need to "make do" in the face of wartime social and economic changes, it provided a potent symbol of the ways in which all Canadians could contribute to the war effort. It did so by providing a direct emotional and material link between work in the home and the work of Canadian soldiers overseas. The imagery of fat transforming into bombs not only made for compelling propaganda, in other words; through its continued repetition and through Canadians' participation in household salvage, it also helped to bring the war home on a daily basis.

Domestic Comforts

Many Canadians found that it was simply not enough to put their homes on a war footing through patriotic activities such as salvage collection and victory gardening. Millions sought to contribute their patriotic enthusiasm and labour in other ways as well. The NWS, which had been established in June 1940 in part to coordinate the activities of charitable and patriotic voluntary organizations, estimated that 3.5 million Canadians were participating in the war-related voluntary activities overseen by its Voluntary and Auxiliary Services Division by the end of the war. By 1944, moreover, 3,745 charitable funds had been organized across Canada – a figure that does not include the voluntary work done by the thousands of branches of existing national organizations, including the Red Cross, the IODE, the Salvation Army, the YMCA, the YWCA, and a wide range of other prominent organizations that shifted their efforts to patriotic purposes during the war.[39]

Women were at the forefront of Canada's wartime mobilization of volunteers. While this in part reflected the long-standing assumption that front-line charity and volunteer work was primarily a feminine domain, it also reflected a distinctly gendered vision of wartime patriotic voluntary work. Wartime propaganda typically defined men's wartime roles in terms of either military service or their primary breadwinner status. It therefore followed that their participation in patriotic and voluntary activities reflected prevailing notions of manliness and masculinity and was, as a result, far more limited in scope. As Jeffrey Keshen has pointed out, men were far more likely to be involved in work that had a "managerial or military dimension," such as serving as air raid wardens or auxiliary police and firemen.[40] Similarly, women's wartime contributions were typically defined in distinctly gendered ways. To a certain extent, this was because wartime voluntary organizations and charities tended to depend heavily on networks of existing women's organizations and on women's well-established fundraising and community-building skills. Women, after all, had been the primary front-line workers and fundraisers in pre-war charities.[41] Now, during the war, they took up similar roles in new patriotic organizations. At the same time, it was equally true that many of the wartime patriotic efforts organized by women reflected a distinctly feminine vision of patriotic citizenship, one that highlighted women's domestic labour in the kitchen as well as their roles as mothers, caregivers, and consumers. Thus, in their wartime voluntary work, many women sought to use the private, maternal virtues celebrated in wartime propaganda in order to contribute to a larger public good. As a result, food preparation and service was often central to the public performance of wartime patriotic citizenship represented by women's voluntary work.

The connection between wartime citizenship and gendered notions of women's domestic duties is perhaps most visible in what was, at the time, typically referred to as "comfort" work. One of the most iconic aspects of women's wartime voluntary contributions on the home front, "comfort" work generally referred to a range of public and private activities aimed at providing soldiers in Canada and abroad with comforts such as food, sociability, companionship, and distraction from military discipline. The idea was to replicate some of the familiar comforts of home for young men and women, many of whom had little experience away from their friends, families, and hometowns prior to enlistment, yet who were being asked to risk their lives on the battlefield. While a range of comforts were provided to soldiers – from sports equipment to donuts, coffee, and magazines and newspapers for soldiers in transit – most of these activities had the common goal of providing a domestic oasis within the highly regimented and often alienating world of the military. This type of war work fit neatly within the "Housoldier" ideal: women could contribute to the war by extending their domestic skills and labour to the country's soldiers in addition to their own families.

Food was the quintessential comfort. It was loaded with emotional and symbolic significance in terms of its connection with the home, family, and community. Particularly for those with family members or friends stationed overseas, regular parcels containing familiar and favourite foods offered one of the most immediate means of maintaining a link to the soldier's home amidst unfamiliar and often unimaginable circumstances. Women's magazines and the women's sections of newspapers regularly offered Canadian women advice on how to best pack such parcels.[42] Janet M. Gibson remembers that as a child, she was often responsible for putting together her brother's monthly care package and that it often "took a month to gather up enough chewing gum, candy, chocolate bars, etc., as these items were scarce and limited in the stores."[43] Soldiers often made specific requests for candies, chocolates, and other store-bought items, but it was baked goods that were particularly popular because they evoked an emotional connection with home. The importance of this emotional connection was stressed in Blanch J. Pownall's sentimental 1941 poem "Box For Overseas":

> Was it but yesterday he shadowed me,
> Snatching the spicy crumbs my hands let fall?
> Pausing, a cookie at his lips, to cry,
> "I love the SMELL of Christmas best of all!"
> The ginger cookies always were his favorites.
> I'll add another dozen! And I knew
> His Christmas wouldn't really be complete
> Without the shortbread and the peanut chew![44]

Clearly, the contents of these packages often said more about the emotional needs of the senders than the desires of the recipients. Even so, they provided sender and recipient alike with at least some reprieve from the emotional trauma of being separated by war.

While the sending of parcels to soldiers was often an intensely private and personal act, some women's organizations and other groups coordinated their efforts to send parcels to local men stationed overseas. The Women's Institute in Fort Saskatchewan, Alberta, regularly sent parcels to local soldiers for Christmas, birthdays, and other special occasions. Groups in other communities set up "Comforts Committees," whose goal was to ensure that "all men enlisting in the community should receive equal treatment insofar as comforts and parcels were concerned."[45] The Canadian Red Cross Society started a national program to supplement Next of Kin parcels sent by family members to soldiers in German POW camps. Recognizing the importance of these parcels to the psychological and physical well-being of captured soldiers, Red Cross volunteers regularly "topped up" parcels sent by families that, because of financial or other constraints, did not contain the maximum allowable weight in permissible items such as dehydrated fruits and berries, dehydrated soups, nuts, coffee, and spices.[46]

Soldiers already overseas were not the only recipients of comforts from Canadian family, friends, and even total strangers. In fact, much of the comfort work done by women on the home front focused on soldiers who were stationed in or passing through local communities before being shipped overseas. At all times of day and night, soldiers were greeted at train stations and ports by volunteers providing them with coffee, donuts, candy bars, cigarettes, and reading materials. In 1943 alone, the Edmonton YWCA greeted more than 2,500 trains in order to provide comforts and help soldiers make their connections.[47] The Women's Institutes of Nova Scotia maintained an "Apples for Troops" campaign throughout the war, which offered fresh fruit to soldiers as they passed through Truro.[48] These efforts were intended to provide soldiers with some of the familiar comforts of home and, perhaps more importantly, to boost morale through what were essentially public performances of support for the war effort. The patriotic aspect became even more apparent during the final years of the war and in the early postwar period, when many of these greeting services transformed themselves into "welcome home" services. Returning soldiers in Halifax, Winnipeg, and other major transportation hubs were often greeted with live bands and tables set out with coffee, donuts, fresh fruit, and ice cream – not to mention gifts of chocolate, candy, soft drinks, games, and reading materials.[49] Although these were simple gestures, many returning soldiers found that the sight of something as ordinary as a banana – which most had not seen in years – could carry a powerful emotional message signalling the promise of abundance and a better life after demobilization.[50]

An important extension of this work – and one of the most intimate and symbolically loaded "comfort" activities – was the common practice of having volunteers invite military personnel stationed in nearby communities to join them for their weekly Sunday dinner or for a holiday meal on Christmas or Thanksgiving. Some families, on their own initiative, sent out open invitations to soldiers at the local military base, but many larger voluntary and charitable organizations acted as liaisons between soldiers and local families. The young female volunteers at the Halifax YMCA, for instance, often invited soldiers staying at the hostel to their own or their friends' homes for Sunday dinners. The Winnipeg Women's Voluntary Service, for its part, organized a more formal service that linked as many as 1,400 soldiers with local families for dinners and weekend leaves each year.[51] By the end of the war, tens of thousands of families had welcomed total strangers from around the country and the Commonwealth into their homes to share a meal.

Home-cooked dinners offered soldiers a welcome respite from military regimentation and the repetitiveness of the not-always-appetizing mess hall. They also had important symbolic value. Margaret Chase Huxford of Halifax remembered that her family's weekly invitations to soldiers were about more than food: "We could offer a hot meal, friendly conversation, a chance to show off at the piano, and the opportunity to flirt with my sister and me as we washed the dishes. Above all, we offered a glimpse of normal family life after so many weeks of danger and discomfort on board ship."[52] The kind of heteronormative sociability discussed by Huxford was often an important aspect of these dinners, but it was the idea that soldiers were participating in "normal family life" that made them so important to both the hosts and the guests. As Amy Bentley has pointed out in the American context, ritualized meals like Sunday or Thanksgiving dinner were often used in wartime advertising and propaganda as representations of the basic cultural foundations of the family, the household, and the nation – all three of which were perceived to be at stake during the war.[53] By inviting complete strangers into their homes to participate in these quintessential "family" meals, volunteers were enacting a vision of the nation as a family bound by ties of military and patriotic service. The fact that such meals typically served expensive, higher-quality, ration-coupon-intensive meats – such as roasts – similarly spoke to families' willingness to sacrifice their own material comfort for the broader good of the men and women in uniform.[54]

As Benedict Anderson argues, nations are always imagined communities whose members will never meet the vast majority of their fellow citizens given the often insurmountable barriers of distance, social inequality, or language but who are nonetheless united by a "deep, horizontal comradeship."[55] These ritualized family dinners therefore acted to make these imagined wartime social bonds much more real for the soldiers and families involved. Canada may have lacked a coherent national food culture, and the menus of these dinners undoubtedly varied with the community where they were held. Even so, their symbolic meaning would have been familiar in ways that crossed regional, ethnic, and linguistic barriers. By combining pan-national rituals with regional and family traditions, these dinners served as important symbolic acts of patriotism that built upon wartime discourses of the nation as a family bound by gendered ideals of citizenship, sacrifice, and duty. And when Canadians invited Allied soldiers stationed in the country as part of the British Commonwealth Air Training Program into their homes, it forged – in the words of one wartime documentary – "new links across the borders," thereby strengthening symbolic and emotional ties within the Empire.[56]

A similar sense of wartime unity was created through the mobilization of volunteers in other large-scale ways. For instance, by far the largest and most important national volunteer efforts to provide comforts to military personnel involved offering communal meals, accommodation, and recreational opportunities to soldiers in their off-duty hours at what, by war's end, would be nearly 245 canteens and recreation centres intended solely for soldiers on active duty.[57] Some of these, like Toronto's Active Service Canteen, Moose Jaw's War Services Club, and Abbotsford's United Services Hut, were operated by local citizens' committees that had been established at a grassroots level in the early months of the war. Most, however, were operated by one of six national voluntary organizations – namely, the Canadian Legion, the Knights of Columbus, the Salvation Army, the YMCA, the YWCA, and the Navy League of Canada. The NWS had assigned these organizations the responsibility for nearly all activities related to the welfare of the armed services. Some of the more targeted sports and recreation facilities were located on the military bases themselves, but most of these canteens, clubs, and recreation centres were off-base in nearby cities and towns.

These centres offered a range of comforts and social services to soldiers, including cafeterias, games, libraries, dance halls, and even "quiet rooms" where "men could think about the more serious things of life or spend a few moments with their loved ones before departing overseas."[58] From the perspective of the military, at least, a principal goal of these establishments was to provide food, entertainment, and companionship in wholesome surroundings. To this end, they offered a variety of services designed to break the monotony of military life, including shops where soldiers could buy items not included in their military mess provisions, such as soft drinks, chocolate, cigarettes, and stationery. The canteens also alleviated homesickness by making available domestic comforts like home-cooked meals and even "mothers' corners" where volunteers would "mend, press, sew on buttons and otherwise look after the clothing of the men."[59]

Even with the large number of services offered by most canteens and recreation centres, food service was often one of their most important functions, both in terms of volunteer labour and their ability to success-fully attract off-duty soldiers. Most canteens offered full meal services or snacks – usually until eleven at night, sometimes even later, and at heavily subsidized prices. They also gave soldiers on leave access to rationed and scarce goods without having to use their ration coupons.[60] Some canteens offered only coffee, soft drinks, and sandwiches, but many more provided full-course meals that drew hundreds of soldiers each day. For instance, Halifax's North End Service Canteen offered full meal service to between 1,500 and 1,800 men per day and went through two hundred pounds of meat, three or four bags of potatoes, one bushel of a second vegetable, eighteen to twenty gallons of canned vegetables, and about one hundred quarts of milk in the course of a typical meal service. Toronto's Active Service Canteen – which attracted more than 3,743,191 visitors over the course of the war – not only provided a full, low-cost dinner service but also, faced with a heavy demand for its hot meal service, opened a separate snack bar serving sandwiches and other, smaller items.[61]

The food services these canteens provided were so popular that they drew more volunteer labour than any other home front campaign. In the Toronto Active Service Canteen, nearly half of the sixty to eighty volunteers working a typical shift – and there were three shifts on most days as well as a fourth "midnight shift" on Saturdays from eleven till two – worked in the kitchen, snack bar, refreshments table, or cafeteria. Over the course of the war, this canteen saw more than 10,000 women volunteer their time, with a peak of 2,911 volunteers per week in April 1945. The Winnipeg United Service Centre was a similarly impressive endeavour and, by the end of the war, was the biggest single volunteer undertaking in that city (see Figure 3.5). The war services operations of the YWCA, which operated dozens of canteens and hostels throughout the country, had drawn the participation of more than 230,000 women by the end of the war.[62] While there is no official total, it is clear that just the canteens required the regular labour of hundreds of thousands of Canadian women, many of whom

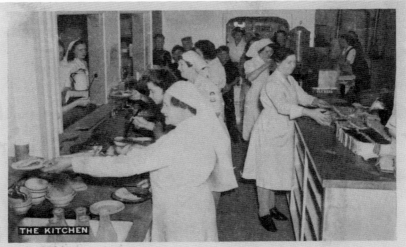

Figure 3.5 Photos of the Winnipeg United Service Centre from a book of postcards produced by the Centre. *Author's personal collection.*

worked nearly full-time hours providing services, comfort, and sustenance to soldiers.

The canteens' food services were popular largely because of their convenience and cost. Many volunteers, though, attributed their success to the fact that most foods reflected a kind of familiar "home cooking." The meals provided were usually simple, hearty dishes of the meat-and-potatoes variety that would have been most familiar to both the volunteer kitchen staff and the soldiers themselves. In most cases, this was a deliberate strategy on the part of the canteen organizers, who knew they were competing with local restaurants, theatres, and taverns for the solders' attention. For instance, inspired by the idea that "the boys would like something really home cooked," the Calgary Women's Voluntary Service established a "Pie Factory" in the basement of a local church, where volunteers were able to produce hundreds of pies for the local Servicemen's Centre.[63] One volunteer at the Winnipeg Airmen's Club – which served an average of two hundred meals daily during the week, and 1,200 to 1,500 on weekends – attributed the success of the food service to the canteen's atmosphere, which they suggested often resembled the family kitchen more than a mess hall or restaurant. As one volunteer recalled, "they watched us do the cooking as they watched their mothers in their own homes. They helped us wash dishes, peel potatoes, and, in fact, did everything but the cooking. Indeed, many the bowl and spoon were licked after the cake was iced."[64] That image may have fit a little too well with the government's broader propaganda narrative but it nonetheless speaks to the mindset that many volunteers brought to their work providing comforts for soldiers. Through their considerable unpaid labour in canteen kitchens, they were seeking to – and, in many cases, were *able* to – recreate a familiar domestic space that served as a refuge for soldiers and as an outlet for civilian volunteers to enact a particularly gendered vision of patriotic citizenship and service.

Overseas Food Relief

Besides providing comforts to soldiers stationed at home, Canadians organized or participated in a range of voluntary and charitable campaigns aimed at sending food and other essential goods to both soldiers and civilians overseas. Although the rhetoric behind wartime conservation efforts like victory gardening stressed the need to save food in order to help free up resources needed to feed Allied soldiers and civilians, many Canadians sought to make more direct and concrete contributions. For instance, thousands of school children, young adult women, and adult women devoted their summers to low-paid agricultural labour on farms in Ontario and British Columbia as members of the Farm Cadets, Farmerettes, or Women's Land Brigades. Created in response to shortages in agricultural labour, these components of the Farm Labour Service represented an impressive mobilization of patriotic enthusiasm to feed Canada's soldiers and allies.[65] But a similar sentiment was also shown in the often overlooked international food relief campaigns that were quickly established as a key part of the nearly four thousand charitable funds organized across Canada during the war.

From the beginning of the war, charitable work was subject to considerable federal oversight through the War Charities Act. That act, which was based on similar legislation passed in 1917, required all charities to register with the federal government and imposed strict organizational and accounting rules on them. It also limited the periods during which fundraising could take place so as to avoid overlap with other campaigns such as Victory Loans and War Savings drives as well as those of established national voluntary organizations like the Red Cross. Other limitations on charities were also set. Early in the war, for instance, a policy was established to register only one fund for each nationality so that food and other relief efforts directed at Allied countries could be coordinated in a more efficient, centralized manner. By the end of the war, a range of funds providing food relief and other essential services to soldiers and overseas allies had been established, including the Aid to Russia Fund, the Chinese War Relief Fund, the Milk for Britain Campaign, and the Save the Children Fund. Tarah Brookfield, Susan Armstrong-Reid, and others have conducted valuable studies of Canadian women's postwar contributions to relief organizations such as UNRRA, UNICEF, CARE Canada, and World Vision. It is clear that many of these postwar efforts built directly on a growing wartime sense of internationalism that was, in many cases, spurred by Canadians' extensive participation in wartime relief efforts.[66]

Canadians contributed generously to overseas relief operations and patriotic charitable funds. Between 1942 and 1945 alone, the funds registered under the War Charities Act collected in excess of $183,000,000 in donations.[67] Part of this success had to do with the fact that during the war, many Canadians saw a significant increase in their real incomes. This, combined with shortages in a wide range of consumer goods, made it much easier for households to increase their charitable giving.[68] Just as important, however, was the massive mobilization of voluntary labour in service of these wartime charities. The NWS estimated that over the course of the war, at least half the Canadian population was linked in some way with work falling under jurisdiction of the War Charities Act.[69] For example, the Winnipeg Patriotic Salvage Corps mobilized hundreds of female volunteers – who often put in long hours of strenuous physical labour – in order to collect a net profit of $112,847 from the sale of locally salvaged goods, with the funds going to a number of charitable activities, including the Save the Children Fund, Chinese War Relief, the Milk for Britain campaign, and the purchase of eight mobile kitchens.[70] While salvage was an important means of fundraising for many groups, much more was collected using well-proven fundraising strategies such as the publication and sale of community cookbooks and the holding of bake sales, dances, and similar events. During the interwar years, women had used all of these strategies to collect funds for everything from the construction of churches to the funding of political campaigns to the maintenance of social service organizations. The Ontario Women's Institutes, for instance, collected more than $700,000 through activities such as (often "tealess") teas, euchre parties, bingos, dances, potluck lunches, and progressive dinners. The money was often put towards the Red Cross or towards causes such as the Seeds for English Gardens and Jam for Britain campaigns, both sponsored by the Women's Institutes.[71]

Although fundraising was an important means of supporting overseas food relief for Allied civilians and soldiers, many Canadian women sought to make more direct contributions, particularly through their work with the Canadian Red Cross Society. By all measures, the Red Cross was the largest voluntary organization in Canada during the war. At its 1945 peak, there were 2,124,189 Canadian Red Cross members. When the Junior Red Cross is added, moreover, the total Red Cross membership exceeded three million – more than one-quarter of Canada's total population.[72] Part of the draw of the Red Cross was its record as one of the most effective outlets for Canadian voluntary and charitable efforts during the previous war.[73] But even more important was the sheer range of war-related work being carried out by Red Cross branches. That work included organizing hospital visitors for injured soldiers, providing troop comforts, purchasing medical supplies and vehicles for use overseas, operating overseas clubs, supplying comforts such as homemade food and hand-knitted clothing for troops, and extending financial and other aid to the dependents of soldiers and returning veterans.

Food often played a key role in Red Cross work, whether it was through the organization's ambitious nutrition education programs or through food relief efforts such as the Jam for Britain campaign, which was launched at a grassroots level by BC women shortly after the war began in 1939 and quickly grew into a nationwide effort.[74] This project, which saw the Red Cross form a national partnership with rural women's organizations such as the Federated Women's Institutes and the Cercles de Fermières, was coordinated by an Ontario Division nutritionist, Mrs. Allan Stephenson. The initial goal was twofold: to make use of surplus fruit that would otherwise have gone to waste, and to support the nutritional needs of Britain in light of the loss of key sources of imported foods. The campaign mobilized individual women's jam-making skills, labour, and surplus fruit in order to close a serious gap in the British wartime diet.

The Jam for Britain campaign was similar in many important ways to the iconic knitting and sewing work done by Red Cross volunteers during the war. Both built on familiar household skills and provided a means for women across the country to link their household production of essential domestic goods to a greater patriotic purpose. And, perhaps just as importantly, both focused on the scientific management ideals of repetition, standardization, and efficiency in their mobilization of women's labour. Most discussion by historians of the oft-repeated trope of women on the home front knitting stockings for soldiers fails to position the act of patriotic knitting within a broader, well-organized system of war production of clothing by individual women either in their homes, with friends, or in communal workrooms. In Toronto, volunteers in a National Workroom developed patterns and samples for a range of items identified as priorities by the military, including sewn items such as pneumonia jackets, dressing gowns, convalescent shirts, bedpan covers, slings, and bandages as well as knitted sweaters, gloves, stockings, caps, mitts, and underclothes.[75] These items were then produced by Red Cross branches and individual volunteers on a national scale and forwarded to the military. All of this highlights the skill, efficiency, and productivity of women's unpaid domestic labour when applied to a larger collective goal.

Similarly, the Jam for Britain campaign focused on the twin goals of standardization and efficiency. To this end, the Red Cross provided volunteers with standardized tins, labels, and packing cases. The campaign also received assistance from the federal government in the form of special ration quotas for branches taking part in the campaign and an instructional pamphlet from the Department of Agriculture outlining the specific methods to be used in producing jam for export.[76] The instructions forbade the use of pectin and encouraged specific fruit-to-sugar ratios, but the country's various regions were allowed leeway to produce their own specialties. Branches in Quebec focused primarily on maple sugar and maple syrup; New Brunswick branches were given permission to ship orange marmalade; areas with less abundant fruit crops either donated money to Red Cross branches in fruit-growing areas or – as was the case in many prairie districts – focused on honey production. The jams this campaign produced therefore reflected the diversity of Canadian fruit production, and included apple, apricot, cherry, currant, peach, grape, gooseberry, orange, pear, plum, raspberry, strawberry, loganberry, thimbleberry, and greengage. In spite of all this variety, the resulting product was impressively consistent and more than 98 percent of the jam produced was deemed suitable for overseas shipment by government inspectors.[77]

By all accounts, the Jam for Britain campaign was a considerable success. Hundreds of Red Cross branches took part, and by the end of the war, approximately 2.5 million pounds of jam, honey, and maple syrup had been shipped overseas, with most of it going to the British Women's Voluntary Services for war nurseries and for homeless victims of the Blitz.[78] All of this food and sugar had been provided by the volunteers themselves, or purchased by them rather than out of Red Cross funds. The jam itself, moreover, had often been produced through the application of assembly-line-like discipline during harvest periods. Mary F.S. Miller, who took part in the Jam for Britain campaign through her local Women's Institute branch near Scarborough, Ontario, remembers that her parents' home "was like a small factory four or five days a week. Each day, five to ten members would show up for work."[79] The Rednersville Women's Institute in Prince Edward County, Ontario, used a local canning factory one day a week to make jam. A "faithful bank of institute members and other volunteers" gathered during the fruit season to oversee the production of jam, which was packed in four-pound pails and shipped in crates supplied by the Red Cross. Ultimately, the Rednersville Women's Institute alone processed and shipped 8,800 pounds of jam.[80]

While the Jam for Britain campaign was impressive in its national scope and in the sheer scale of its production, by far the most important overseas food relief effort undertaken during the war was the Red Cross prisoner-of-war parcel program. More than any other wartime voluntary effort, this program reflected the ambitious efforts of the Red Cross to mobilize the voluntary labour of Canadians to preserve the health and morale of soldiers, their families, and Canada's international allies. And at war's end, it was shown to have had a direct and measurable impact on the physical and emotional survival of Allied soldiers overseas. The packages themselves had been designed by a prominent Canadian nutrition expert, RCAF Wing Commander Dr. Frederick Tisdall, who was a pediatrician at the Toronto Hospital for Sick Children as well as a co-inventor of Pablum. His goal had been to make up for the deficiencies in fat, protein, calories,

Figure 3.6 Volunteers packing Red Cross POW parcels in an assembly line in Hamilton, Ontario, March 1943. *Hamilton Public Library.*

vitamins, and minerals experienced by POWs surviving on German rations alone. The parcels, which were limited to eleven pounds each by an international agreement, were carefully packed in a way that ensured maximum nutritional content in the space allotted. They therefore contained items such as powdered milk, butter, cheese, canned meats, dried fruit, sugar, jam, pilot biscuits, chocolate, salt and pepper, tea, and soap.[81] Because of the near-starvation allowances provided by the Germans, the POW parcels became a major priority for the Red Cross, accounting for up to 47 percent of the organization's total wartime budget.[82]

This was a massive undertaking that required the establishment of POW packing plants in Toronto and Montreal in January 1941. Soon afterwards, additional plants were opened in Hamilton, London, Windsor, and Winnipeg. Each plant was run on an assembly-line model and was expected to meet a specific quota of standardized POW parcels (see Figure 3.6). The vast bulk of this work was carried out by women, thousands of whom regularly volunteered their time in large enough numbers to keep the plants running full-time throughout the war. By the end of the war, the Winnipeg plant alone was depending on the labour of nearly eight hundred regular volunteers and was producing upwards of 24,000 parcels a week. At its peak, the combined production of all plants was an impressive 100,000 parcels per week.[83] By war's end, 16,310,592 parcels had been sent to POWs through the International Committee of the Red Cross, and because of the volunteer labour, the cost for packaging and shipping had been a remarkably low $2.50 per parcel.[84]

From its inception in July 1941, the POW food parcel program was a potent symbol of the voluntary contributions of Canadian women to the war effort. Like other voluntary efforts, it spoke to a domestic, feminine ideal of caring and self-sacrifice through the provision of nutritious food. But while other food-focused wartime efforts such as the active service canteens and weekly home-cooked meals for soldiers focused mainly on morale, the POW parcels were linked specifically to the actual survival of soldiers overseas. Freed POWs regularly reported that they "were sure they would not have lived without the Red Cross food parcels."[85] One former prisoner told *Saturday Night* in 1945 that "food parcels are not just parcels to prisoners of war, they are the gift of life itself."[86] The POW parcel program, perhaps more than any other, lived up to the promise made by wartime propaganda that women's individual efforts on the home front would save the lives of soldiers overseas. The sheer scale of the program, moreover, meant that volunteers were contributing directly to the survival of thousands of soldiers in a way that was more easily quantified than other forms of wartime participation on the home front.

Volunteers, Womanpower, and the State

As the POW parcel program showed, women's wartime voluntary work was more than just "busy work" and more than just an impressive mobilization of patriotic sentiment. These voluntary activities often made essential material contributions to the war effort that would otherwise have been much more expensive and much more difficult to achieve, given Canada's wartime "manpower" shortages. NWS officials recognized that this was true of the hundreds of volunteer-run canteens and recreation centres, which department officials described as a "labour of love" that had an "incalculably beneficial" effect on morale.[87] This was given official acknowledgment when, in 1942, the NWS began to fund the work of the Canadian Legion, the Knights of Columbus, the Salvation Army, the YMCA, the YWCA, and the Navy League of Canada directly from the public treasury rather than through charitable appeals. Only a year earlier, the fundraising apparatus of each organization had been subsumed under the umbrella of the Canadian War Services Fund. Yet, soon after this, government officials realized that the services these organizations provided were too important to the maintenance of morale to be left up to charitable collections alone. By the end of the war, roughly $55,000,000 had been dispersed by the NWS Funds Advisory Board for the operation of these services. The state, in other words, was subsidizing volunteer efforts to shore up the inadequate military infrastructure for food, leisure, and social needs.[88]

This direct state funding of voluntary war services was just one part of a much larger official effort to harness and direct women's voluntary labour as a means to fill important (wo)manpower gaps in wartime programs and operations on the home front. The government's heavy utilization of women's unpaid labour during the war has been somewhat eclipsed in the historical literature by accounts of women's unprecedented wartime participation in both the military and the industrial workforce. As a number of historians have documented, women had been drawn into these previously "male" forms of labour in response to national "manpower" shortages caused by the movement of large numbers of working men into military service. Officials in the military and National Selective Service bureaucracies tended to view single women – and, later on, housewives – as a potential "female labour reserve" that could free up more men for frontline service.[89] But the Canadian government also viewed women's voluntary labour as another, separate reservoir of "womanpower" that could be marshalled to meet specific wartime goals through patriotic appeals to the "Housoldier" ideal of women as wives, mothers, and consumers.

This was particularly true of the Canadian Nutrition Programme, whose wartime advocacy and education work was made possible by hundreds of volunteers who organized a range of both small and large community nutrition campaigns. Driven in large part by warnings from the scientists and in the media that malnutrition was threatening both their families and the war effort more generally, many women took up Byrne Hope Sanders's 1941 call to action that "every woman should study diet and nutrition seriously; if there are no classes available in your community – agitate and educate until there are."[90] Soon after its founding in 1941, the Nutrition Services Division of the Department of Pensions and National Health began receiving hundreds of letters from concerned Canadian women seeking information on how to improve their own or their community's nutritional status. Mrs. Marion Spencer of Chilliwack, BC, wrote to Ottawa after reading about Canada's high rate of military rejections, and with the help of the Nutrition Services staff, she and other interested women formed a local nutrition committee in order to launch a "quiet" campaign focusing on "small gatherings and expert advice."[91] Mrs. William D. Tucker of Port Credit, Ontario, appointed herself "as a one-man, or one-woman, committee to assist Canada's campaign for better national health in our community" and sought out educational materials that she and her local Home and School Association could use to improve the eating habits of local children.[92]

It was through hundreds of similar requests to Nutrition Services that women throughout the country began their own nutrition programs either within their local women's organizations or on a broader community basis. By the end of the war, dozens of community nutrition councils were in operation throughout the country. Most were run by volunteers in co-operation with municipal and provincial departments of health as well as with charitable organizations like the Red Cross, Women's Institutes, the National Council of Women, the Société Saint-Jean-Baptiste, and the Health League of Canada. It was these voluntary nutrition committees, rather than the "official" efforts of the Nutrition Services Division, that formed the heart of the Canadian Nutrition Programme. The Nutrition Services Division had a limited staff and limited resources to get the message about good nutrition out to the general public. To fill this gap, these local committees therefore adopted a range of strategies for promoting public knowledge of nutrition. The Kingston Community Nutrition Council, for example, conducted surveys, distributed educational materials, sponsored public lectures, created downtown nutrition displays, produced children's radio plays, and even launched a fundraising campaign to pay the salary of a municipal nutritionist.[93] The Nutrition Council of Windsor, for its part, spearheaded a pilot school lunch project in a few local schools that grew so popular that it was expanded throughout the school district.[94]

The most popular approach of local nutrition committees, however, involved organizing large-scale educational campaigns that, over the course of a few weeks, offered lectures, classes, displays, and other nutritional materials to local women. In many cases, the success of these campaigns reflected both the impressive organizational skills of local women as well as the popular desire among women to improve their own nutritional knowledge in light of a perceived national malnutrition crisis. Montreal's "Food For Health, Health For Victory – La Nourriture Pour La Santé, La Santé Pour La Victoire" campaign in January and February 1942 was, by most accounts, a highly successful collaboration among a variety of French and English organizations – including the Women's Canadian Club, the Société Saint-Jean-Baptiste, and the Red Cross – as well as local social service agencies, the city's nutrition professionals, and all levels of government. The campaign ultimately saw thousands attend a series of public lectures in English and French, whose audiences ranged in size from 17 to 450. There were also a series of four nutrition courses run by trained dieticians and home economists, whose attendance exceeded five thousand for the English-language courses alone.[95] A similarly successful campaign was launched by women's groups in Winnipeg, where more than eight thousand women attended nutrition courses as part of the city's "Health for Victory Campaign."[96]

Perhaps the most important way in which the state sought to manage and utilize the deep reservoirs of voluntary "womanpower" was through the Women's Voluntary Service (WVS), established by the NWS in October 1941. The stated purposes of the WVS were to coordinate the voluntary efforts of the women of Canada and to encourage the organization of women's voluntary services on a community basis.[97] The WVS was loosely based on its British counterpart and, perhaps more directly, on grassroots efforts by women in Manitoba and Ontario. The idea was to encourage communities to create recruiting offices where women could register as volunteers and be matched with a local patriotic campaign. In practice, local WVS branches often more closely approximated existing charitable and voluntary organizations such as community councils, councils of social agencies, or citizens' committees than the British WVS, which was devoted primarily to civil defence activities and assisting victims of Nazi bombing raids.[98] The Canadian WVS was also unique in that it reflected a much broader conception of voluntary work. For its organizers, the broad mandate of the WVS was its strength, given that their stated goal was "to encourage the organization of women's voluntary services on a community basis with the emphasis on the 'community'" as well as to "cover all voluntary effort, whether for war services or community health and welfare services."[99]

By 1944, there were forty-four active WVS centres in Canada, with thousands of registered volunteers in most of Canada's major cities. Individual WVS centres set their own priorities and activities. Their campaigns therefore ranged from fundraising for charitable causes to conducting immunization drives and nutrition programs to organizing educational and vocational programs. They also provided a pool of unpaid labour that various government departments could access for their own purposes.

For instance, through a "Block Leader Plan" developed by the WVS leadership, individual volunteers delivered information on state-sponsored programs to anywhere between ten to thirty families. These volunteers sometimes even conducted large-scale, national surveys of public attitudes towards new food products such as Canada Approved Breads. In 1944, WVS volunteers even conducted a national Victory Garden survey that examined the productivity of 1,613 wartime gardens in seven cities.[100]

Perhaps the most impressive example of how government departments used the unpaid labour of WVS and other volunteers to meet essential wartime economic and social goals was in relation to rationing. As discussed earlier, given the WPTB's extremely limited enforcement capacity, the success of rationing heavily depended on the voluntary participation of consumers, producers, and retailers. At a more basic level, though, the actual machinery of rationing depended heavily on the voluntary labour of the thousands of women who were organized largely through the efforts of the WVS. For instance, the implementation of coupon rationing in 1942 required the assistance of nearly eighty thousand volunteers, who filled out (by hand) and distributed nearly twelve million ration books in 106 regional centres in only fourteen days (see Figure 3.7).[101] Without volunteers, this particular task would have been prohibitively expensive. Indeed, given the "manpower" shortages faced by the civil service, it would have been nearly impossible. And this broad mobilization of volunteers was repeated for the release of each new ration book well into the early postwar period.

Especially in larger urban centres, much of this ration book work was organized through the local WVS branch. The Toronto WVS, for instance, marshalled 4,500 registered volunteers to help distribute the first ration book on short notice, while eight thousand volunteers took part in the Winnipeg ration book distribution scheme over the course of the war.[102] According to Byrne Sanders, the director of the Consumer Branch, women's participation in ration book distribution provided a highly public demonstration of the kind of "organizing ability and co-operative genius" that was the cornerstone of most local and national women's organizations and thereby showed the whole country that women "can measure up to an emergency with dispatch and ability – and skill."[103] Perhaps just as importantly, however, it was a prime example of how the state had come to depend on the unpaid patriotic labour of Canadian women to ensure that key wartime priorities were met. Much of the wartime propaganda of the "Housoldier" and "Mrs. Consumer" variety portrayed women's

Figure 3.7 Ration books. The time and effort involved
in filling out each book by hand required thousands of
volunteers. *Author's personal collection.*

contributions primarily as private acts of patriotic service within the home.
Yet by the end of the war it was clear that more public mobilizations of
women's skills and labour had played an even greater role in meeting key
wartime social and economic priorities.

The type and scale of the volunteer work carried out by Canadian women
during the war highlight the limits of the "Housoldier" ideal of private

patriotic citizenship that was promoted in so much of the wartime propaganda. Many women found decidedly public outlets for their patriotism, even when it required considerable sacrifices of time and labour. As many of the jobs described above attest, wartime voluntary work often involved long hours of hard, repetitive labour of the kind that – although often done in groups – reflected the drudgery of housework and factory labour rather than the pleasures of leisure and sociability. Carolyn Gossage remembers the long hours her mother spent washing dishes at the local service canteen. As a child, she thought it "sounded like a very boring and horrible way for her to 'contribute to the war effort.'"[104] The WVS publication *Volunteer Voice* noted in its December 1943 issue:

> Many of the projects ... are hard, strenuous and tedious work, without glamour or excitement. Yet none of the women feel their work is superfluous or unnecessary. Each seems to realize that although her job may appear small and unimportant, it is part of a plan that can be completed only if all jobs are well done.[105]

Budge Wilson, who was a child during the war, did not remember her mother's extensive volunteer activities as a source of pleasure or leisure. "[Our mothers] worked long hours each week at the hostels and canteens for the people in the armed forces, handing out coffee, mending rips and tears, making sandwiches, hoping they'd get home in time to look after their own families. My mother, frail and nervous at the best of times, seemed to be tired more often than not."[106]

Accounts like these suggest the ways in which the state's wartime mobilization of women's voluntary labour contained some important parallels with paid labour. From the perspective of government officials, women provided a dependable reservoir to be tapped to meet wartime labour market shortages. In fact, many of the iconic voluntary and patriotic campaigns organized by women more closely resembled the paid workforce than the domestic ideals often used to rally women's participation in patriotic causes. Joy Parr contends that the war "intensified, reinvigorated, and ratified household production of more clothing and food, affirming that the work factories did, what was called production, homemakers also did within the household."[107] The work done by volunteers in active service canteens, communal jam-making operations, and POW parcel packing plants, however, often made this connection even more explicit by transforming familiar domestic tasks such as food preparation into a kind of household mass production that borrowed as much from the industrial discipline of the factory as it did from women's work in the home.

Conclusion

As one of Canada's most important contributions to the war effort and as one of the focal points around which women's domestic responsibilities for household production and reproduction were situated, food played a key role in the mobilization of Canadians' patriotic efforts throughout the war. Ideas about patriotic duty on the home front were based, in part at least, on the notion that food, the kitchen, and other organizing principles of domestic life needed to be mobilized in service of the nation, whether it involved victory gardening, fats and bones salvage, or other conservation efforts. Even when these efforts were more symbolic than materially important, they did much to rally Canadians in support of larger changes taking place in the wartime economy and in society more generally. And as many women showed through their considerable contributions to various wartime voluntary and charitable campaigns, it was mainly through these public expressions of support for the war effort that many Canadians came to define the parameters of their wartime citizenship. By pooling their labour with other women from around the country and sacrificing many of their short leisure hours to efforts like jam making, cooking for soldiers, and packing POW parcels, Canadian women rallied their domestic skills and labour in ways that highlighted their productive and economic value as key engines of the Canadian economy and of the war effort more generally.

4

Tealess Teas, Meatless Days, and Recipes for Victory

Transforming Food Culture and Culinary Practice in Wartime

In January 1943, entrepreneur George Hebden Corsan wrote to the *Globe and Mail* to relay his housekeeper Miss Elizabeth Hoffman's exciting discoveries in the field of butter substitutes. In addition to a sandwich spread of boiled beans – which were run through a colander to deprive them of their "gas-forming properties" and flavoured with raw onion – Corsan enthusiastically described Hoffman's recipe for potato butter: "Slice and boil potatoes in as little water as possible to keep them from burning, salt and mash. Then add finely chopped raw onions, celery and parsley." "Was it good!" Corsan added. "Try this with the children and war workers' lunches, and note how exceedingly well they will be."[1] *Globe* readers might have been forgiven for thinking that these butter substitutes were unlikely to taste, smell, look, or spread anything like actual butter, but Corsan and Hoffman were not alone in experimenting with new and unusual ways of making do with less as rationing and shortages forced significant changes in how Canadians shopped, cooked, and ate. Newspapers, magazines, and the more than two hundred cookbooks published during the war years were filled with experimental ideas for substitutes, stretchers, and "patriotic" alternatives for any number of familiar staples that had gone missing from Canadians' pantries and iceboxes by the middle of the war.[2]

Building on a growing feminist literature on cookbooks and the construction of popular ideas about gender, citizenship, and nation, this chapter examines multiple genres of wartime food writing – ranging from ordinary Canadians' contributions to newspapers and community cookbooks to the avalanche of wartime prescriptive literature produced by food experts, government officials, and advertisers – as a means of exploring the different ways in which profound wartime social, economic, and political changes were translated into the language of food culture and culinary practice.[3] It also examines how rationing and other wartime controls – in combination with near-constant patriotic appeals for Canadians to transform their diets – created a space for a number of common, distinctly "wartime" pan-Canadian culinary practices. In doing so, it argues that although "war" recipes marked a clearer break from the past for some, Corsan's "Potato Butter" was nonetheless very much part of a larger national conversation on how Canadians could meet the challenge of wartime controls and shortages in new and creative ways.

This chapter also acknowledges that wartime culinary change was driven by more than just food rationing. For many, in fact, the war years were marked less by austerity than by the end of Depression-era hunger and want. It therefore explores not only the contradiction between the rhetoric of sacrifice and the reality of abundance that characterized wartime cuisine, but also the ways in which Canadian women, in particular, used wartime cookbooks and recipes to articulate a range of distinctly postwar culinary visions that built on their very different experiences of the social, economic, and political transformations that characterized this period. This chapter, then, argues that the national experience of the war facilitated attempts to articulate a decidedly "Canadian" form of culinary practice. In this regard, wartime cookbooks, recipes, and other forms of culinary literature provide a unique insight into the often contradictory ways in which popular ideas about both wartime and postwar citizenship were articulated through the gendered language of domestic practice and culture.

Recipes for Victory

The emergence of a pan-Canadian, "patriotic" form of culinary practice during the war in many ways reflected the extended reach of the wartime state. The federal government therefore played a key role in defining "patriotic" cuisine, and, by the end of the war, a number of federal departments were actively encouraging Canadians to change their eating habits through propaganda, consumer education, and other means. Leading the way in this effort to change how Canadian women in particular shopped for and cooked food was the Consumer Section of the Department of Agriculture. Prior to the war, this agency had focused on using tools such as educational demonstrations and pamphlets, booklets, and newspaper articles to encourage the consumption of foods produced on Canadian farms. But after September 1939, it quickly turned to publishing wartime materials with titles such as *Foods for Home Defence* and *Wartime Sugar Savers* as well as to other forms of popular education.[4] By 1942, moreover, it had been joined by a number of newly formed agencies, including the Consumer Branch of the Wartime Prices and Trade Board (WPTB) and the Consumer Section of the Wartime Information Board (WIB). These agencies, with the WIB's propaganda network at their disposal, produced a torrent of recipes, radio scripts, articles, and other food-related press materials, many of which were translated into Ukrainian, Polish, and German for Canada's foreign-language press.[5]

Early in the war, much of the federal government's effort in this area focused on providing assistance to domestic agricultural producers who found themselves holding large surpluses after they were cut off from European markets. The Departments of Agriculture and Fisheries, in particular, began heavily promoting the domestic consumption of these surplus foods as a patriotic duty. Apples were the first food to be declared "patriotic," and as early as December 1939, full-page advertisements began to appear in Canadian magazines telling Canadians: "Serve apples daily and you serve your country too." Similarly, the collapse of the export market for lobster by early 1940 saw these shellfish quickly added to the list of patriotic foods through a ubiquitous advertising campaign sponsored by the Fisheries Department[6] (see Figure 4.1). Both campaigns found an enthusiastic partner in the country's food columnists. Ads in women's magazines were typically accompanied by articles reminding readers that eating lobsters and apples was "a matter of patriotism to your country as well as profit and pleasure" and included recipes for newly "patriotic" dishes such as Apple Pie, Baked Apples, Lobster in Aspic, and Lobster à la King.[7] In 1940, for instance, *Chatelaine* described a "Patriotic Christmas Dinner" that included lobster in a "tangy tomato sauce" partly for the "Christmas color" and "partly because we're asked to use this good Canadian fish."[8] Even the women's section of *Le Devoir* regularly provided readers with patriotic recipes supporting local food producers and, in 1941, went so far as to encourage readers to serve a patriotic Christmas dinner of foods "préparés d'une façon attrayante, produits au Canada," including Salade de Pommes et de Celeri Croquant, Moules de Tomates, and La Dinde Rotie à la Canadienne.[9]

By the second year of the war, the language of patriotic consumption had begun to embrace the themes of thrift, sacrifice, and restraint that had

Figure 4.1 Canadian lobster advertisement sponsored by the Department of Fisheries. *Canadian Home Journal,* June 1941.

characterized the previous war.[10] This was initially tied to Canada's overseas commitments. As Canada began to supply a larger proportion of the British diet, producers struggled to meet commitments for items like pork, cheese, and butter. Canadians were therefore regularly asked to reduce their consumption of items like these in order to ensure that their allies would not go hungry. One *Maclean's* editorial, for instance, scolded that Canadians could "get all the steaks, onions and butter they want" while British visitors to Canada "are appalled at our waste of food and other commodities."[11] By the summer of 1941, however, Canadians themselves were beginning to feel the pinch as rising domestic consumption, shrinking imports, and growing commitments to supply food to Canada's allies led to skyrocketing prices and periodic shortages of a number of basic foods. Calls to stop hoarding and to take only one's fair share became more and more strident, but ultimately, it was the establishment of a broad range of price and supply controls by the WPTB that led to the most significant changes in Canadians' eating habits.

Rationing and price controls would eventually become the prominent aspects of wartime controls on food, but these restrictions at the consumer level were also accompanied by the introduction of hundreds of WPTB regulations governing the production and sale of a wide range of foods. Many familiar foods began to disappear from stores as the food industry became subject to quotas on scarce ingredients such as sugar or cocoa, as well as packaging materials like tin and paper. By June 1942, for instance, the number of tin can sizes that could be used by food processors had dropped from 116 to only nine standard sizes, and foods like carrots, beets, apples, and spaghetti had been removed from the list of foods that could be sold in cans.[12]

Restaurants and bakeries were similarly regulated. The WPTB established quotas on foods purchased from wholesalers based on pre-war sales, and strict regulations were placed on the types of foods that could be sold in this way. In bakeries, prohibitions were placed on everything from iced cakes to hot dog buns to sliced bread, in order to reduce waste and streamline production. In restaurants, restrictions were placed on the amount of rationed and scarce goods that could be served, and customers were limited to no more than one-third of an ounce of butter and to no more than one cup of tea or coffee per person. Between 1943 and 1944, during the first round of meat rationing, restaurants were also required to make Tuesdays "meatless days." Later, between 1945 and 1947, meatless days were extended to both Tuesdays and Fridays. This meant that restaurants and cafeterias across the country – with the exception of industrial canteens, work camps, and hospitals – could serve only meals that used unrationed proteins like chicken and fish or meat substitutes like eggs, cheese, and beans.[13]

But for most Canadians, it was coupon rationing that truly came to define their wartime culinary practices. Regardless of region, ethnicity, language, or social class, everyone was required by law to use less sugar, drink less coffee, and put less butter on their morning toast (see Figure 4.2). Many, of course, bent or broke the rules by hoarding foods in short supply, by bringing home an extra cup of tea from the corner store, or by shopping for extra tea, butter, and meat on the black market. But as noted earlier, most available evidence suggests that a sense of fairness, patriotic

Figure 4.2 Navigating the coupon rationing of meat, 1941. *Library and Archives Canada/Department of Finance, e01094498.*

support for the war effort, and the threat of legal sanctions meant that the vast majority of Canadians tended to follow the rules. And when the rules were considered unfair or unreasonable, Canadians made their displeasure known. The public outcry against a 1943 WPTB order prohibiting the exchange of rationed commodities among neighbours, for instance, forced the board to quickly reverse itself, and in October of that year the order was rescinded to much media fanfare.[14]

Overall, Canadians tended to simply make do with shortages and rationing. Most adopted a range of novel strategies to conserve scarce foods. These included simply putting a much smaller spoon in the sugar bowl so that the morning coffee ritual of one or two scoops could go on unimpeded, and – as was the practice with one family – dividing the day's butter ration among family members each morning so that each could decide what to do with the daily allotment.[15] A larger effect of rationing was that it united Canadians around the fact that each shopper across the country needed to keep track of which ration coupons had become valid and of whether individual ration allotments had changed. Also, all Canadians needed to carry both their and their family members' ration books with them whenever they went out for groceries. Rationing also meant that the "Magic Butter Spread" recipe from *Globe and Mail* columnist Ann Adam – which stretched your butter ration through the addition of gelatine, cold water, and evaporated milk – was useful for housewives across the country, not just in Toronto, after the weekly butter ration declined from eight ounces per person in December 1942 to only four ounces between March and April 1945.[16] The same was true for Mrs. Frank Schmidt of Abbotsford's "Sugarless Raspberry Pie," for Mrs. James R. Mullen of Cornwall's "Butterless, Eggless, Milkless Cake," and for Helen Campbell of *Chatelaine*'s suggestions for "Tealess Teas" – all of these recipes met a need that cooks across Canada could relate to based on their common experience of rationing and wartime controls.[17] This was also why the post-1942 period saw an explosion in "war" recipes.

Wartime recipes, as it turned out, were an easy way to sell newspapers, magazines, books, and food products. Well-known home economists like *Chatelaine*'s Helen Campbell, the *Montreal Standard*'s Kate Aitken, the *Globe and Mail*'s Ann Adam, and the *Vancouver Sun*'s fictional food writer Edith Adams all regularly featured ration-friendly, nutritious menus, which were often flanked by ads offering the same. For instance, Swift Canadian Co. ads often took the form of "Weekly Wartime Nutrition Hints" from its own ersatz home economist Martha Logan and included ration-stretching recipes such as "Tongue Rolls Florentine" and "Spaghetti with Meat."[18] Similarly, nutrition became an easy way to sell a range of products. Ads for Crown Brand Corn Syrup claimed that their product was a "nourishing food for growing children," and Ganong contended that its chocolates were "essential for their dietetic value and uplifting morale."[19] For food writers, the message that Canadians should eat more "protective" foods was similarly easy to adapt to almost any column. Recipes for everything from a vegetable casserole containing peas, lima beans, carrots, onion, dripping, eggs, milk, and chili sauce to nearly any type of dessert containing milk and/or fruit – including Chocolate-Chip Fluff, Cinnamon Eggnog Pudding, Maple Noodle Custard – were therefore recommended by magazine and newspaper food columnists simply based on the presence of one or more of the food groups recommended in Canada's Official Food Rules.[20]

The line between food columnist, advertiser, and the federal government often became rather blurred. Recipes from the *Globe and Mail*'s Ann Adam, for instance, were regularly included in ads for companies like Bee

Hive Syrup. But Adam also published a number of wartime cookbooks in conjunction with both the federal government and partners in the food industry. Titles sponsored by Appleford Waxed Paper included *The Lunch Box and Food Saver Book* – published "in support of the Canadian Nutrition Programme" – as well as the *Meat Extender Book,* which was produced "in support of the Gov't Meat Rationing Plan" and included a cooking guide from the Department of Agriculture.[21] US-based food corporations like Coca-Cola, Campbell's, and Kraft – many of which had come to dominate the ad space in Canadian newspapers and magazines, not to mention grocery-store shelves, by the 1940s – had little trouble adapting their American advertising materials to Canadian conditions. The coupon rationing of sugar was introduced in the United States in May 1942, and in subsequent months it was extended to meat, coffee, tea and other foods. Although American controls differed in their specifics from their Canadian counterparts, much of the advice regarding both ration stretching and healthy eating applied on both sides of the border.[22] Swift easily adapted its 1942 publication *Eat Right to Work and Win* – a full-colour, sixteen-page booklet illustrated with popular characters like Blondie, Flash Gordon, and Popeye – to a Canadian audience. The foreword, directed "to Americans, and especially to American housewives," was replaced with a message from Dr. L.B. Pett, the director of Canada's Nutrition Services Division. Similarly, the page instructing readers to "Eat Nutritional Food" because the "US Needs Us Strong" was replaced with the message "Eat Right, Feel Right – Canada Needs You Strong" and an illustrated version of Canada's Official Food Rules.[23]

The food industry responded to the war in other ways as well. Pre-war products were often rebranded as wartime ration extenders and time savers for the busy – and, increasingly, working – wartime mother, who was offered recipes such as the bright orange "Kraft Dinner Platter," whose namesake had first been introduced to consumers in 1937.[24] At the same time, as familiar consumer goods began to disappear from stores, a range of novel, ersatz foods emerged to take their place. In part, this reflected the fact that the war was a boon for Canadian food processors and engineers, who were trying out new and often experimental methods of dehydration, freezing, preservation, enrichment, and flavour enhancement in their efforts to improve the field rations of Canadian soldiers and their overseas allies. Some of these new products therefore also began to appear in stores. Soybeans were sold as a substitute for salted peanuts, peanut butter, and chocolate while saccharine, an artificial sweetener that had long been used in diabetic diets, was experimented with by everyone from industrial food producers to home canners hoping to stretch their sugar rations.[25]

This public desire for new foods to fill the gaps left by familiar staples that were either rationed or in short supply sometimes led to problems. Journalists, the food industry, and government officials worked closely together to promote the state's wartime food policies but did not always act in concert. In the case of meat, for instance, the WPTB tended to ask Canadians to use extenders, not substitutes. Because the goal of meat rationing was to reduce overall consumption, officials worried that substituting non-rationed meats like chicken in place of more familiar meats like pork or beef would have a "pyramiding" effect whereby shortages of one substitute would lead to a run on other substitutes. So they pushed recipes that called for the use of abundant foods like macaroni, bread crumbs, and dried beans as extenders.[26] Food writers, though, often failed to heed this advice. In one instance, the WPTB traced a shortage of condensed milk in Winnipeg to a recipe for mock whipped cream that had been promoted by the home economics editor of the *Winnipeg Tribune*.[27] In 1943, the promotion of recipes containing canned evaporated milk, such as Anne Adams's "Magic Butter Spread," compelled the government to restrict purchases of that product to mothers of infants (it was a common ingredient in infant formulas of the period) and to those requiring it for health reasons.[28]

Canadians were clearly eager to test out new wartime recipes and conservation strategies – and, like Corsan and Hoffman, to share their own "recipes for victory" as a way of contributing to the war effort and displaying their commitment to the national priorities of thrift, sacrifice, and conservation. Canadian women, in particular, were not simply passive recipients of wartime food propaganda but, instead, often used wartime recipes and community cookbooks to contribute to the war effort and to articulate their own wartime vision of patriotic citizenship. Women therefore found numerous public outlets for their tried and tested war recipes. The *Windsor Daily Star*, like many newspapers of the period, called for readers to send in submissions to its popular "This Week's Best Wartime Recipes" column.[29] But even newspapers without a wartime recipe section often featured readers' contributions. Many contributors traced these recipes back to the previous war. For example, one *Globe and Mail* reader had purchased her "War Cake" recipe for five cents from a neighbour who had been selling recipes and cake samples to raise funds for the Red Cross. Others wrote in to let fellow readers know about their recent experiments in substitutions and ration-stretching recipes. These ranged from

Corsan's creative bean-and-potato-based butter substitutes to M.E.
Coleman of Vancouver's marshmallow-based "Mock Whipped Cream."[30]

Among the most significant outlets for such recipes were local community cookbooks. According to Elizabeth Driver's invaluable bibliography
of Canadian cookbooks, these accounted for most of the full-length cookbooks published during the war. Community cookbooks were published
mainly to raise money, whether for new wartime charities or for the long-
standing charitable drives of church groups and welfare organizations.[31]
For instance, *Cook to Win,* published in 1943 by the Calgary Wesley United
Church's Good Cheer Club as part of their annual fundraising drive,
claimed to be "your ever ready help until the day returns when 'Freedom
From Want' is realized throughout the world." Its recipes focused on ration-
stretching items and included contributions from local and national ce-
lebrities like Nellie McClung (Wartime Stew) and Mrs. John Bracken (Meat
Loaf).[32] Most cookbooks could not claim a similar level of celebrity content.
But many, like the *Willing War Workers Cook Book* from Moore's Mills,
New Brunswick, the *East York Schools Win the War Cook Book,* and Regina's
Knox United Church's *Victory Cook Book,* featured similar recipes and
helped raise funds for a range of patriotic and charitable causes.[33]

It was not just the explicitly patriotic cookbooks that focused on adapting to wartime conditions. Most cookbooks produced during the war
included sections dealing with the problems of the wartime kitchen, such
as guides to meatless, sugarless, and eggless cooking. Many others also
included sections on nutrition, home canning, and Canadian produce.
The 1944 *Canadian Favourites: CCF Cookbook,* for its part, had no specifically "wartime" sections but did include dozens of member-submitted
"war" recipes, including Soy Bean Succotash, Victory Icing, and Cucum-
ber Saccharine Pickles.[34] As these and the thousands of other recipes
submitted by ordinary Canadians to local newspapers and community
cookbooks seemed to attest, the shared language of cooking provided
women with an important means for engaging in a dialogue with their
neighbours – whether they were next door or on the other side of the
country – on how to best deal with their common wartime experiences in
the kitchen. And when these efforts were combined with the flood of recipes
produced by advertisers, food writers, and government home economists,
this meant that by the final years of the war, Canadians increasingly found
themselves presented with something approximating a wartime cuisine.
Or, if not an actual cuisine, at the very least a kind of makeshift patriotic
wartime culinary practice defined largely by the restrictions Canadians

shared regarding food consumption and the vast culinary literature this had created.

Sacrifice and Abundance

Although thrift, conservation, and sacrifice became the watchwords of patriotic eating, the reality of many Canadians' wartime experiences was often quite different from this austere ideal. This was most true for the more than one million Canadians who saw some form of military service during the war. As veteran William Patrick recalled of his first military meal, "They had so much food on the platter that my poor little shrunk stomach couldn't handle it ... I thought it was such a shame to throw all that good food away and, of course, we'd just come out of the – well we were in the midst of the deepest of depressions."[35] Indeed, all three military services provided impressive quantities of food in their mess halls. In 1943, the Royal Canadian Air Force's (RCAF) standard ration scale was based on the consumption of nearly 3,900 calories per day. Meat consumption ranged from between seven pounds per person per week in 1939 to four pounds ten ounces later in the war. Perhaps unsurprisingly, then, the average RCAF enlistee gained five pounds in their first six months in the services.[36]

Although the nutritional needs of soldiers were frequently stressed in order to justify sacrifices on the home front, most civilians were also eating better than they ever had before. Overall, Canadians increased their consumption of nearly every known nutrient. By 1945, per capita consumption of dairy products, fruit, and meat had risen 23 percent over their 1939 levels, and poultry and egg consumption had risen 12 percent.[37] The reason for this was largely economic: by 1942, Canada was experiencing nearly full employment and the average pre-tax income for waged workers had increased by an astonishing 42 percent.[38] While not all Canadians shared equally in this economic prosperity, these changes dramatically increased the demand for all kinds of food – and this was despite increases to federal income taxes and the introduction of mandatory savings. By 1942, grocery sales had risen by 64 percent. Between 1939 and 1945, restaurant sales nationwide rose from just under $50 million to $210 million.[39]

These improvements in Canadians' diets caused inflation to surge and shortages to develop in the early years of the war, and these developments eventually led to WPTB intervention through price controls and rationing.

This causal relationship was particularly apparent in the case of meat rationing, which, unlike other rationed items, was introduced as much in response to increased domestic consumption as to Canada's overseas food commitments or import restrictions. In fact, when meat shortages began to appear in the months leading up to the May 1943 introduction of rationing, Canada's meat production was actually at an all-time high. Hog production alone had doubled thanks to federal subsidies and price guarantees. Even with Canada's major commitments to feeding its own armed forces and its British allies – which amounted to more than 700 million pounds of meat in 1943 – there was still 33 percent more meat available for domestic civilian consumption than there had been before the war.[40] But even this increase only barely kept up with rising domestic meat consumption. Rationing had been introduced in order to achieve an overall reduction in meat consumption from its wartime high, yet it still promised a level of consumption well above typical Canadian pre-war norms. Even during the first two years of meat rationing, annual per capita domestic consumption of meat remained between 30 and 36 percent higher than in 1939.[41]

This is not to say that wartime controls did not require significant changes in Canadians' cooking and eating habits. Rather than eating less, though, they often simply ate different foods. Unrationed foods like fruits, vegetables, dairy products, eggs, and poultry, for instance, were all being consumed at levels well above pre-war norms. But few at the time viewed this as a permanent or necessarily desirable change. Although rationed foods like meat, sugar, butter, tea, and coffee were not completely necessary from a nutritional standpoint, most Canadians considered them essential to their diet and found it genuinely difficult to make do with less. Meals were typically structured around the presence or absence of meat and sweets. And, given that margarine had been banned during this period and that other vegetable-based fats were rare in Canadian stores, butter was a central component of most families' diets.[42] Anthropologists, for their part, have long argued that the symbolic meanings of foods often play as important a role as physical necessity in defining culinary patterns and popular tastes. Because meals are ordered events that have essential religious and secular meanings related to larger social structures such as gender, class, age, and ethnicity, disruptions to their familiar patterns and elements tend to be difficult and subject to considerable resistance.[43]

It is no surprise, then, that Canadians took rationing very seriously. Meat and sugar were especially important determinants of social status during this period, and their consumption was closely tied to popular gendered ideas about identity and class.[44] This partly explains why ration allotments for these two items, in particular, encountered considerable protest when they were perceived to be unequal. Here it is important to note that despite an overall increase in food consumption, consumption levels for rationed foods (with the notable exception of meat) either stayed close to their pre-war levels, which were themselves well below wartime highs, or – in the case of butter, sugar, and tea – dropped to levels well below even pre-war norms. Sugar saw the most significant drop: its per capita consumption had fallen to 70 percent of its 1939 levels by 1945. Butter consumption also saw a significant overall decline as a result of rationing, with per capita consumption falling to a low of 83 percent of pre-war levels by 1946.[45]

These changes had very different effects depending on one's experience of the Great Depression. Although the wartime economic boom did not reach everyone, the war's early years saw the dramatic improvements at the bottom of the income scale. Wartime controls therefore not only helped to protect these early wartime gains but also required the greatest reductions in consumption from middle- and upper-income families. Sugar rationing was the exception in that it required significant reductions in consumption by *all* Canadians. The rationing of items such as butter, though, had a far smaller impact on low-income households. While Dominion Bureau of Statistics (DBS) studies indicated that later reductions in the butter ration resulted in consumption well below pre-war levels for Canadians of all income groups, the initial eight-ounce weekly ration required roughly a 20 percent decrease for middle- and upper-income Canadians, which simply brought them down to the Depression-era average of a typical low-income family. The same was true of the tea ration, which required a much smaller reduction in consumption for low-income earners than for their middle-income counterparts.[46]

The impact of social class on the experience of rationing was most apparent in the case of meat. The initial ration of approximately two pounds per person per week had a very different impact depending on one's experience of the Great Depression. A 1936 study had found that for low-income families, weekly consumption of meat ranged between 1.6 pounds per person (for families on relief) and 2 pounds (for low-income families). Middle- and upper-class families, by contrast, consumed between 2.7 and 3.3 pounds per person.[47] And given that during the 1930s, higher-income families not only consumed more meat but also higher-quality cuts, rationing had the added effect of levelling out these differences and, as one WPTB official noted, creating "an abnormal demand for the more expensive cuts of meat."[48] Even though such cuts required more coupons – with weekly rations of only one pound for higher-quality cuts as opposed to two-and-a-half pounds for lower-grade cuts with higher fat and bone content – butchers complained that falling demand was forcing them to throw away large quantities of lower-quality rationed meats like sausage, ground beef, and flank cuts.[49] In part this reflected the fact that Canadians were using their improved purchasing power to buy what they saw as better-tasting and higher-status foods. But during the first round of rationing, the trend towards buying higher-quality cuts of meat also reflected the fact that a number of non-rationed alternatives were available that could be used to supplement a smaller ration of higher-quality meats. While fish and chicken were expensive and difficult to find in most cities, other non-rationed "fancy" meats like kidneys, heart, liver, and tongue – as well as jellied meats, bologna, hot dogs, and other prepared meats – were often readily accessible and saw high sales during the first round of rationing. Many of these cuts had been familiar staples of the working-class diet during the 1930s and were not typically seen on the tables of middle- and upper-income households. This meant that wealthier Canadians who wanted to maintain pre-war levels of meat consumption were being forced to change their cooking and eating practices.

The levelling effects of rationing and other wartime controls were also apparent in the kinds of "wartime" recipes and cooking advice that began to appear more frequently after 1941. This popular literature, which focused on developing strategies for "winning the war in your kitchen" by avoiding waste and intelligently stretching your ration, borrowed heavily from Depression-era advice on how to stretch a dollar. During the 1930s, advice manuals developed by social agencies such as the Canadian Welfare Council, for instance, advised families to save money on meat by consuming cheap alternatives such as organ meats and to extend small amounts of more expensive meats "by combining them with macaroni, rice and other cereals."[50] This was remarkably similar to the advice given in a May 1943 article in *Maclean's*, which suggested using unrationed organ meats and stretching better-quality meats with starches or proteins like beans, cheese, peas, and eggs. Even the recipes looked as if they had been culled from Depression-era manuals – their suggestions included Baked Corn and Sausage, Oatmeal Beef-Liver Loaf, and Branburgers.[51] *Chatelaine's* advice to "Try Kidney" and *Canadian Home Journal's* assertion that "Variety Meats Give the V-Sign for Vitamins, Value and Availability" may not have convinced middle-class Canadians to eat low-status foods. Even so, they reflected the major effort then under way to recast the foods of poverty as nutritious and patriotic wartime dishes.[52]

The interchangeability of wartime and Depression-era cooking practices was also often visible in the names given to these recipes: "economy" or "economical" recipes quickly became recast as "war" or "victory" recipes. Examples include the popular recipe for "War Cake" or "Canada War Cake" – a typically eggless, milkless, butterless, and sugar-stretching dessert that appeared in newspapers and cookbooks across the country throughout the war. While there were a number of variations on the cake, the recipe typically consisted of a few basic ingredients, including (like the recipe submitted by Mrs. John Brownell of Farrans Point, Ontario, to the Cornwall *Standard Freeholder*) hot water, brown sugar, lard, raisins, flour, baking soda, cinnamon, and cloves.[53] The recipe for this dense, slightly sweet cake seems to have been reproduced in some form or another across Canada in both cookbooks and newspapers. The variations on it adjusted some components depending on the availability of other scarce items, and, to that end, at times included eggs, molasses, mace, nutmeg, or cocoa.[54]

Although many women traced their own recipe for War Cake all the way back to the Great War, many had continued to eat War Cake – albeit often by a different name – throughout the interwar years. In March 1930, for instance, S.H. Green of New Westminster, BC, won a one-dollar prize from the *Vancouver Sun* for her recipe for something called "Poverty Cake," which, under a different name, would have been indistinguishable from most War Cake recipes. The Health Service and Federated Agencies of Montreal's 1942 cookbook, *Food and the Family Income: Low Cost Recipes,* which was distributed to families receiving social assistance, included a recipe for what it called "Economy Cake." With the exception of replacing nutmeg with chopped figs and allspice, the cake was clearly in the same family. The CCF cookbook, *Canadian Favourites,* perhaps provided the best example. In it, "Canada War Cake" and "Raisin Economy Cake" appeared on the same page and listed much the same ingredients. The latter, though, called for two beaten eggs and white instead of brown sugar.[55]

The interchangeability of "Economy" and "War" cake pointed to the different ways in which Canadians experienced wartime eating. For those who had managed to maintain even a moderate income during the 1930s, this would have been a very foreign dish that harkened back to the previous war because, during the Depression, they would have found little need to skimp on milk, sugar, eggs, or butter. But because rationing and short-ages required significant changes to some of the basic staples of their pre-war diet, wartime cooking truly *did* mark a break with the past and a novel culinary experience. For those who had suffered through unemploy-ment and chronically low wages during the Depression, however, these kinds of recipes would have been more than familiar. They had already experienced the much more restrictive but informal "rationing by price" for nearly an entire decade. Wartime rationing and shortages simply were continuous with recent eating practices.[56] This meant that, for some at least, wartime calls for patriotic thrift, sacrifice, and conservation in the kitchen likely seemed almost insulting, given their recent experience. As one woman told Barry Broadfoot in the 1970s:

> You remember those Sunday supplements, they were jammed with war stuff. How to cook cabbage, make cabbage rolls and then drink cabbage juice. Or carrots. Swiss chard. Spinach. Did they think we didn't know that stuff, like how to make a dollar do the price of ten? You'd think the idiots in their big offices in Toronto and Ottawa didn't know about the Depres-sion we just went through — ten years of nothing.[57]

But for many who had suffered through low wages and unemployment during the 1930s, the war also offered a kind of unity with other women across the country and a chance to be recognized for the skills they had developed during the hard years of the Depression, particularly their creativity in making the best of a bad situation. For thousands of women, then, submitting "War" and "Victory" recipes to the local newspaper or community cookbook was not a simply patriotic gesture. It was also a badge of their own resilience through depression and war alike.

Cookbooks, Community, and Nation

Yet "War" recipes were only one part of the wartime eating experience. These culinary novelties rarely marked a permanent change in Canadian tastes or expectations. In part, this was because many of the recipes pro-duced by food writers, home economists, and government agencies were somewhat experimental and thus not always successful. Catherine Carroll remembers her attempt to make a healthy, ration-friendly recipe she heard on the radio:

One [recipe] which I decided to try was carrot sandwiches – shredded carrots mixed with mayonnaise and raisins. I took these delicacies with me to one of the dances. The soldier I was dancing with after lunch asked me in the most puzzled tone if I'd ever heard of anyone making carrot sandwiches! He thought someone in the group must be very weird. I didn't confess – just agreed![58]

The same was true of other "war" recipes. The recipe for "War Pie" that appeared in the Cornwall *Daily Standard-Freeholder*'s annual "1943 Cook Book Edition" was especially bleak. Essentially consisting of mashed potatoes and parboiled onions – laid out in a baking dish in "alternating layers," seasoned with salt and pepper, dotted with lard, and topped with a layer of pastry – it was a particularly austere meal that few were likely inclined to reproduce.[59]

To a certain extent, the frequency with which reader-contributed re-cipes began to appear in local newspapers and community cookbooks after rationing was introduced in 1942 suggests that Canadians were often will-ing to go to great lengths to adapt their recipes and diets to wartime cir-cumstances.[60] At the same time, though, the community cookbooks of the period also suggest that such recipes were typically seen as simply temporary stand-ins for more desired and familiar dishes. While a number of cookbooks produced during the war focused exclusively on wartime ration-stretching recipes, most contained a range of recipes suitable to both war and peacetime conditions. Although most did include a fair number of distinctly "war" recipes – whether in a separate section or inter-spersed throughout the cookbook – these were typically outnumbered by other recipes designed for periods with more abundant meat, butter, sugar, and other goods then in short supply, such as bananas, rice, or cocoa.

Cookbooks, of course, are never simply snapshots of the culinary prac-tices of a given individual or group. Best-selling, mass market cookbooks are primarily prescriptive texts, in which a trusted expert tells readers how to prepare a range of dishes. And while it is difficult to tell how often readers actually use particular recipes from even best-selling cookbooks, we do learn something about the tastes and aspirations of home cooks in any given period from reading those books.[61] Community cookbooks, for their part, often provide historians with a far more intimate look into the actual cooking practices of a given time or place. They are among the only written sources actually produced by ordinary women about their own culinary practices, and, as such, they provide unique insights into women's lives and work. As Laura Shapiro, Lynne Ireland, and others have suggested, the recipes in these books are not necessarily the best indication of what women cooked on a day-to-day basis, but the very fact that contributors were willing to attach their name to their submissions suggests that they felt that these recipes somehow represented their own personality, style of cooking, and place within the community. As Susan Leonardi has pointed out, moreover, cookbooks and the recipes they contain should not be read simply as lists of ingredients and cooking instructions. Instead, they need to be approached as a kind of "embedded discourse" that employs a range of narrative strategies and individual meanings that go well beyond mere descriptions of culinary practices.[62]

Being attuned to the multiple narratives and meanings contained in any given community cookbook therefore means recognizing the ways in which these cookbooks are often self-conscious representations of the "communities" responsible for producing them. The Edmonton Ukrainian Ladies' Good Will Organization's 1941 cookbook, *Tested Recipes,* provides a particularly instructive example of how multiple "embedded discourses" are contained in wartime community cookbooks. On the surface, *Tested Recipes* is a fairly typical fundraising cookbook. Besides the usual sections on cakes, cookies, meat dishes, and vegetables, there is a section titled "War Time" recipes that includes, among others, recipes for "Canada's War Fruit Cake" and "Honey Lemon Cake." What makes this particular cookbook unique, though, is that it includes additional sections for "National Recipes" – which are predominantly Ukrainian but include Russian, Czech, Hungarian, and Slovak recipes – as well as a section outlining a traditional "Ukrainian Christmas Eve Dinner" that includes dishes such as kootia, borscht, stuffed jellied fish, holopchi, pyrohy, and kolachi.[63]

It is perhaps unsurprising that a Ukrainian Catholic organization would produce a cookbook that celebrated its own culinary traditions. While ethnic community cookbooks would become much more common in the postwar period, a small number were published by Jewish, Ukrainian, and German organizations during the 1940s.[64] In many ways, though, such cookbooks were an important means for ethnic and linguistic communities to navigate the uncertain terrain of national identity and Canadian citizenship. Ethnic community cookbooks often helped community members share strategies for adapting ingredients and methods to Canadian conditions, and they also recorded what was often unwritten knowledge about culinary practices and rituals that went to the heart of the community's identity. Most immigrant groups were divided generationally, politically, and economically. In this regard, the articulation of a shared culinary tradition and common "national" dishes was a means of main-taining cohesion in the face of both internal divisions and external pres-sures to assimilate to Canadian linguistic and social norms. And, as Donna Gabaccia has suggested, such cookbooks were often intended for a younger, second- and third-generation audience and therefore often served to "re-cover and celebrate the past and to teach lost culinary skills to descendants of enclave cooks."[65]

There are, however, a number of indications that this particular cook-book – like many other ethnic and community cookbooks of the period – was also directed at an audience beyond the Ukrainian community. The war was a unique time during which Canadians, like their American neighbours, were encouraged to experiment with ration-stretching recipes and practices that were already familiar to a multitude of ethnic groups.[66] Some of this built more on cultural stereotypes than on actual practices. For instance, a December 1944 advertisement for the American Can Company suggested to *Chatelaine* readers, "Not all Chinese customs are 'quaint' or 'queer.' Some are very practical." This ad, illustrated with a large caricature of a smiling "Chinese" man eating from a bowl with chop-sticks, argued that even though the Chinese subsisted on a "monotonous diet" of rice, "bird seed" (millet), wheat, and soy beans, Canadians could nonetheless learn from their practice of eating "ALL of their food. Every last grain."[67] Canadians were also often encouraged to experiment with actual "ethnic" recipes. In November 1943, for instance, *Le Devoir* published an article outlining the different ways in which various ethnic groups stretched their meat dollar. The article included recipes for Chinese Chow Mein, South American Chili Con Carne, Italian Spaghetti "á la viande," Russian Galoubtzy, and Hungarian Goulash.[68] Similarly, a 1942 *Saturday Night* article suggested to readers that "the Hungarians are supposed to be masters of the stew situation so here are a couple of recipes from that bit of Eastern Europe." These recipes included, among other things, a Hungarian Stew – which included beef, onions, tomatoes, paprika, and cumin seeds "if you can get them" – as well as a Transylvania Stew of cab-bage, beef, fresh herbs, vinegar, and sour cream.[69] Clearly, liberties were being taken with the actual content of these ethnic recipes, but as their frequent appearance during the war suggested, rationing and shortages had made culinary adventurousness a patriotic act.[70]

In many ways, the Edmonton Ukrainian Ladies were trying to take advantage of this fact, and, to that end, their cookbook appears to be directed at readers outside the Ukrainian community. In part, this is reflected in the naming of the recipes in the "National Dishes" section.

The nationality of most of these recipes is part of the name itself – as in "Russian Perishke" and "Houlupchee (Ukrainian)" – and the European names are provided with additional English descriptors. Pyrohy, for instance, are described as a "sort of Filled Dumpling," mundelen as "soup nuts," and kolacky as "nut rolls." These naming practices are clearly aimed at a non-Ukrainian (and non-Eastern European) audience and thus enable the cookbook to serve multiple purposes. While the separation of "national" dishes from the kinds of recipes that typically appeared in most Canadian cookbooks, magazines, and newspapers reconfirmed the separateness of these culinary traditions from the Canadian norm, they also highlighted some similarities. The fact that the vast majority of recipes were non-Ukrainian suggested to readers that Ukrainian women cooked many of the same kinds of modern dishes as other Canadian families. And by translating unfamiliar names and drawing parallels between various "ethnic" dishes and their North American counterparts, the cookbook also suggested that Ukrainian and other "national" dishes were not as foreign as they might at first seem and, therefore, could easily coexist with other Canadians' own culinary practices and traditions. Given that *Tested Recipes* sold at least five thousand copies and went into multiple editions during the 1940s and 1950s, this message likely resonated with cooks outside as well as within the Ukrainian community.[71]

As Sherrie Innis, Janet Theophano, and others have argued, cookbooks can provide important insights into how ordinary women articulated and enacted different ideas about gender, work, and citizenship.[72] Because they are written primarily by women and are one of the most widely read genres of women's literature, cookbooks reflect an interesting range of visions of gender and domesticity. Given the extent to which the war destabilized gendered norms relating to work and domesticity following women's unprecedented entry into the previously "male" domains of military service and the industrial workplace, then, it may seem surprising that most wartime cookbooks tended to reinforce the prescriptions of a familiar "Housoldier" domestic ideal that made defending the hearth and home while men went off to war part of women's "sacred duty."[73] The slippage of workplace gender roles, as discussed in the previous chapter, was by no means accompanied by calls for a similar role reversal in the domestic sphere. For the most part, working women were expected to do the double duty of mother *and* breadwinner. But while few wartime cookbooks offered a radical challenge to the status quo, some did attempt to reframe the social, economic, and political importance of women's household labour. CanLit icon Margaret Laurence, in her foreword to *Food from*

Market to Table (1940) by popular *Toronto Star* food writer Marie Holmes, attempted to place cooking "at the very centre and heart" of women's "great racial work in the home." She made much of the renewed attention that the scientific study of the home had brought to women's work more generally:

> The home is now considered the laboratory of the race and women are realizing more deeply every year the vast amount of brain power and study, as well as devotion, homemaking demands ... The tending of a home properly is the most important work there is in the world – the accent being on the word properly. For, as we know now, the relation between the home and human character and also between the home and healthy human beings is very close.[74]

"Armed with her cook book," Laurence argued, "the woman can remake the human race and send it out healthy and with quiet nerves to take in its stride all the problems it meets."[75]

In many ways, Laurence's "racial" argument for greater respect and recognition for the economic and social value of women's work was a familiar one. It reflected a strategy that was already prominent in the domestic science and home economics movements in the decades leading up to the war – albeit one that, as Laura Shapiro has pointed out, did little to challenge women's exclusion from other areas of public life.[76] Other cookbooks, however, made a more direct case for women's involvement in broader political movements seeking more specific social and economic changes. For instance, while cookbooks had long been a key source of fundraising for a range of church and social service organizations with broader political goals and aspirations, they could also be used as a means of advocating on behalf of specific political causes. The 1940 *Cook Book* of the Saskatchewan Women's Section of the United Farmers of Canada (UFC) made its goals explicit, stating that its organization's members were committed to seeking "legislative and economic changes which will make the improvement in our home life possible":

> We believe that every farm home should be equipped with all available modern conveniences; that social, educational and health services should be within the reach of every farm family; that our boys and girls should have equal opportunity with others to enter the higher educational institutions, and that there should be a place for them upon the farm where they can establish their home.[77]

They stressed that this political work was up to the women of the province, and they expressed regret that "so many farm women are content to accept present deplorable conditions without an endeavor on their part to join with others in association to remedy this situation."[78]

Clearly, the UFC cookbook, like the Ukrainian Ladies' *Tested Recipes*, was more than simply a fundraising exercise or an effort to share recipes. Much more important was its use of the shared language of recipes to foster a sense of community united, in this case, around a shared politics, geography, and occupation. As Paul Magee has argued, an advantage of the recipe format is that – when the proper ingredients are available – it provides a unique and surprisingly effective means of transmitting culture across time and space.[79] For organizations like the UFC, cookbooks offered a means of bridging cultural gaps. Regardless of their ethnicity, for instance, farm women throughout Saskatchewan could try to understand their neighbours' tastes by trying Mrs. J. Sample's "Bakemian Haska," Mrs. G. Dyak's "Vereniky," Mrs. J. Bonitz's "Oliebollen," and Mrs. G.B. Street's "Gnocchi." Although the inclusion of such recipes was a small gesture, the recipes were nonetheless meaningful in that they showed a very real attempt to communicate across social and linguistic barriers using the more universal and shared language of food.

Making a Canadian Cuisine

In recent years, the important role that cookbooks play in defining the social and cultural boundaries of different communities has received considerable attention from historians, especially in relation to the development of "national cuisines." As Benedict Anderson has argued, the modern nation-state is an "imagined community" that became possible only after the emergence of a form of modern print-capitalism, which transformed the traditional spatial, social, and linguistic boundaries that defined community membership.[80] In his analysis of the relationship between food and the making of Mexican national identity, Jefferey Pilcher has expanded on Anderson's ideas by suggesting that cookbooks, in particular, helped sustain this process by enabling ordinary women to "begin to imagine their own national community in the familiar terms of the kitchen, rather than as an alien political entity formulated by men and served up in didactic literature."[81] As Arjun Appadurai has argued in the context of the development of an Indian national cuisine, the use of food to foster and sustain nationalism in hierarchical societies that are highly segregated by class, caste, region, and language is often particularly effective because "recipes sometimes move where people may not."[82] Although such national cuisines are, themselves, highly contested cultural constructions rather than "authentic" reflections of popular culinary practice, their articulation through cookbooks, recipes, and other forms of culinary literature provides an important glimpse into the role of ordinary women in transforming and enacting popular notions of national identity and citizenship.

In the Canadian context, food has played a much different role in maintaining ideas about nation and citizenship than in Mexico, India, and other countries where deliberate efforts have been made to construct a unified national cuisine. In the postwar years, Canadian culinary nationalists would try to articulate a kind of "hybrid" cuisine reflecting Canada's regional and immigrant culinary traditions (or, in Quebec, a distinct and separate Québécois cuisine). Such attempts, however, were rare during the war years.[83] But as will be shown through an examination of *Canadian Favourites: CCF Cookbook* (1944), Kate Aitken's *Canadian Cook Book* (1945), and the Women's Voluntary Service's (WVS) *Canadian Cook Book for British Brides* (1945), even in the absence of a nationalist culinary consensus, cookbooks were able to articulate a number of very different and decidedly gendered wartime visions of Canadian food culture, citizenship, and postwar reconstruction. These three cookbooks are singled out here in part because they all either aimed at a national audience or attempted to describe authentically "Canadian" eating habits. At the same time, because all three differ quite substantially in tone and approach – one was compiled from hundreds of individual recipe contributions, another was written by a well-known food expert, and another was produced on behalf of a government agency and directed at recent immigrants – they provide an instructive example of how cookbooks were used to articulate three very different visions of Canada and its future.

Canadian Favourites: CCF Cookbook was, perhaps, one of the most interesting articulations of "Canadian" cuisine to be produced during the war. Although most community cookbooks from the period were aimed at a local or provincial audience rather than a national one, *Canadian Favourites* was a notable exception. It was published in a year when the CCF had just won a historic election in Saskatchewan and was widely believed to be on the cusp of a major federal breakthrough. Its preface describes the book as a fundraising effort, but also as the first national project by the female membership of the CCF. Spearheaded by Marian Nicholson and a group of CCF activists in Ottawa, the project quickly became national in scope; in the end, it totalled more than 250 pages and included nearly two thousand recipes. According to the second (1947) edition, it sold out its first run of ten thousand copies "in record time," making it one of the best-selling publications ever produced by the party.[84]

There are, of course, many ways that historians can read *Canadian Favourites*. The very fact that it was the first national project undertaken by CCF women since the party was formed in 1932 suggests that it was very much informed by the gender politics within the CCF during this period. As Joan Sangster and others have argued, although the CCF was home to some of Canada's pioneering feminist politicians, including Agnes McPhail and Grace MacInnis, the party was nonetheless structured along patriarchal lines, much like Canadian society more generally during the 1940s. National and provincial women's committees struggled to make their voices heard, and in general, women were rarely in positions of leadership within the party. More often, they were relegated to grassroots activities such as fundraising, administrative support, and education.[85] Clearly, *Canadian Favourites* did little to advance the broader feminist cause of women's social and political equality. Like many cookbooks of the period, moreover, it seemed to reinforce a patriarchal vision of women's social roles and responsibilities. Yet at the same time, it reflected a genuine attempt by CCF activists to use quite literal "bread and butter" issues to reach out to "housewives" and thereby increase the party's appeal to Canadian women. This connection between the household politics of food and the CCF's broader political goals is most explicit in the cookbook's chapter on "Nutrition and the Canadian Diet," in which Margaret S. McCready – the director of the McGill School of Household Sciences – praises wartime controls on the price and distribution of food for improving Canadian diets and calls on the government to introduce additional postwar controls and subsidies in order to spur the consumption of nutritionally important foods such as Canada Approved Breads.[86]

But perhaps the most interesting way to approach *Canadian Favourites* is to look beyond its explicit political aims so as to glean its implicit message about the party's vision of itself and of Canada as a whole. From the start, the book makes clear its national ambitions and postwar vision. Although it was published at the height of the war, the editors emphasize that they do not intend it to be a "wartime" cookbook. In part, this is because "in a country the size of Canada, the shortages are not uniform," but it is also because "before long we shall enjoy peace again and [hope] this book will continue to be used."[87] The editors also highlight the book's national character by identifying each contributor by both name and place of residence. *Canadian Favourites* is therefore a fascinating glimpse into the favourite recipes of the party's members, who include Lucy Woodsworth (Marshmallow Salad), Agnes Macphail (Cherry Cottage Cheese Salad), and Mrs. David Lewis (Fried Brain Patties). But the recipes also give some sense of the party's internal dynamics. Although there are recipes from nearly every province and territory, there are decidedly fewer from the Maritimes and Quebec (particularly outside Montreal), and only one recipe is published in French. These weaknesses would only be further highlighted by the party's struggles to attract supporters east of the Ottawa River in the 1945 federal election.

Perhaps most striking about *Canadian Favourites* is that, besides being one of the most ambitious cookbooks of the period, it is one of the most ethnically diverse. Recipes representing more than two dozen ethnic, national, and regional cuisines are included, ranging from French Canadian to Chinese, Aboriginal, Italian, Ukrainian, Polish, and Spanish. This seems to reflect a conscious strategy by the editors. The cookbook has dozens of recipes whose ethnic origins are made explicit, including "Pemican (North American Indian)," "Norsk Julekake (Norwegian)," "Pilaff with Lamb (Greek)," and "Russian Cabbage Rolls." At times, there are multiple recipes for a single dish: three for borscht, five for curry, five for spaghetti. And, despite the editors' explicit claim to publish one recipe from each contributor, they chose to publish multiple recipes from contributors of certain ethnic backgrounds, including four Italian recipes from Mrs. A. Fossati of Montreal (among them, Chicken Alla Cacciatora and Risotto Alla Milanese) and seven Chinese recipes from Charlie Quan of Toronto (including Lobster Egg Foo Yung and Yok Gar Mein). Quan, moreover, appears to have the most recipes of any single contributor.

Clearly, *Canadian Favourites* was more than simply a "wartime" cookbook or even a static snapshot of the CCF in 1944. Instead, it presented a distinctly "national" vision of the party and its future. Besides laying out the CCF's economic and political goals in the preface and throughout the cookbook, *Canadian Favourites* was clearly more ethnically diverse and inclusive than most cookbooks of the time. It was also far more diverse than the party itself, and this suggested that *Canadian Favourites* was making an intentional nod to a more cosmopolitan and pluralistic ideal of citizenship – an ideal that by the 1970s would became official government policy and would be celebrated in most efforts to define a distinctly "Canadian" cuisine.

The CCF was not alone in its attempt to create a truly "Canadian" cookbook in the absence of a coherent national cuisine. In 1945, popular *Montreal Standard* food editor and national food salvage spokeswoman

Kate Aitken published her best-selling *Canadian Cook Book*. Aitken was already a household name throughout Canada, and her *Canadian Cook Book* was in many ways the culmination of decades of experience as a nationally recognized food expert.[88] Unlike its CCF counterpart, therefore, her cookbook was published as a "handy, inexpensive guide to healthy daily living." To that end, it often addressed the inexperienced cook directly through the frequent "Notes to Brides" that accompanied the recipes. Although mainly a prescriptive text, Aitken's cookbook was similar in many important ways to *Canadian Favourites*. Both made their national ambitions clear in the title, and although both were published in the context of continued rationing, price controls, and shortages, neither was an explicitly "wartime" cookbook. Aitken's book suggests substitutions as well as a number of eggless, sugarless, butterless, and milkless recipes, but it makes no explicit reference to rationing, shortages, or the war. Instead, it offers a vision of a postwar future free of wartime and early postwar constraints.

Where the two cookbooks differed fundamentally was in their vision of Canada and its food culture. Aitken's *Canadian Cook Book* is much more reflective of the kind of middle-class, Anglo-European culinary vision regularly presented to Canadians in magazines and newspapers and by the food industry. This is perhaps no surprise given that, by 1945, Aitken had published a number of instructional cookbooks for corporations like Ogilvie Flour Mills and Canada Starch Ltd.[89] To a certain extent, this emerging corporate, middle-class cuisine was the closest thing Canada had to a national food culture in the decades leading up to the war. This cuisine was defined largely by the kinds of (multi)national brands whose standardized and mass-produced products filled the ads in the women's sections of newspapers and magazines; thus, it rarely strayed from its conservative, largely Anglo-European culinary roots and was mostly indistinguishable from its American equivalent. As Valerie Korinek and Franca Iacovetta have noted about *Chatelaine* during the postwar period, when "ethnic" recipes did appear they were often modified to the point of unrecognizability in order to become acceptable to "timid North American palates."[90]

Aitken's *Canadian Cook Book,* whose nearly three hundred pages contained upwards of a thousand recipes, reflected a 1940s vision of modern culinary practices. The recipes drew heavily from the author's own Anglo-Protestant culinary roots – Aitken at one point referring to the British as "our Old Country friends" – and from the middle-class, corporate culinary vision represented by most of Canada's major newspapers and magazines. Throughout the book, for instance, the recipes stress the importance of up-to-date knowledge about the science of nutrition, and they are often designed specifically for the kind of modern kitchen that many Canadians, in 1945 at least, could still only dream of, with its gas or electric oven and electric refrigerator. The recipes also often call for decidedly "modern" ingredients – a constantly shifting concept that at least during this period would have meant industrial, mass-produced "convenience foods" of the sort that would become staples of postwar dining. To this end, most of the recipes in the salad section are for gelatine mould salads, which had already come to define the emerging corporate food culture. They included, among others, a lettuce-free "Green Salad" that calls for pickles, horse-radish, gelatine, mayonnaise, and green food colouring. Even a decidedly ethnic or regional recipe like "French Canadian Braised Beef," moreover, includes a can of condensed mushroom soup as a key ingredient.

Aitken's *Canadian Cook Book* was less an explicit commentary on Canadian cuisine than an indicator of a number of broader culinary trends that would come to dominate postwar food writing. Although she sometimes makes assertions such as that Canadians dislike mutton and that pie is the "most popular dessert in Canada," she defines Canadian food culture more in terms of what it is *not* rather than by any specific characteristic. Although this was common to most cookbooks of the period, a notable and important exception was the *Canadian Cook Book for British Brides*. Published in 1945 by the WVS in cooperation with the WIB and the Department of Agriculture, this full-colour, thirty-two-page cookbook and instruction manual, which contained around fifty recipes, was one of the period's most decidedly "official" efforts to codify Canadian eating habits. It described itself as a "practical form of welcome to the Canadian way of life," and, to this end, its stated goal was to provide "a guide to the things that are different [from Britain] and to give you recipes for dishes that are likely to be among your husband's favourite things to eat."[91]

The cookbook consistently reinforces perceived notions about the similarities between Canadian and British culinary practices by repeatedly drawing the reader's attention to minor differences between the two. Many of these are noted as being purely semantic: "treacle" in Britain is molasses in Canada, "scrag end of lamb" is neck of lamb, and "shortening" is "a general term for cooking fats and includes butter, lard and the various blended shortenings." Significant contrasts between the two countries are also noted – there is no "afternoon tea" in Canada – but generally, the book highlights differences in food preferences rather than in culinary practices. Canadians are described as an "informal people, [who] will never criticize you for what you haven't got," and as "very fond of all sorts of pickles and relishes." The typical Canadian also generally "dislikes boiled fresh meat almost as much as he dislikes suet pudding" and would prefer cakes to be "lighter and richer than most British cakes." The recipes therefore tend to reflect these supposed characteristics of Canadian cuisine and include kitchen basics like meat loaf, potato salad, fruit crumble, pumpkin pie, pancakes, and donuts.

The *Canadian Cook Book for British Brides* is perhaps most notable for what it does not include. There is little discussion of regional culinary differences, no discussion of what cooking would be like for women moving to French-speaking areas, and little recognition of the presence of non-British foodways. To a large degree, this was because the war bride cookbook was, fundamentally, an exercise in what Franca Iacovetta has termed "culinary gatekeeping." The postwar food and nutrition gatekeepers examined by Iacovetta were attempting to reshape newcomers' cooking and eating practices "to promote a pro-capitalist and pro-democracy ideal of family and kitchen consumerism." In a similar vein, the war brides cookbook was suggesting that even "preferred" immigrants were in need of education regarding their duties and obligations as both wives and Canadian citizens.[92] It was, in that sense, as much a prescriptive text about "normal" practice in an ideal, male-breadwinner-centred household as it was a description of Canadian food culture. Immigrant women, it made clear, were to learn to be savvy shoppers and the "good cooks" who carefully followed recipes and owned all the right equipment. Most importantly, the goal was less about teaching these newcomers to adapt to Canadian food culture than it was about outlining the skills necessary to meet the expectations and desires of their new husbands.

Conclusion

The war's culinary legacy proved to be a mixed one. For a brief time, Canadians could claim something approaching a "national" eating experience defined by their shared efforts to creatively adapt to wartime controls and the ideals of thrift, conservation, and sacrifice in the kitchen. But the war's levelling effect was short-lived. Postwar inflation and the relaxation of controls led to the re-emergence of the income gap that had characterized pre-war consumption patterns, and it was not until well into the 1950s that wartime peaks in the per-capita consumption of milk, fruit, vegetables, meat, and eggs were regained.[93] Even so, the central role that food played in the construction of Canadians' day-to-day experience on the home front did provide a brief window of time during which cookbooks and recipes could be used, not simply to show one's support for the war effort, but to promote a new vision of community, citizenship, and nation. L.B. Kuffert has argued that the final years of the war were pervaded with a kind of optimistic "culture of reconstruction" that saw Canadians engage in a collective dialogue about the direction of the country's postwar social, economic, and cultural order.[94] Wartime cookbooks were a distinctly feminine contribution to this national conversation, and as such, they provide unique insights into the ways in which Canadians' visions of the postwar future had been transformed by their wartime experiences.

While "wartime" recipes ultimately had little impact on postwar culinary practices, the competing national visions articulated by the CCF, Kate Aitken, and WVS cookbooks would be reflected in the later efforts of postwar nationalists to define a Canadian cuisine. Ultimately, the multi-ethnic *Canadian Favourites* and Aitken's more modern vision – rather than the much more rigid war brides cookbook – would come to characterize postwar attempts to define a distinctly "Canadian" food culture. Canadians would come to embrace corporate, mass-food culture in profound ways after the war and by the 1960s had become heavily invested in the fast and convenience foods associated with the "Golden Age of Food Processing."[95] But the culinary aspirations of postwar nationalists were also affected by changing ideas about Canadian citizenship. As Rhona Richman Kenneally has argued, Canadian cuisine would soon be redefined as a reflection of the "broad assemblage of the food habits, tastes, aesthetics, and experiences" of Canada's ethnically diverse population.[96] Although these efforts were not particularly successful in defining even the basic components of a recognizably national cuisine (the only restaurants advertising "Canadian" foods typically being small-town Chinese restaurants "Specializing in Chinese and Canadian Food"), they formed an important element of postwar Canadian nationalism. Even Canada's culinary "gatekeepers," according to Iacovetta, typically "endorsed, mined, and appropriated ethnic foodways as part of their nation-building strategy of promoting national unity through an embrace of cultural diversity."[97] While this was done within limits imposed by existing hierarchies that established the perceptions about new Canadians' ethnic and racial suitability, it nonetheless showed the ways in which the CCF's pluralistic wartime portrait of Canadian foodways was gaining acceptance as a truly national culinary vision.

5

The Politics of Malnutrition

Nutrition Experts and the
Making of Canada's Postwar Welfare State

A s planning for postwar social security and reconstruction became a primary focus of national debate during the final years of the war, the political implications of Canada's wartime malnutrition crisis also became the subject of considerable debate and controversy, both within and outside Canada's fledgling nutrition professions. This was particularly true during the often-heated debates over the introduction of Family Allowances, which was announced by Prime Minister W.L. Mackenzie King's Liberal government in 1944 as Canada's first universal welfare payment program. While opponents attacked family allowances for their cost relative to more targeted, means-tested welfare programs, many of the most vocal supporters of the program publicly defended it largely on nutritional grounds. Citing recent studies by prominent Canadian and international researchers, proponents of family allowances contended that as many as six in ten Canadian children were suffering unnecessarily from malnutrition. They argued that more than 65 percent of households did not have sufficient income to purchase the "protective" foods required to maintain a healthy diet and that, as a result, permanent damage was being done to the physical and mental well-being of Canada's next generation of soldiers, workers, and mothers. *Toronto Star* columnist Margaret Gould perhaps put the economic and nutritional argument for family allowances most succinctly: "The Family Allowances Act declares that all children have a claim on the country's surplus revenue; that good nutrition for children is important; that the welfare of the nation depends on the children; that Canada's future depends on the physical and mental quality of the population."[1]

This chapter explores the ways in which the science of nutrition transformed – and was itself transformed by – these kinds of wartime and early postwar debates over social security and reconstruction. Earlier chapters examined the ways in which new methods of measuring the nature and extent of malnutrition among large populations produced dramatic changes in the perception of nutrition as a public health priority – and, as a result, brought renewed legitimacy to nutrition professionals more generally. This chapter, however, explores the social and political limits of this newfound scientific consensus. The war not only saw proper nutrition based on Canada's Official Food Rules emerge as a wartime responsibility of patriotic citizenship (and patriotic motherhood in particular) but also saw a growing number of Canadians insist vocally that the state's responsibility for preventing malnutrition extended beyond public education. The Food Rules were by then the most visible representation of the optimal dietary standards that had been used to identify Canada's malnutrition crisis. By the end of the war, though, it became clear to nutrition experts and policy makers alike that these same dietary standards could also be mobilized as a powerful tool of social criticism. Critics of the social and economic status quo therefore began to make extensive use of the Canadian Dietary Standard as a seemingly objective yardstick for challenging the adequacy of everything from wages to unemployment relief rates.

Although earlier chapters highlighted some of the ways in which nutrition professionals were internally divided (often along gendered lines) in their interpretations of the five Canadian Council on Nutrition (CCN) surveys, this chapter shows the ways in which the growing reliance on nutrition as a scientific and moral rationale for major wartime and postwar social and economic reforms such as family allowances brought these divisions even closer to the surface, thus contributing to the breakdown of the tenuous scientific consensus that had produced warnings of a wartime malnutrition crisis in the first place. Nutrition, as it turned out, would prove to be a less reliable ally to supporters of an expanded postwar welfare state than it had first seemed during the early years of the war. By 1945, moreover, these changes within the scientific community would bring into question not only nutrition's usefulness as a tool for generating scientifically grounded public policy but also the very meaning and measurability of basic concepts like "health" and "malnutrition."

The Cost of Living

During the middle years of the war, Canadians were constantly reminded that the country was facing a wartime malnutrition crisis. The newly appointed director of nutrition services, L.B. Pett, warned readers of the 1942 cookbook *Wartime Recipes and Food Rules* that recent Canadian studies had found "definite evidence" of malnutrition and, even more shockingly, that "only about 40 percent of the people studied could be considered adequately nourished." For Pett, the message was clear: "This means that there is a serious saboteur in our midst which must be combated in every way possible."[2] As noted in earlier chapters, the wartime malnutrition crisis identified by the five CCN-sponsored dietary surveys published between 1939 and 1941 had very quickly transformed popular perceptions of malnutrition as a public health threat as well as the professional status of Canadian nutrition experts. Although the CCN itself was, from its creation in 1938, often fractured by internal divisions between many of the mostly female front-line nutrition professionals like dieticians, nutritionists, and home economists and the largely male, university-based research scientists who ultimately took control of decision making within the organization, Canadian nutrition experts nonetheless all tended to agree on one thing during the early years of the war: Canada was facing a malnutrition crisis that required significant government intervention.[3] Where they often disagreed was with regard to what form this intervention should take – specifically, whether the priority should be placed on education or income as the leading cause of malnutrition. These professional and political divisions, which had their origins in Depression-era debates over the adequacy of unemployment relief rates, would only become sharper in the aftermath of the CCN dietary surveys.

The first major Canadian dietary survey using the newly created Canadian Dietary Standard highlighted some of these internal divisions within the CCN. The survey – conducted in Toronto between 1937 and 1939 to examine the nutritional adequacy of the diets of one hundred low-income families – had actually been launched prior to the creation of the CCN. Its instigator had been a special committee of Toronto's Child Welfare Council (CWC), a pioneering social planning organization representing a range of charitable organizations as well as the city's front-line social workers. From the beginning, the survey was politically charged. Throughout the 1930s, the social work profession had often been divided along political lines between what Alvin Finkel describes as "conservatives who emphasized techniques for changing individual behaviour and humanists who focused on the need for social change."[4] The CWC was strongly associated with the left wing of the profession, so much so that shortly after the 1937 Toronto nutrition study was initiated, it was disbanded in part as a result of accusations that its executive secretary, Margaret Gould, was a communist. While responsibility for the survey was ultimately taken over by the Toronto Welfare Council (TWC) – a new social planning body formed to replace the CWC shortly after it was disbanded – both the survey and the TWC itself retained something of their original activist agendas.[5]

As Gale Wills has argued, many of the leaders of the CWC and, later, the newly formed TWC were aligned with a distinctly Fabian strain in Canadian social work. Their professional values were grounded in a belief that a more humane system of social welfare and security could be established if a scientific approach to social policy reform was adopted.[6] This movement was exemplified during the 1930s by the social democratic League for Social Reconstruction (LSR) – formed in 1932 and considered the "brain trust" of the newly created Co-operative Commonwealth Federation (CCF) – as well as by the work being done at McGill University by Leonard Marsh and other researchers aligned with the McGill Social Sciences Research Project. Like their British counterparts, the Canadian Fabians advocated a scientifically planned welfare state that guaranteed a national minimum standard of living. And they believed that this goal could only be achieved by making a rational and scientific – rather than simply moral – case for social reform. Marsh stressed the need for a scientifically rigorous research methodology, arguing that the methods "which have been applied so successfully in the fields of the natural sciences should be refashioned for service in the attack on social disorganization."[7] For Marsh and other social scientists, nutrition therefore proved to be an ideal tool because it enabled them not simply to emulate but also to adopt some of the research methods of the natural sciences.

Nutrition's increasing prominence as a tool of social criticism became particularly apparent during the Great Depression. Up through the 1930s, Canadian social welfare policy had long reflected the liberal, laissez-faire doctrine of less eligibility. This concept had its origins in Britain's 1834 Poor Law Report, which established the principle that relief for able-bodied workers ought to be kept below the income of an "independent labourer of the lowest class" so that workers would have an incentive to find paid employment. Application of this principle, it was believed, would reduce the threat of "dependency." Relief was therefore always viewed as a temporary expedient, and as a result, policy makers typically devoted little attention to its long-term effects on the health and well-being of families that relied on it.[8] But as the Depression deepened and parts of the country began to see prolonged unemployment levels of between 20 and 30 percent, it quickly became clear that relief was no longer temporary for hundreds of thousands of Canadians. Rather, it had become their primary means of subsistence.[9]

Increasingly, critics began to ask whether the long-term psychological effects of "dependency" really were worse than the effects of malnutrition caused by the meagre unemployment benefits being provided to workers and their families. In Ontario, this issue was raised in separate reports by Harry Cassidy, a young professor of social science at the University of Toronto and founding member of the LSR, and by a special committee of the more politically neutral Ontario Medical Association (OMA) led by Dr. Frederick F. Tisdall, a pediatrician at Toronto's Hospital for Sick Children as well as one of Canada's most prominent nutrition researchers. Cassidy found that many relief officers readily admitted that they "did not consider the food allowances adequate for the maintenance of health," and this was confirmed by the OMA report, which, using a modified version of an early dietary standard developed by prominent American nutrition expert Hazel Stiebeling, found that the minimum cost for a nutritionally adequate diet was far in excess of the value of relief diets being offered by the vast majority of municipalities in Ontario and in Canada as a whole.[10] As OMA committee member Marjorie Bell – a prominent dietician and the Director of the Red Cross Visiting Home-makers Association – would go on to argue, such findings challenged the basic assumptions behind Canadian social welfare policies:

> There is the general impression that ambition and energy, with the desire to work and be independent, are qualities which everyone should possess and are personally to blame for lacking. The science of nutrition has shown that these qualities in an individual will vary in proportion to the adequacy and balance of the diet. If the unemployed are showing lethargy towards returning to work, it is the inevitable result of the treatment we have given them. They can no more be blamed than a man for drowning if we held his head under water.[11]

This message would be forcefully repeated by Leonard Marsh at McGill in his 1938 study *Health and Unemployment*, which – despite often being remembered only for its argument in favour of a system of national, state-run health insurance – also included detailed nutritional studies of

Montreal families. These studies included complete physical examinations of thousands of individuals, the analysis of heights and weights of school-children and infants, and clinical examinations of the nutritional status of families receiving unemployment relief.[12]

It was, therefore, no surprise that reform-minded social workers within the CWC (and, later, the TWC) sought to conduct a nutrition survey among low-income Toronto residents. Their goals from the start were, first, to examine the objective conditions of poverty among low-income families, and second, to develop a political lever for welfare reforms and higher wages by helping establish a measurable basic standard of nutritional adequacy. To this end, the TWC made the study as scientifically rigorous as possible by forming a survey committee made up of national leaders in the fields of social work, public health, and nutrition – a number of whom would become prominent members of the CCN. In addition to Tisdall, Bell, and Gould, these people included A.E. Grauer, Lois Fraser, and E.W. McHenry. In 1937, the committee received a $2,000 grant from the London Life Insurance Company. With this funding in place, it began one of the most comprehensive nutrition surveys ever to be conducted during the 1930s – one, moreover, that would have a major impact on the subsequent CCN-sponsored dietary surveys in Edmonton, Quebec City, and Halifax as well as on Canada's national nutrition policies more generally.

After serious internal deliberations as well as correspondence with leading international researchers, the CCN chose to model its survey methodology primarily on widely publicized surveys conducted by Sir John Boyd Orr in Britain and Hazel Stiebeling in the United States. As discussed in greater detail in Chapter 1, this meant that whereas Marsh's McGill researchers had looked primarily at clinical indicators of mal-nutrition, the CCN chose instead to compare the diets of individuals and families against a pre-determined dietary standard that outlined daily requirements for nutrients based on factors such as age, gender, and oc-cupation. As was the case in Britain and the United States, this new research methodology generated rather alarming results: widespread nutritional deficiencies were found, and virtually all of the low-income Toronto fam-ilies examined were consuming insufficient quantities of calories, proteins, vitamins, and minerals.[13]

Yet when E.W. McHenry, a leading member of the CCN's Scientific Advisory Committee and University of Toronto School of Hygiene bio-chemist, published the results of the survey in 1939, his conclusions sur-prised many on the survey committee. This was because, despite a relatively clear correlation in the results between income and nutritional status,

McHenry concluded that "from the data available in this survey we cannot provide a clear-cut conclusion regarding the effect of income." Instead, using an example of two families with the same per person weekly income but with significantly different nutritional outcomes, McHenry argued that the real lesson was that "mothers should be given training in the essential principles of nutrition and in economical purchasing."[14]

Given the survey's original motives, it was perhaps unsurprising that other committee members took serious issue with McHenry's conclusions. Some of the front-line social workers involved in the study, such as Bell and Gould, had long maintained that income, not education, was the primary barrier to adequate nutrition, and they saw little in the Toronto survey results to alter their conclusions. The main planning body responsible for the survey similarly rejected McHenry's conclusions. In a 1939 report released shortly after the publication of McHenry's findings titled *The Cost of Living: Study of the Cost of a Standard of Living in Toronto which Should Maintain Health and Self-respect,* the TWC insisted that the Toronto nutrition study provided "concrete evidence" that low-income families were genuinely suffering as a direct result of their insufficient income. And in what could be interpreted as a thinly veiled refutation of McHenry's conclusions, the TWC dismissed the idea that some families were able to "get along very well" on a low wage, instead arguing that "those who have detailed knowledge of the situation are convinced that the ability to manage well, while valuable, is not sufficient and they have constantly before them the evidence of the harm resulting from the low standard of living made necessary by inadequate income."[15]

The TWC's *Cost of Living* was, in many ways, one of the most complete articulations of a scientifically grounded minimum standard of living developed in Canada during the 1930s. As such, it had an impact well beyond Toronto. The study was part of a larger effort by the TWC to educate the public and policy makers on the need for improved relief allotments and minimum wages by scientifically establishing the minimum cost of securing sufficient food, shelter, clothing, utilities, and other basic necessities. The TWC's estimates on minimum levels of family expenditure sufficient to maintain "health and self-respect" were therefore calculated through collaboration among social service agencies, front-line social workers, and nutrition experts. The results of this analysis showed that the minimum weekly budget for a family of five was $28.35 – a figure "far above prevailing wages" and one that excluded nearly 67 percent of Ontario families with an employed breadwinner, not to mention virtually all families on relief. Perhaps unsurprisingly, nutrition played a central role in these calculations, not simply because food was shown to be the single greatest cost incurred by families, but also because it was the one calculation that could be estimated with scientific precision. And because the TWC's figures represented one of the earliest attempts to translate the newly developed Canadian Dietary Standard into specific foods, it carried the added legitimacy of reflecting the consensus of Canada's leading nutrition professionals and the federally mandated CCN.

Social Nutrition

The TWC's *Cost of Living* report clearly contradicted McHenry's earlier assertion that there was no "clear-cut" connection between levels of malnutrition found in the Toronto survey and the incomes of the families surveyed. Given that the average size of the families that took part in the survey was 6.2 and that their average income was $19.64 per week, income was clearly a serious barrier to meeting the requirements set out by the Canadian Dietary Standard. Even if families cut back on the other expenses outlined by the TWC, the fact that a nutritionally adequate grocery bill was estimated to be $8 for a family of five suggested that many of the low-income families surveyed simply could not afford nutritious foods. Critics of local relief policies also pointed out that, according to the TWC's report, the situation was even worse for families on relief, a group who had been intentionally excluded from the Toronto dietary survey but were clearly surviving on far smaller incomes than even the survey's low-income sample base.[16]

The clear connection that had been drawn between income and nutritional status in the TWC's *The Cost of Living* report put McHenry on the defensive. He was forced to admit that there were, indeed, economic barriers to good nutrition, but he nonetheless continued to stress the primacy of education:

> In this country there are two principal causes [of malnutrition]: financial inability to buy an adequate diet and a lack of knowledge of the basic principles of nutrition and of how to buy foods economically. I am not particularly optimistic that much can be done to overcome the first obstacle but I believe that much can be accomplished by education.[17]

In part this attitude reflected McHenry's politics. He was willing to admit that relief rates in Toronto were, at best, only 80 to 85 percent adequate.

Nonetheless, he rejected the notion that they should be raised to meet
the requirements set out in the Canadian Dietary Standard, arguing that
"the relief allowance is not sufficient to provide an adequate diet but it
can furnish nutrition more adequate than is being secured by working
families." For McHenry, the doctrine of less eligibility clearly applied to
nutrition as much as it did to wages, and he insisted that "the diets of
many families could be improved without increasing the allowance by
training mothers how to buy food."[18]

Clearly, McHenry's report on the Toronto survey contradicted the dietary standard that he, personally, had played a key role in constructing.
This was in large part because, when the Canadian Dietary Standard was
translated into specific foods, it drew a clear line between those who could
and could not afford a nutritionally adequate diet, with most Canadian
families falling into the latter category. In large part, this critique – whether
it was recognized at the time by the CCN members or not – was built
into the definition of malnutrition that formed the scientific basis for the
dietary standard itself. Although key changes were introduced in order to
make the Canadian Dietary Standard "applicable to Canadian conditions"
– most notably, lower energy requirements were adopted for women –
requirements for minerals and, later, for vitamins included the kinds of
considerable "margins of safety" that were the hallmark of the "optimal"
dietary standards in use by Stiebeling, Orr, and the League of Nations
Health Organization (LNHO).[19] The outcome of defining "normal" health
in terms of an ambitious nutritional ideal saw the results of Canadian
studies mirroring the alarming malnutrition predictions of their international counterparts, but it also meant that an adequate diet was now
financially out of reach for most Canadians.

For many of the most vocal international proponents of optimal dietary
standards, their implicit critique of the existing social and economic order
was part of what made them attractive. While these scientific standards
enabled nutrition experts to account for the kinds of "in-between" or
"sub-clinical" states of nutrition that were more difficult to measure, many
prominent nutrition experts, including Sir John Boyd Orr, saw them as a
rejection of the social uses to which dietary standards had been put in the
past. Orr was a leading proponent of optimal nutrition and saw within
its definition of health a much more egalitarian vision of social relations.
The point of normalizing the goal of optimum nutrition was to ensure
that all individuals could meet their own biological potential in terms of
growth, strength, intelligence, and health. This meant that, whereas the

architects of minimal dietary standards believed they could define the amount of food needed to keep the poor alive and able to work, proponents of optimal nutrition argued that their standards promised to remove the physical inequalities that typically resulted from inequalities of wealth.

Orr, in many ways, exemplified the Depression-era movement among nutrition experts towards what James Vernon describes as "social nutrition." According to Vernon, the 1930s saw the growing prominence of social nutritionists like Orr who "sought not just to ground nutritional science in social realities but to make it an effective tool of social transformation."[20] Not only did the use of optimal standards in Orr's British dietary studies produce alarming malnutrition estimates that drew greater public attention to the problems of malnutrition and its direct relationship with income; it also held up the science of nutrition as the solution to larger social and economic problems, such as what to do with the undistributed agricultural surpluses that characterized the Depression-era economies of many Western nations. For Orr, in particular, malnutrition was fundamentally an economic problem and therefore required government intervention to ensure that "the great wealth of food which we have or can produce will be brought within the purchasing power of the poorest." This, he believed, would likely also spur a broader, agriculture-based economic recovery in Britain and elsewhere.[21]

Orr was not alone in his support for the social uses of nutrition. When the LNHO published the final report of its Mixed Committee on the Relation of Nutrition to Health, Agriculture and Economic Policy in 1937, it stated unequivocally that "the basic cause of malnutrition is poverty" and that "where resources fall below the limits of reasonable living standards, adequate nutrition cannot be secured even by the most scientific expenditure of those resources."[22] This finding was related to the fact that the committee had adopted one of the most ambitious optimal standards in use – one that, when translated into dollar terms, was significantly more expensive than those used by Stiebeling, Orr, and the CCN. It was perhaps unsurprising, then, that the policy solutions the committee offered to ameliorate both the Depression and the world malnutrition crisis included higher wages, centrally planned agriculture, and redistributive social security measures such as unemployment insurance, children's allowances, and school lunches.

As the debate between McHenry and the TWC supporters showed, however, Canadian nutrition experts were decidedly mixed in their support for the social politics of nutrition being promoted by Orr and the LNHO. Following the 1941 publication of the alarming results of the CCN's dietary

studies of low-income families in Edmonton, Quebec City, and Halifax
and of wealthier families in Toronto, there was still widespread disagreement within the CCN over whether malnutrition required primarily
economic rather than educational solutions. While Bell, Tisdall, and others
began to push for more generous unemployment relief rates and other
reforms, many within the CCN executive continued to stress the need for
an educational, public health–focused approach. Yet however serious these
internal divisions were within the profession, it was clear that the Canadian
Dietary Standard had become a powerful tool of social criticism and would
be playing an increasingly important role in wartime debates over social
security and reconstruction planning.

A National Social Minimum

The official response to the malnutrition crisis uncovered by the CCN
surveys largely reflected a public health–focused approach to the problem
that – through government sponsored efforts such as the Canadian
Nutrition Programme – stressed education, regulation, and expert intervention in the diets of ordinary Canadians. Meanwhile, however, the
political possibilities of the kind of "social nutrition" espoused by Orr
began to attract influential proponents. A.E. Grauer's two widely discussed
1939 reports, *Public Assistance and Social Insurance* and *Public Health*,
developed for the Royal Commission on Dominion–Provincial Relations,
were indicative of this shift in attitudes towards malnutrition. Grauer's
report on public assistance, for instance, included a detailed discussion of
the nutritional adequacy of relief rates, comparing them with the OMA
and LNHO dietary standards. His report on public health, however, made
little mention of nutrition except to highlight the limits of the most common kinds of public health interventions:

> Malnutrition, poor and crowded housing, and overwork, especially on
> the part of the mother are causes of illness beyond the limits of medicine
> in the accepted sense and link up the field of public health with the general
> field of welfare. Thus any steps – legislative, social or economic – that
> help do away with poverty are fundamental contributions to the field of
> public health.[23]

The 1939 publication of TWC's *Cost of Living* also did much to transform the politics of nutrition, in part because it was quickly adopted as a

key tool in the wartime arsenal of the political left in Canada. Its initial print run of five hundred copies sold out quickly, and a 1944 revision went so far as to become a national best-seller, selling more than five thousand copies. The report was ultimately dubbed the "Red Book" because of its cover – if not for its politics – and became especially popular with labour activists, who used it to show that despite wartime gains, an adequate standard of living remained out of reach for most Canadians during the war years.[24] But the TWC study's influence extended beyond the political left and the labour movement. During the war, the federal government used its figures when calculating Dependents' Allowances, and the BC government used them to calculate its Foster Home Maintenance Rates.[25] However, it was one thing to use the social minimum outlined in the *Cost of Living* as the basis for programs directed at so-called deserving recipients such as soldiers' families and foster parents. It was another altogether to challenge the basic assumptions that had guided welfare policies throughout the pre-war period – particularly the assumption that adequate relief rates resulted in psychological dependency. For many both within and outside the TWC, the real test of the report was whether it would spur reforms to existing social welfare programs like unemployment relief and mothers' allowances.

At the federal level, at least, there were encouraging signs of changing attitudes among policy makers. One of the most important of these was the 1940 passage of the landmark Unemployment Insurance Act. Attempts at creating a viable unemployment insurance system during the 1930s had been hampered by long-standing disputes over federal and provincial jurisdiction as well as federal concerns about the costs associated with such a program. The wartime emergency, combined with the achievement of nearly full employment around the country, allowed enough of a consensus to develop between the provinces and the federal government that a constitutional amendment could be passed allowing for exclusive federal jurisdiction over the newly created program. The Unemployment Insurance Act was widely hailed as an important step towards a more comprehensive social security system, but it was nonetheless deeply flawed. Its contributory nature meant that, instead of being based on financial need, benefits were provided on average at 50 percent of an individual's wages without taking into account whether this would be sufficient to meet basic needs such as for food, shelter, clothing, and fuel. Moreover, only 42 percent of workers even qualified for the plan in 1940 due to eligibility criteria that excluded seasonal workers, farm labourers, small-business people, domestic servants, and working women more generally.[26]

Given the apparent limitations of this new program, Canadians quickly began to make it clear that they were no longer satisfied with the status quo and that many of them considered unemployment insurance to be just a first step. Polls showed that an increasing majority of Canadians supported large-scale government intervention in the economy after the war, and the growing popularity of the CCF suggested that its calls for economic planning and universal welfare programs such as children's allowances and national health insurance were finding wider appeal among Canadian voters.[27] This leftward political turn reflected a desire among Canadians to avoid any return to Depression-era social and economic conditions. But, as was noted earlier in relation to food rationing and price controls, the war also saw a transformation in what Canadians considered fair in light of the enormous sacrifices they had made for their country at home and overseas. This produced a growing consensus that the state needed to intervene more directly in the economy in order to ensure that citizens were accorded much broader social and economic rights. As a culture of reconstruction took hold of Canadians' imaginations and as planning for the postwar future became a major point of debate and political mobilization on the home front, the rights of children, in particular, to basic levels of nutrition, housing, education, and health care became an especially potent force in the political discourse of the period.[28] To capture the broader public desire for postwar reform and, more importantly, to outflank its political opponents on the left, Mackenzie King's Liberal government was therefore forced to develop its own comprehensive postwar social security and reconstruction plans.

Leonard Marsh's *Report on Social Security for Canada*, tabled in early 1943 at the request of the federal government, was perceived by many as an important turning point in debates over Canada's postwar welfare state. The Marsh Report, as it became known, came on the heels of Britain's 1942 Beveridge Report, which had already made waves across the Atlantic. The Beveridge proposals were widely interpreted as a blueprint for a comprehensive "cradle to grave" postwar social security system designed to guarantee a national social minimum to all British citizens. Marsh, a former student of Beveridge, had been appointed the research director of the federal Advisory Committee on Postwar Reconstruction in 1941, and he had been assigned to produce a similar type of blueprint suitable for Canadian conditions. Aided by a number of prominent economists, social scientists, and social workers – including Bessie Touzel of the TWC, a key figure in the development of the *Cost of Living* report – he completed a draft of his own report in less than two months. The speed with which it was written led many at the time (and indeed, since) to criticize his proposals for being virtual copies of Beveridge's. It would be more accurate, though, to say it reflected a summary of Marsh's work at McGill in the 1930s and that it included many of the insights and recommendations of earlier works like *Health and Unemployment* and *Canadians In and Out of Work.*[29] Consequently, nutrition also ended up playing a prominent role in Marsh's *Report on Social Security.*

As with the Beveridge Report, the concept of a social minimum lay at the heart of Marsh's proposals for a comprehensive, cradle-to-grave welfare state. But while historians have tended to focus on the details of specific social security programs outlined in the Marsh Report (such as unemployment insurance, children's allowances, health insurance, workmen's compensation, and pensions), Marsh himself made the case that these proposals would be effective only to the degree that they contributed to a national minimum standard of living. A key recommendation of the report, then, was that means-tested social assistance programs be replaced by a comprehensive system of employment-based social insurance measures as well as universal benefits that would provide "a national minimum of coverage against major causes of poverty and insecurity."[30] For Marsh, this national minimum was not a vague ideal so much as a specific benchmark that could be calculated "by reference to the minimum quantities of the essentials of life sufficient to maintain the nutrition, health, and decency of the family as a unit."[31] He therefore began the report with an attempt to calculate a social minimum that met these basic goals for health, efficiency, and affordability in the context of a broader national policy of full employment.

In *Health and Unemployment,* Marsh had singled out nutrition as being "at the root of poor health standards." "Inherited organic strength, housing and clothing, the types of work which individuals do and their related strains, all play their part," Marsh argued, "but sufficiency of food and balance of diet are fundamentals."[32] Nutrition therefore also had a central place in the 1943 report's attempt to define a social minimum. Like the TWC's *Cost of Living,* Marsh began his calculations by examining basic necessities such as food, shelter, fuel, and clothing. But he drew a distinction between food and other necessities, arguing that "the most authoritative work on living standards has been done with special reference to food." He suggested that "there is to-day enough authoritative understanding as well as actual experience of food requirements to enable them to be discussed with a reasonable degree of confidence," adding that "the physical requirements of such matters as housing, fuel, and clothing do not require the same degree of scientific knowledge."[33] Nutrition, in other words, was the scientific, and therefore objective, backbone of any kind of national social minimum.

For his report, Marsh adopted the food budget that the TWC had developed for the *Cost of Living*, which was itself based on the 1939 Canadian Dietary Standard. While he acknowledged that there were more recent budgets based on the recommended dietary allowances (RDAs) developed by the US National Research Council – intakes that, in 1942, had been adopted as the new Canadian Dietary Standard – he suggested that the *Cost of Living* recommendations were sufficient to maintain an adequate level of health and that they also reflected "the knowledge of social workers, of the purchasing habits and requirements of low-income families, and the limits to the adjustments they can reasonably be expected to make." Moreover, because the foods in the TWC budget ultimately cost less than the ones on the lists developed by nutrition experts in Canada and the United States, the TWC budget could not be labelled as an "excessive variation of the 'minimum adequate' level."[34]

In Marsh's final calculation of an adequate social minimum, he distinguished between the kinds of "short-term" or "emergency" budgets used to calculate rates of social assistance and a "desirable" minimum for working families. As a consequence, he produced two separate budgets: a "Desirable Living Minimum" budget set at $1,577.40 per year for a family of five based on the *Cost of Living*, and an "Assistance Minimum" set at $1,134.48 based on reductions from the TWC budget following his own "careful assessment."[35] Marsh defended the apparent double standard for unemployed and employed Canadians by arguing that even his assistance budget far exceeded the highest minimum wage that had been legislated in the country and that 33 percent of urban and 50 percent of rural families were already subsisting on wages that fell below the "Assistance Minimum" budget. By comparison, a majority of Canadian families – 65 percent in urban areas and 73 percent in rural areas – failed to meet the "Desirable Living Minimum." But what is most interesting about Marsh's "Assistance Minimum" and "Desirable Living Minimum" budgets is that, while the former assumes "more crowded housing accommodation and the absence of any allowance for advancement expenditures or savings at all," he maintains the same food budget for both on the grounds that "there is least room for safe economy on food."[36] Nutrition, in other words – because its health outcomes are more easily and objectively measurable – emerged as the primary anchor of Marsh's national social minimum.

Marsh was not alone in directly linking social security and a national social minimum to nutrition. Harry Cassidy's proposals – published shortly after the Marsh Report as *Social Security and Reconstruction in Canada* – offered an alternative route to social security that focused largely on reforms to existing welfare services and their administrative machinery. But, like Marsh, he also pointed to the need for minimum standards of public welfare. Cassidy's "social balance sheet" therefore included four "basic indices of social well-being": nutrition, health, housing and delinquency. Moreover, after discussing the dietary standards adopted by the TWC, Orr, and Stiebeling, he concluded that a typical family of five required at least $1,500 per year "for bare maintenance of health and physical efficiency" – a figure strikingly close to Marsh's own "Desirable Living Minimum" and clearly influenced by the TWC's *Cost of Living*.[37]

Mackenzie King, a more recent (and, many have argued, half-hearted) convert to social security, recognized that the public was demanding reforms of the sort being called for by Beveridge, Marsh, Cassidy, and others.[38] In outlining his government's objectives for a national social minimum, he suggested that they would include "useful employment for all who are willing to work; standards of nutrition and housing adequate to ensure the health of the whole population; social insurance against privations resulting from unemployment, accident, the death of the breadwinner, ill health and old age."[39] The Liberal government's first tentative step in this direction – the Family Allowances Act of 1944 – was likely motivated more by a fear of a leftward movement of Canadians following the surprising electoral success of the CCF in provincial elections in Ontario and Saskatchewan as well as in key federal by-elections than by genuine support for Marsh's proposed social security state. It was nonetheless viewed by many as an important step towards something approximating a national social minimum as outlined by Marsh. In this way, nutrition came to the fore in a fierce debate over the program both within and outside parliament.

Marsh himself saw children's allowances as the "key to consistency" in a properly functioning social security system because they were universal and, therefore, addressed the income deficiencies faced by families with children. This meant that, without requiring the introduction of a "living wage," they went some way towards contributing to a social minimum on a truly national basis by providing for the basic needs of all children without the stigma of charity. Critics attacked the proposed legislation on a variety of grounds: fiscal conservatives pointed to the sheer cost of the program, and organized labour contended it justified continued wage controls and undermined demands for a living wage. There was also the more racially based criticism that the program was being used to "buy" the votes of Catholic Quebecers with larger families.[40] Conservative feminist and social work pioneer Charlotte Whitton was perhaps the most vocal opponent of the program, and at various times she invoked all of these criticisms of Family Allowances. At the heart of her critique, however, was her rejection of the concept of a social minimum.

Although Whitton conceded that welfare reforms were necessary, she argued that Beveridge-style reforms offered by Marsh were unsuited to Canada's federal division of powers as well as to the Canadian character and temperament. For instance, in response to Marsh's proposal that social security measures combine new social insurance measures with universal benefits, she called instead for the strengthening of Canada's existing welfare institutions – in particular, for a greater focus on Canada's "social utilities," which, according to Whitton, were composed of "such essential public services as the schools, hospitals, children's services, etc., and the wide variety of agencies, designed to serve in the impairment or breakdown of physique, mentality or character."[41] Where Marsh called for a minimum standard of living to be calculated in terms of income, Whitton argued for a "general minimum standard of the public services" buttressed by a "living wage policy" and by means-tested, locally administered social as-sistance programs. Although Whitton acknowledged that the state had some responsibility for "assuring to all its citizens at least the means of subsistence at a level not degrading to human decency," she argued that this was best achieved "by affording such conditions of gainful occupation within the country as make it possible for all willing workers to maintain themselves and those dependent upon them through the proceeds of their own gainful occupation, whether by sale of their products, or of their labour or of their skill for wages."[42] In Whitton's view, family allowances not only undermined the principle of a living-wage policy and of remunera-tion based on skill and individual initiative, but also provided little guar-antee of "adequacy or fitness of the child's guardianship, or of the physical or mental competence of the child and similar related factors, which might question the efficacy of a cash allowance when treatment of another type might be required."[43]

Defenders of the Family Allowances program were quick to attack Whitton's distinction between existing "social utilities" and the kinds of social security measures outlined by Marsh by arguing that these social utilities were half-measures that would do little to address the root causes of Canada's malnutrition problems. The Canadian Association of Social

THE POLITICS OF MALNUTRITION

Workers and family allowance proponent Margaret Gould – an editorial writer for the *Toronto Star* and former executive secretary of the CWC – both argued that Whitton was proposing a false alternative because nutrition-related social utilities such as school lunches did little to meet a child's entire nutritional needs in the face of inadequate income. They argued that such programs could only guarantee one meal a day and that they did little to help children who were too young for school or who had to spend much of the year doing farm work.[44] These limitations were also pointed out by Family Allowance supporter Dorothy Stepler, who argued that malnourished children

> will not have enough energy either to learn or to enjoy modern playground facilities. If a hot lunch is provided at school, well and good, but lunch won't make up for a scanty breakfast and dinner, or a cold house, and it won't help at all on Saturday or Sunday ... Finally, the effects of malnutrition and neglect during childhood can never be wholly corrected by free health services, dental care, and so on in later life.[45]

Pointing to the work of the TWC in Canada and of Orr in Britain, Stepler argued that nutritional surveys had shown conclusively that, for low-income families, an adequate diet "is impossible, and no amount of education on correct foods for health can be successful if the housewife has not enough purchasing power."[46]

For those who supported family allowances and the "cradle to grave" social security measures outlined by Marsh and Beveridge, nutrition seemed to be a powerful ally. Given the apparently close correlation between nutritional status and income, the prevention of malnutrition could easily be invoked as a justification for expanding the welfare state. The innocence of children added to the case for universal rights to a national social minimum. Many Canadians may have continued to view individual breadwinners as primarily responsible for their own unemployment and poverty, but it was harder to make the case that children should be punished for their parents' failings. While Stepler made the case that poverty was by no means the parents' fault, given that most Canadians lacked sufficient income to secure nutritious foods, she added that "even when it is, to punish the children by malnutrition is the surest way of reproducing the same faults in the next generation."[47] Gould took this line of argument even further. Citing the CCN studies, military rejection figures, and more recent studies of the relationship between nutrition and infant mortality, she argued that the nutritional improvements promised by family allowances would have profound effects on children's physical and mental development:

> Much ability and talent is suppressed because of poverty. The Family Allowances Act will help to release creative energies. It will help to improve the quality and efficiency of the Canadian people. Research in nutrition has shown that mental alertness and the learning ability of children depend upon proper nutrition ... Children who eat better food, who do not miss school, who do not enter "blind alley" occupations, who receive vocational and cultural training will, in one generation, become efficient, benefactors of this country.

She even added that nutritional studies "among races with a reputation for laziness showed that for generations they were simply hungry."[48] In the end, the arguments of both Gould and Stepler boiled down to a question of citizenship, defined in terms of the rights, responsibilities and, perhaps most importantly, future capacities of the population. "This measure" Gould promised, "will raise the quality of the population. It will increase the physical and mental health of children, [and] thus improve their learning ability and increase the number of efficient, talented and skilled citizens."[49]

Reforming Relief Diets

As the debates over the Family Allowances program and the Marsh Report showed, many Canadians believed that nutrition provided a compelling moral and scientific justification for sweeping social and economic reforms. In the context of a perceived wartime malnutrition crisis, the idea of a nutritionally defined, basic standard of health and decency for all found increasingly broad appeal as a more humane alternative to the patchwork of largely inadequate welfare systems in place throughout the country during the war. One of the earliest tangible victories for the kind of nutrition-based social nutrition envisioned by Marsh and his supporters was the City of Toronto's decision in early 1943 to base its food relief schedule on a scientifically determined and nutritionally adequate weekly food list.[50] This reform of the municipal welfare system marked the culmination of the TWC's efforts in the aftermath of the 1939 Toronto low-income dietary survey. And because it sparked very public debates between leading figures in Canadian nutrition research and policy, not to mention some of the founding and most senior members of the CCN, this development in Toronto helped precipitate a profound rethinking of the nature and extent of malnutrition on a truly national scale.

The main impetus for Toronto's new relief policy was a concerted lob-bying effort by the TWC and other advocacy groups following the 1939 publication of the *Cost of Living* report. The city's official response to the report in the months after its publication had largely echoed McHenry's conclusions. The outbreak of war, however, brought about a decided change in attitude at City Hall.[51] Spurred in part by the election in 1941 of a more progressive city council and by the election of former Welfare Council of Ontario president Fred Conboy as mayor (and in part by a significant drop in relief rolls following the return of full employment in the early years of the war), the city agreed to a request by representatives of the Women Electors' Association of Toronto that a Committee on Public Welfare be appointed to examine the adequacy of Toronto's food relief allotments.[52] As one of its first actions, the committee requested that the TWC prepare a brief on the question. Prominent TWC committee members Marjorie Bell and University of Toronto nutrition professor Alice Willard prepared material for the brief by attempting to secure an adequate diet on relief allotments provided in Toronto using two methods: one in which foods were purchased in the most economical and scientific way possible, and another trying to mirror the actual shopping habits of families based on Bell's front-line experience. In both cases the foods purchased fell far short of nutritional requirements set out by the Canadian Dietary Standard.[53] Willard and Bell's experiment received wide local and national coverage, and by showing that even trained dieticians could not maintain a nutritionally adequate diet on existing relief allowances, it directly refuted the notion that education, rather than income, was the primary cause of malnutrition.[54]

In September 1941, Toronto City Council responded to the committee's brief by passing a motion authorizing an immediate increase of 20 percent in municipal unemployment relief allowances. At the same time, it ap-pointed leading nutrition experts Tisdall, Willard, Bell, and McHenry as a committee to write a report on the nutritional value of municipal food relief. McHenry ultimately declined to take part in the work of the com-mittee, likely due to his ongoing disagreements with Bell over the results of the first Toronto survey and the structure of the CCN.[55] Even so, the formation of the Tisdall–Willard–Bell committee can be seen as the cul-mination of years of efforts by local social welfare and labour activists to reform the city's relief schedule along nutritional lines. Tisdall and Bell, in particular, had been key figures in the creation of the OMA and TWC reports, and by the 1940s both were committed to welfare reform. Tisdall had become convinced that the setting of appropriate relief rates was an important wartime function, particularly in light of the high rejection rates of Canadian soldiers and experiments in the United States that showed that men on relief were unable to perform their jobs efficiently when they returned to work as a direct result of their years of deprivation.[56] Also, Tisdall and Bell were both researchers on a 1941 University of Toronto study of low-income pregnant women that showed that, when provided with as little as $5 extra per month to purchase protective foods, they were able to achieve significantly lower rates of infant and maternal mortality than a control group.[57]

In November, Tisdall, Willard, and Bell submitted their report to Toronto City Council. Their methodology had closely resembled that of the OMA and TWC studies. This time, however, they applied the newly created US RDAs rather than the 1939 Canadian Dietary Standard. The RDAs had been adopted in June 1941 by the Canadian Dietetic Association on the recommendation of Willard and Bell, and the following year they were also adopted by the CCN as the basis for the new Canadian Dietary Standard. As discussed in Chapter 1, the RDAs contained the most complete set of requirements for vitamins and minerals yet produced, but they were also based on an ambitious definition of "optimal" nutrition. When translated into weekly food lists, the result was dramatic: recommendations for a family of five, for instance, called for a relief rate increase of between 50 and 70 percent.[58]

In one of the first genuine victories for advocates of a nutritionally grounded social welfare state, the City of Toronto adopted the relief schedules recommended by Tisdall, Willard, and Bell in March 1943 after months of fierce debates in and out of council. These debates hinged on two very different visions of social policy and practice. On the one hand, the doctrine of less eligibility was premised on the assumption that the market should set relief rates based on the wages of the lowest paid workers. On the other hand, the growing support for an alternative vision – one defined by minimum standards of living established objectively by scientists, social workers, and other experts – reflected a growing sense among Canadians that the market had failed them during the Depression and that they had a right to a certain basic standard of living, which should be underwritten by the state in light of their wartime sacrifices.[59] Because so many had either experienced or witnessed the hunger and want of the Depression first-hand, this latter argument became increasingly powerful during the war and helped produce broad support for the Tisdall–Willard–Bell recommendations.

The Ontario government responded to these changes in Toronto by launching its own investigation of the adequacy of provincial contributions to food relief payments. Since the early years of the Depression, the province's contribution to municipal relief costs had been defined in large part by a schedule set out by a provincially appointed Advisory Committee on Direct Relief in 1932. The committee's report – later dubbed the Campbell Report after its chair, Ford Motors General Manager Wallace Campbell – established a set of maximum relief ceilings to which the province would contribute funds. The schedule of food allotments used as the basis for the Campbell Report had been established with little reference to nutritional adequacy and with no meaningful input from nutrition professionals. Although the dollar values of these ceilings were periodically increased to reflect changes in the cost of living, provincial relief allotments between 1932 and 1944 were based largely on the approach outlined in the Campbell Report.[60] Critics of that report had long used nutritionally derived relief allowances such as those produced by the OMA and the TWC to argue against the continued use of that report's food schedule, but the province was only pushed to assess the nutritional adequacy of its relief policies after Toronto had adopted the Tisdall–Willard–Bell Report's recommendations. But instead of taking the recommendations of that report at face value, the province appointed McHenry to produce his own recommendations for how relief food allowances could be adapted to meet basic nutrition requirements in the context of wartime rationing and shortages.

The outcome of this investigation was the *Report on Food Allowances for Relief Recipients in the Province of Ontario*, which was officially adopted as the basis for a reformed schedule of relief allowances in Ontario in September 1944. This was a turning point in the political debate over nutrition and social policy that had long divided the country's nutrition professionals. McHenry's report applied a methodology similar to that of the TWC and of Tisdall, Willard, and Bell, but it was also coloured by McHenry's different vision of the relationship between nutrition and income. From the outset, for instance, he was careful to stress the limitations of cash allowances in securing proper nutrition by arguing that a "liberal cash allowance cannot, in itself, guarantee an adequate diet" and that a family's health depended "as much, if not more, upon the wisdom with which the allowance is spent and upon cooking methods used as upon the money supplied."[61] He suggested that it would probably be more economical to return to a direct relief system based on the "central, large-scale purchasing of foods" or even by establishing state-run restaurants directed at relief recipients. While acknowledging that cash allowances were likely to be continued by most municipalities well into the future, he emphasized the importance of nutrition education for families on relief through cookbooks and other means, repeating his usual argument that "housewives should be trained to spend the food allowance to the best advantage."[62]

In many ways, the McHenry Report's focus on the ignorance of mothers as a leading cause of malnutrition contrasted with its actual findings. Like the Tisdall–Willard–Bell and TWC reports, the McHenry Report was based mainly on a detailed analysis of the minimum cost of a nutritionally adequate weekly shopping list for families of different sizes and age ranges. And like these earlier reports, McHenry's found that, with the noticeable exception of cash allowances for single adults, the existing maximum relief ceiling based on the Campbell Report was largely inadequate. But while McHenry's analysis in many ways supported the findings of the Tisdall–Willard–Bell Report, there were a number of important differences. The most significant of these was that McHenry chose to use the Canadian Dietary Standard as more of a guideline for, rather than as the primary determinant of, his suggested weekly shopping lists. This meant that, with the exception of children under three years old, the report's suggested weekly diets generally failed to meet the standard's requirements for one or more nutrients set out in the 1942 standard. Adults, for instance, would receive only 87 percent of their recommended allowances for thiamin and riboflavin, while nursing women would secure only 71 percent of the requirements for ascorbic acid and 75 percent for thiamin. In terms of the actual dollar value of relief allotments, these changes represented cuts of up to 36 percent for single men in comparison with the new Toronto relief schedule and, for a family of five with older children, between 17 and 28 percent.[63]

McHenry justified his decision to adopt lower nutritional standards than the Tisdall–Willard–Bell and TWC reports in part based on his perception of supply conditions, which he suggested had never been sufficient to provide an optimal diet to all Canadians. He therefore argued that it would be "unwise to recommend that all persons on relief in Ontario at present be given food supplies which are not available to all citizens." But McHenry devoted the bulk of his explanation to a much broader critique of the optimal requirements set out in the Canadian Dietary Standard itself. Although he himself had sat on the committee that developed both revisions of the Canadian Dietary Standard and had recently spoken in favour of basing Canada's Food Rules on an unambiguously optimal set of requirements, his official report on Ontario's relief diets was quite frank in its discussion of the limitations of nutrition research in the 1940s.[64] In particular, he admitted that "requirements for the various vitamins are, at present, only approximations which later research may show to be quite erroneous." He went on to suggest that "there is little evidence that people will suffer if they fail to secure the precise amounts of the various nutrients listed in the [1942 Standard]." While he argued that the Canadian Dietary Standard represented "the best information available at present on which to base dietary recommendations," he nonetheless cautioned that "a supply of foods sufficient to meet these recommendations will not necessarily guarantee a state of optimal nutrition."[65]

The McHenry Report once again highlighted long-standing divisions within the nutrition professions over social and political questions while, at the same time, challenging the very basis of the optimal consensus that had governed Canadian nutrition science and policy up to that point. It did, nonetheless, mark a genuine victory for critics of Ontario's relief policies and for supporters of a scientifically planned welfare state more generally. Even though the new relief guidelines adopted by the Ontario government were decidedly less generous from a nutritional standpoint than Toronto's – and also represented a maximum ceiling, rather than a minimum baseline, for relief payments – the fact that the province had decided to base its relief rates on nutrition at all showed how far the debate had come since the 1930s. While nutrition-based critiques had little effect on the value of relief diets during the Depression, wartime public opinion had shifted to the extent that all levels of government felt pressure to justify their welfare policies as humane, reasonable, and scientifically grounded.

Reconstructing Malnutrition

The debates over relief diets in Ontario were, in many ways, the culmination of what had, up till then, been a significant expansion of the influence of nutrition experts in discussions over the future of Canada's welfare state. But they also highlighted some of the major weaknesses inherent in using nutrition-based arguments for a scientifically grounded minimum standard of living. The differences between the Tisdall–Willard–Bell, TWC, and McHenry reports suggested that, even using the same basic data, leading nutrition experts could arrive at significantly different conclusions regarding the components of a nutritionally adequate diet. More important, they also exposed the rather tenuous nature of the social, scientific, and political compromises that formed the basis of the CCN's nutritional research during this period. The usefulness of nutrition as a social-policy planning tool had largely been derived from its ability to objectively quantify the dietary needs of individuals, but the final years of the war would see a transformation in the consensus around the nature and extent of malnutrition in Canada. This changing consensus would not only bring into question the kinds of social uses to which the Canadian Dietary Standard had been put but also, as a consequence, challenge many of the CCN's earlier warnings of a wartime malnutrition crisis.

McHenry would emerge as a leading figure in the transformation of the postwar scientific consensus among Canada's nutrition experts. After tabling his report on relief diets, he expanded on his critique of the physiological bases of the Canadian Dietary Standard and began to pressure the CCN to discontinue its use. In particular, he argued that the nutritional requirements in the existing standard were much too high and that, as a consequence, they were producing "unnecessarily exaggerated statements about the prevalence of malnutrition." These statements, he argued, were being used by advocates for the "widespread use of vitamins, as in the enrichment of flour and other foods" and also as "evidence of iniquities in the present social order."[66] Conceding his own "considerable responsibility" for claims that malnourishment was widespread in Canada in the aftermath of the CCN surveys, he argued now that the lack of correspondence between the dietary surveys and clinical evidence of disease since that time called for a rethinking of how dietary standards were constructed and applied. For instance, his own research examining schoolchildren in the Toronto suburb of East York had shown that even children consuming less than 70 percent of the dietary standard for nutrients such as ascorbic acid and thiamin – a figure used by the CCN to differentiate between "markedly deficient" and "borderline deficient" diets – showed little evidence of overt deficiency states following thorough clinical examinations. Based on these findings, McHenry concluded that optimal standards with considerable margins of safety should never have been treated as a rigid standard of nutritional adequacy in the first place but, instead, should have been treated more as "guides in supplying optimal supplies of food."[67]

McHenry's critique of the Canadian Dietary Standard posed a number of fundamental challenges to the nutritional orthodoxy of the day. He was not only calling for a lower standard for the purposes of drawing up minimum relief schedules but also, and perhaps more importantly, bringing into question the very existence of the national wartime malnutrition crisis that had rallied Canadians around the CCN's nutritional message in the first place. Indeed, the "unnecessarily exaggerated statements" about malnutrition rates that McHenry identified in his critique of the Canadian Dietary Standard (such as one newspaper editorial's claim that 60 percent of Canadians were potentially malnourished) were remarkably similar to the kinds of alarmist conjectures made by his CCN colleagues only a few years earlier. Moreover, McHenry himself had played a key role in uncovering this malnutrition crisis, not only as a principal architect of the research methodology used in the CCN surveys, but also as one of the leading members of the Scientific Advisory Committee that had developed the 1939 Canadian Dietary Standard and that later voted unanimously to adopt the US National Research Council's RDAs in 1942. Overall, then, his stance at the end of the war in many ways represented a rejection of the CCN's earlier research program as well as his own earlier findings on the nature and extent of malnutrition in Canada. He admitted as much in 1944, although he continued to defend the usefulness of the CCN surveys, which, he argued, may have exaggerated overall rates of malnutrition but nonetheless "provided abundant proof of the prevalent need for nutrition education."[68]

Eventually, McHenry succeeded in recruiting other allies to his cause, and in June 1945 the CCN issued an official statement concerning the "Construction and Use of Dietary Standards." Citing a "lack of correlation between the results of dietary surveys and the physical condition of the subjects," the CCN announced that "because of the accuracy which is falsely conveyed and because of the seriousness of their misuse, it would be advisable to discontinue the use in Canada of the Allowances adopted by the [CCN] in 1942." The CCN then outlined a set of more modest requirements for most of the nutrients included in the 1942 standard, cautioning, however, that until more accurate measures became available, "the kinds of approximations represented by standards should be limited to planning food supplies and not as a criteria of the adequacy of individual intakes."[69]

The CCN's announcement signalled a significant break with its international counterparts. When McHenry and others on the CCN executive approached leading American nutrition experts with their concerns about the RDAs and with their own proposal for a new dietary standard that would recognize multiple states of nutrition – including excess nutrition, optimal nutrition, and deficient nutrition – their ideas were given "a very poor reception" because American scientists remained wedded to the optimal requirements set out in the RDAs.[70] Moreover, in 1945 Sir John Boyd Orr – a champion of the optimal consensus – was named the first director of the UN Food and Agriculture Organization on an ambitious platform of global nutrition-based agricultural planning through a proposed World Food Board.[71]

The CCN's decision to part ways with the international community and its rather remarkable about-face regarding the measurement of malnutrition were not, however, simply responses to new scientific research indicating that evidence of nutritional deficiencies was lacking. In important ways, this decision also reflected much larger changes in ideas about the social uses of nutrition, particularly given the changed circumstances facing Canada in the aftermath of the war. Some especially useful insights into this shift away from the optimal consensus were provided in a June 1945 article on the construction of dietary standards written by the director of the federal Nutrition Division, L.B. Pett, and his colleagues C.A. Morrel and F.W. Hanley. In attempting to explain the rather dramatic shifts in thinking about nutritional requirements in recent years, this article provided some historical context for the scientific and social changes that had led to the creation of many of the international dietary standards that had been developed up to that point. Their argument hinged on the idea that many of these standards had been created, not because of specific scientific discoveries, but "as a direct result of certain national or international situations of a critical nature in which food played a decisive or important role."[72] In particular, they identified four specific crises that served as catalysts for the most widely accepted standards: the unemployment of English cotton workers in 1862, the Great War, the Great Depression, and the Second World War.

In perhaps one of the more revealing statements on the social determinants of nutritional knowledge during this period, Pett, Morrel, and Hanley argued that the purposes assigned to these particular standards – "and hence the standards themselves" – tended to "reflect not only the contemporary level of scientific knowledge but also, consciously or not, the manner chosen to deal with the problems necessitating them." For instance, the first English dietary standard – established in 1862 by Edward Smith – was produced specifically in light of widespread unemployment and was designed to describe a diet adequate to prevent outright starvation, although not necessarily to prevent hunger. While the 1930s saw considerable advances in nutrition through important discoveries of new vitamins and minerals, Pett, Morrel, and Hanley argued that it also saw a significant change in thinking about the broader social purpose of dietary standards.

Many of the standards developed during this period were at least partly motivated by a growing need to deal with similar problems related to scarcity and unemployment. But, they continued, most of these standards ultimately utilized a much higher threshold of adequate nutrition, in part because of the "existence of huge undistributed surpluses of food in a world where inadequate nutrition of all degrees abounded" and in part because "the advance in productive capacity and related social thinking during this period had been such that the later standards had a considerably higher objective than the mere prevention of starvation."[73] The most socially and nutritionally ambitious standard of all, they argued, was the RDAs adopted in 1941 by the US National Research Council and in 1942 by the CCN. Pett, Morrel and Hanley suggested that while philosophically similar to their Depression-era optimal predecessors with their large "margins of safety," these RDAs were a product of the Second World War in that they "represent[ed] the response of nutrition specialists in that country to the need for a program of action to mobilize all the nation's resources for large-scale and protracted warfare." The standard, that is, had been produced for the purpose of building up the population "to a level of health and vigour never before attained or dreamed of," and this was done by setting all standards based on the highest theoretical optimum for "*any* individual under any normal circumstances."[74]

The main conclusion to be drawn from the history of dietary standards up to that point, for Pett, Morrel, and Hanley, was not that the science of these standards had been proven wrong over time by new research. Instead, they were arguing that "a standard set up for one purpose, for a specific problem, may not be applicable to the solution of another problem." For instance, while critical of optimal dietary standards of the 1930s and, in particular, of the RDAs for being too high and thereby overestimating the incidence of malnutrition, Pett, Morrel, and Hanley also admitted that, even in 1945, it was still impossible to create a definitive standard "on the basis of well-established evidence (as distinct from opinion and compromise)." They therefore called for a new compromise between the limitations in the available scientific knowledge and the anticipated social utility of that knowledge, arguing that new standards must be developed that were "adapted to the provision of freedom from hunger in the immediate post-war world."[75]

The idea that a new standard needed to be developed to better meet the realities of a new postwar world reflected a key weakness in the wartime optimal consensus. On a regular basis, images of starving Greek, Dutch, Indian, and Chinese children were featured in Canadian newspapers and

magazines as the increasingly dire situation in the liberated countries of
Europe and Asia following the near total destruction of their agricultural
and industrial output became apparent. Growing attention was similarly
being paid to relief efforts by the United Nations Relief and Rehabilitation
Administration (UNRRA), the Red Cross, and other international aid
organizations to prevent future humanitarian crises in liberated countries
and to provide a buffer against the spread of fascism and communism.
The cumulative effect of these repeated images of hunger abroad, however,
was to bring into question much of the wartime discourse of malnutrition
at home. Pett's own assertion that 40 to 60 percent of the population was
malnourished, in other words, seemed increasingly problematic in the face
of genuine starvation abroad.

When the CCN finally agreed on a new Canadian Dietary Standard,
the standard partially reflected these concerns with hunger abroad. But,
at the same time, it also represented a very different social vision, one that
had clearly been developed in response to the changing political uses to
which nutrition had been put during the final years of the war. The new
standard, now rebranded the Dietary Standard for Canada, had been in
development throughout the early postwar period and was officially
adopted in 1948. One of the most immediately apparent differences between the new standard and its two predecessors was its increased com-
plexity. Whereas earlier standards simply provided recommendations based
on the categories of age, gender, and occupation, the new standard added
an additional layer of analysis by basing its recommendations on an individual's body size. This reflected a growing consensus that nutritional needs
differed significantly between individuals and were more closely related
to physical size and activity than to categories such as age or gender. This
focus on the specific needs of the individual signalled a rejection of the
tendency of the RDAs to define "normal" in terms of the requirements of
the largest, most active individual. As a result, overall requirements for
most nutrients were on average lower in almost every category in the 1948
standard than they had been previously.

The introduction of body size eliminated some of the more obvious
excesses of the 1942 standard. But the most fundamental philosophical
change to be found in the 1948 standard was that it divided malnutrition
into two categories: one set of requirements was provided in order to
measure the minimum nutritional needs of an individual; the other provided optimal requirements. The former were termed the "nutritional
floor" and essentially described a nutrient intake below which "the maintenance of health in people cannot be assumed."[76] While the requirements

for some nutrients, such as calcium and ascorbic acid, were constant across all levels of activity, the requirements for others, such as thiamin, riboflavin, and niacin, offered a "maintenance" requirement that was less than half that of the "sedentary" requirement outlined in the 1942 standard. Besides the nutritional floor there were various optimal requirements for categories including work, pregnancy, and lactation. The idea was for these optimal figures to be added to the "maintenance" requirements in order to calculate the nutritional needs of a "normal" or "active" person. Although these optimal requirements were somewhat lower than those in the 1942 standard, they were still based on an arbitrary physiological ideal, and in that regard, CCN scientists readily admitted that "there is difficulty in defining health in the nutritional sense" and that "there are no quantitative experimental data bearing on the question of how much more than enough is better."[77]

Ultimately, the 1948 Dietary Standard for Canada was a complicated document that was, in many ways, less a reflection of any specific advances in scientific research during this period than the product of a renewed compromise within the CCN concerning the social, political, and scientific uses of nutrition. The introduction of the nutritional floor, in particular, meant that the 1948 standard managed to reflect the priorities of both optimum and minimum standards of health. And, as a result, it also clearly rejected Orr's vision of social nutrition. Whereas nutrition experts, both domestic and international, had to a certain degree adopted optimal requirements in the 1930s in recognition that there were broader, and more difficult to measure, health effects of improved nutrition – effects that extend beyond the simple prevention of overt nutritional deficiency states – the CCN's new standard created a kind of two-tiered definition of nutritional health. Although the nutritional floor could theoretically be used to assess individual risk of nutritional deficiency states more accurately than could previous standards, it could also be used in the calculation of relief or institutional diets in a way that, unlike earlier purely optimal standards, did less to challenge the existing social and economic order. The "optimal" requirements provided in the standard, on the other hand, could still be used as the basis for prescriptive materials such as Canada's Food Rules, because they reflected a set of aspirational goals for health, industrial productivity, and agricultural planning.[78] Ultimately, however, the decision as to which of these guidelines constituted adequate "health" was left to individual nutrition experts. This meant that the new standard could be adapted to a much broader range of social, political, and medical purposes than its predecessors.

In effect, the Dietary Standard for Canada allowed nutrition experts to straddle the line between the social, political, and medical uses of nutrition in a way that consciously reflected the new socio-political circumstances of a postwar international order. This transformation was made explicit when, for the first time in a Canadian dietary standard, the recommendations included warnings that "excess ingestion of nutrients should not be confused with an adequately nourished state such as is sometimes referred to as 'optimal nutrition'" and that the "ingestion of more of a nutrient than serves a clear physiological purpose is undesirable in the face of the world scarcity of food and may even be harmful to the individual under certain circumstances."[79] McHenry, for his part, went so far as to warn that as many as 15 to 20 percent of Canadian adults were overweight and that it was causing "more harm to adults than any deficiency state found in this country."[80] The fact that such warnings were quickly echoed by Pett and others in the CCN suggests that, rather than being chastened by their wartime exaggerations regarding the scale of malnutrition, nutrition experts were eager to open new areas of intervention into Canadians' dietary practices.[81] And, perhaps unsurprisingly, overweight was a threat that reflected the CCN's increasing focus on malnutrition as an individual problem rather than the result of structural social and economic inequalities.

School Lunches and the Limits of Nutrition

After the war ended, it quickly became clear that nutrition would be a less reliable ally to those seeking to challenge the political and economic status quo than it had been only six years earlier. Ontario's successful efforts to significantly improve unemployment relief had in many ways been the product of perceptions of a national wartime malnutrition crisis and of the ambitious and generous optimal dietary standards adopted by the CCN in 1939 and 1942. But by the war's end, hunger abroad and a transformed scientific consensus had seriously weakened nutrition-based arguments for broader political and economic reforms. Not only had the 1945 abandonment of the Canadian Dietary Standard signalled a rejection of the more activist vision of social nutrition that had been implicit in the earlier standards; the uncertainty it engendered also had the side effect of undermining efforts to develop more modest and targeted nutrition-based welfare programs. This became particularly apparent when nutrition professionals within the CCN and the federal Nutrition Division tried to build institutional support for a national school lunch program modelled on its American and British counterparts.

Some within the CCN were uncomfortable with the wartime political uses of nutrition by social critics on the left. But many also saw the public desire for new universal social programs as an excellent opportunity to develop more targeted, nutrition-focused efforts. School lunches emerged as a top priority for many of Canada's leading nutrition experts in part because – unlike family allowances and other universal, income-based programs – it was a program that would provide them with greater control over planning and long-term operations. Like family allowances, school lunches spoke to the increasingly prominent political discourse around children's rights that had been popularized in discussions about postwar reconstruction, both in Canada and abroad. More importantly, however, the program reflected a compromise between those who viewed malnutrition as primarily resulting from inadequate income and those who viewed it as more of a public education problem. A national school lunch program had become unpopular among many on the political left in Canada because of its strong association with Charlotte Whitton's more conservative proposal for national "social utilities." Such a program was nonetheless attractive to a broad range of nutrition experts because it promised to supplement inadequate incomes while, at the same time, potentially training an entire generation in the principles of nutrition-based meal planning.

Canadian nutrition experts also hoped to build on the success of similar efforts in Britain and the United States. Britain, in particular, had become a model for many in the CCN, in that it had introduced a wide range of nutrition-based social services during the war. These included a "National Milk Scheme" offering subsidized milk to expectant and nursing mothers and children; a "Milk-in-Schools" program offering free and low-cost milk to children; a "National Vitamin Scheme," which offered fruit juices and cod liver oil to children; and a number of nutritionally determined rationing policies.[82] The most important innovation, however, was the creation of a national school lunch program in 1944, which by 1946 saw 43 percent of British students receive free midday meals. The government subsidy ranged from 70 to 95 percent of the cost of food, and the estimated annual cost of the program following its national implementation was pegged at over $260 million.[83] And although the June 1946 US National School Lunch Act was, perhaps, less comprehensive than the British model, it nonetheless saw more than $55 million per year being spent on a national program intended to improve children's health and to encourage consumption of domestic agricultural goods.[84]

The CCN began working on its own proposal for a Canadian program in 1943 following the formation of a Committee on School Lunches and a survey of existing school lunch policies and programs conducted with the assistance of the Canada and Newfoundland Education Association (CNEA). It quickly discovered that school lunch programs were by no means new in Canada. Between 1903 and 1939, the Ontario Department of Education provided grants to rural schools to support school lunch programs, and by 1930, hot lunches were being provided in 1,800 rural schools through the program.[85] Ontario had cancelled these grants prior to the war, but other provinces, including Manitoba, Saskatchewan, and BC, were providing grants to schools to cover the costs of the equipment for school lunch programs, albeit with the actual administration of programs and the purchases of food largely done by volunteers. While local school boards in larger centres like Montreal, Vancouver, and Toronto offered subsidized school lunch programs during the war, a range of surveys conducted during the 1940s found that the practice was unevenly spread throughout the country. Provincial and municipal governments generally lacked the resources to operate such programs, and as a result, the vast majority of Canadian schools had no school feeding programs at all. Most Canadian teachers also had little training in food and nutrition. In general, moreover, schools simply lacked basic facilities such as electricity, kitchen appliances, and running water required to operate a school feeding program.[86]

The School Lunch Committees of the CCN and the CNEA completed their joint proposal for a national school lunch program in July 1944. Building largely on the federal model of school lunches already proposed in the United States, the program was promoted as "one of the most valuable of all contributions to the health and fitness of Canadians, and toward school health education."[87] Funding was to be based on a federal subsidy to schools that were able to meet certain nutritional and sanitary standards, with costs being borne equally by all three levels of government. The primary goal was to stimulate the creation of programs that would be operated locally and administered by provincial education ministries. The proposal also suggested three types of lunch programs that schools could offer depending on their capacities: complete meals, incomplete meals, and nutritional supplements such as milk, hot cocoa, or cod liver oil. Based on the estimated $55 million cost of the very similar US program, the proposed cost to the federal government was pegged at somewhere near $5.5 million per year – far less than the Family Allowances program, whose costs in the first year alone were over $250 million, and only one-tenth the cost of the WPTB's wartime subsidies on milk.[88] The report was well received and gained a number of vocal supporters, ranging from provincial governments to organizations such as the Red Cross and the National Committee for School Health Research.[89]

Perhaps the most fervent and dedicated supporter of the national school lunch plan was L.B. Pett. In presenting the proposal to the Deputy Minister of Pensions and National Health, Pett repeatedly made the case that "no single step could be more valuable for the health of Canadians of the future." In correspondence with his superiors and with potential supporters of the plan, he stressed the importance of the school lunch program as a preventative public health measure, as an educational program aimed at overcoming faulty dietary practices in the home, and finally as a form of economic stimulus that would "assist in stabilizing the utilization of farm products."[90] In a letter to a supporter of the program, he acknowledged that as a civil servant, he was "not supposed to advocate actively specific action by the public in order to influence the government," but he nonetheless drafted petitions supporting the program for the National Council of Women and other interested groups.[91]

Despite these efforts, the plans for a national school lunch program were not well received by federal politicians. By 1945, Mackenzie King's Liberals were already backing away from many of the ambitious promises of the Marsh Report in light of the significant costs associated with the new Family Allowances program and the generous benefits being provided to returning soldiers and their families as part of the postwar Veterans Charter. In his official response to the proposal in February 1945, National Health and Welfare Minister Brooke Claxton stated that he was "all for school lunches" but insisted that they needed to be "considered in relation to the whole problem of dominion provincial relations." In particular, he argued that it was "hardly conceivable that until we have worked out health insurance and contributory old age pensions, which have a definite place on the programme, that we could secure consideration for a conditional grant in aid for school lunches."[92] Claxton and other federal officials, moreover, felt that they had gone far enough to address the problem of malnutrition. At one point, Claxton suggested that in light of the generous nature of Family Allowance payments, "there should be no possible excuse for all Canadians not having the right food. If they do not have it, it will be due to ignorance alone."[93]

In many ways, Claxton's argument reflected the heavy emphasis that supporters of family allowances had placed on its potential nutritional benefits. And to at least some extent, when the first Family Allowance cheques were sent out to Canadians in July 1945, they marked what seemed to be a major victory for proponents of a nutritionally based national social minimum. Stripped of the stigma of charity and means testing, these monthly payments of $5 to $8 per child per month initially represented a significant increase in the spending power of low-income families, and could mean up to $228 more per year for a family of five.[94] While these rates were less than those proposed by the Marsh Report and were insufficient to move the annual income of most Canadians up to Marsh's "Desirable Living Minimum" of $1,577.40, they nonetheless meant a significant increase in income for the approximately 40 percent of Canadian families living on less than $1,000 per year.[95] Although the monthly payments did not quite meet the minimum food costs set out in the Tisdall–Willard–Bell report or in the updated 1944 revision of the TWC's *Cost of Living*, they nonetheless made up for between 70 and 90 percent of the cost of an adequate diet as described by both reports, a development that appeared to many to constitute a significant move towards a nutritional minimum.[96]

As many have argued, however, family allowances did not mark a significant departure from the past but were, rather, meant to serve a much more conservative economic purpose than the program's loudest supporters had envisioned. King had never been a strong supporter of the kind of comprehensive welfare state envisioned by Marsh, and he was less concerned with underwriting a minimum standard of living than he was with outflanking his political opponents on the left, keeping the labour peace, and providing a Keynesian stimulus program as a buttress against the threat of a postwar depression.[97] The fact that the Family Allowances program was not indexed to inflation, for instance, is compelling evidence that it was never intended to be the foundation for a national social minimum. After all, Marsh and others had found the work of nutrition experts useful because it had allowed a social minimum to be calculated with some degree of scientific precision, independent of larger inflationary changes. The rates set out in the 1944 Family Allowances Act, however, were fixed and were not set to keep pace with food, clothing, and shelter cost increases. And the rapid inflation of basic food prices that characterized the late 1940s and early 1950s meant that, in many areas, payments were no longer sufficient to purchase even the quantities of milk outlined in Canada's Food Rules, let alone the minimum cost of a child's basic nutritional requirements.[98]

By the early postwar period, it had become increasingly clear that the Liberal government had little intention of subsidizing a permanent, nutritionally derived national social minimum for Canadian children. But it was also clear that the failure of the CCN and other groups to promote more direct, nutrition-focused programs like School Lunches could not be blamed solely on federal intransigence. Although family allowances provided an immediate excuse for rejecting the CCN's proposed national school lunch program, nutrition professionals themselves began to find it increasingly difficult to make a compelling case for new nutrition-focused social programs in the aftermath of the revelations that their earlier warnings of the nature and extent of malnutrition in Canada had likely been exaggerated.

When Claxton officially rejected the CCN's original school lunch proposal, for instance, he did leave open the possibility that such a program might be launched in the future. Perhaps in order to test the CCN's wartime hyperbole, Claxton suggested that further studies be conducted throughout the country comparing the health outcomes in schools with subsidized school lunch programs to those in control schools that lacked them. "If the results [of these experiments] are as striking as the proponents of this would expect them to be," he argued, "then that will be the best way of securing the support of public opinion so as to have this measure adopted more widely."[99] Many nutrition experts took Claxton's suggestion to heart, and starting in 1945, they began a series of pilot projects intended to prove the value of school lunch programs in achieving a wide range of health, educational, and other improvements. These projects were carried out by local nutrition councils in Montreal, Windsor, Kingston, and Orillia, in conjunction with the federal Nutrition Division. Plans were also put in motion to start a large-scale, controlled experiment on the effectiveness of free school lunches in Toronto.

In many ways, the Toronto study highlighted the newly apparent limitations of nutrition as a lever for social and political change. This study, which began in 1947, examined two hundred children receiving free school lunches in Toronto's Moss Park neighbourhood, comparing them with a second "control" group of two hundred students. This project, organized primarily by Tisdall and funded through a large grant from the Canadian Red Cross, was one of the most detailed of its kind ever conducted and involved IQ tests, dental and physical fitness exams, a range of physical and biomedical exams, studies of absenteeism, and home visits to determine family dietary practices and to gain parents' voluntary cooperation with the research team. Preliminary studies showed that the children being examined did not have unusually high rates of malnutrition. Researchers nonetheless believed that their focus on a decidedly working-class neighbourhood would lend itself to a useful case study on the long-term health effects of school lunches in an urban setting, more generally. Yet despite considerable international attention devoted to the study, the Red Cross chose to discontinue it after only two years. In part, this was due to the unexpected death of Tisdall in 1949. As Chairman of the Red Cross Nutrition Services Division and a nationally recognized figure in light of his widely hailed work on Red Cross prisoner-of-war parcels and his key role in the invention of the infant food Pablum, Tisdall had spear-headed the project, intending to use it to promote an expansion of Red Cross involvement in more nutrition-based projects. These included an ambitious plan for a national prenatal nutrition program aimed at low-income families.[100] While Tisdall's death meant the loss of one of the leading advocates of school lunches and of nutrition-based economic interventions more generally, the Red Cross also justified the abandon-ment of the study in large part because it "had revealed, so far, no startling improvements in nutrition between the test and control children."[101] While the preliminary findings of this study and of others like it suggested some improvements, none were of the dramatic nature promised so often by the CCN's nutrition experts. Supporters of the study maintained that two years was simply not enough time to track many of the long-term benefits of free school lunches for children. By 1949, however, the cost of the study had ballooned to $124,000 – nearly double the initial $65,000 estimate, making it one of the most expensive nutrition studies of the early postwar period. Not only had the promised effects of an improved diet beyond the simple prevention of deficiency diseases become increas-ingly difficult to pin down in an objective manner, but the cost of attempt-ing to do so had also become a serious barrier to nutrition-based social programs such as free school lunches.[102]

The failure of the Red Cross school lunch study suggests that the trans-formation of the wartime consensus regarding the measurement of mal-nutrition had a lasting effect on the scientific and social uses of malnutrition research. It had been relatively easy in the late 1930s and early 1940s to produce population-level studies showing dramatic levels of malnutrition using optimal dietary standards. But by the end of the war, it proved to be much more difficult to show the physical, medical, intellectual, and psychological benefits of the kinds of dietary interventions that had been proposed by nutrition experts over the previous decade. The new, more complicated Canadian Dietary Standard not only made confident estimates of national malnutrition rates nearly impossible, but also made it increasingly difficult to diagnose even individual instances of more subtle, subclinical forms of malnutrition. Given their confessed uncertainty regarding the use of dietary standards in the early postwar period, nutrition experts began to argue that malnutrition could only be confirmed in an individual based on a combination of physical exams, dietary records, and laboratory tests.[103] But as the Red Cross study had shown, the need for multiple confirmations of malnutrition had made the cost of such studies increasingly prohibitive. Researchers now struggled to prove the efficacy of diet-based social and public health interventions and shifted their focus to smaller groups already showing clinical or other signs of malnutrition. As a consequence of all this, findings of genuine malnutrition in Canada were increasingly treated less as causes for social and economic intervention than as a means of filling the considerable gaps in their knowledge about the relationship between the intake of specific nutrients and their physical consequences.

The newfound limits of postwar nutritional research in Canada were nowhere more apparent than in its increasing use among First Nations, Metis, and Inuit peoples. Aboriginal peoples not only were denied many of the basic rights of Canadian citizenship – including voting rights – but also were among Canada's most economically disadvantaged populations. As a result, Aboriginal peoples became a major focus of postwar nutritional research. This came about, in large part, after many of the military personnel, civilians, and scientists who entered the North in greater numbers during the war returned with alarming accounts of hunger and even outright starvation among Aboriginal peoples.[104] The response, however, was often not to provide immediate economic and nutritional relief to malnourished First Nations but, instead, to use their hunger as an opportunity for further research.

This was clearly the case even during the war when, in 1942, researchers including Tisdall and Indian Affairs Branch Superintendent of Medical Services Dr. Percy Moore discovered widespread malnutrition in a number of Cree First Nations in northern Manitoba. The conditions were, to say the least, shocking. After visiting the Norway House and Cross Lake First Nations, for instance, the research team reported that "while most of the people were going about trying to make a living, they were really sick enough to be in bed under treatment and that if they were white people, they would be in bed and demanding care and medical attention." And when they visited the homes of some of the elderly residents of Norway House at the request of the Chief and Council, researchers found that "conditions were deplorable where the old people were almost starved and were plainly not getting enough food to enable them to much more than keep alive."[105] Yet instead of calling for immediate emergency food relief, the researchers first attempted to take advantage of the research opportunity with which they had been presented. As Moore would tell a House of Commons Special Committee in May 1944: "As a result of the survey one of the first steps considered necessary in any program to improve the health of the Indian through better nutrition was to demonstrate whether provision of some of the food substances or food factors found to be lacking in their diet would result in an improvement in their health."[106] Moore and the rest of the research team therefore almost immediately set about organizing a scientific experiment on the effectiveness of vitamin supplements, to be conducted primarily by the resident physician for the Indian Affairs Branch at Rossville, Dr. Cameron Corrigan. Over the next few years, 125 of the individuals identified as malnourished were provided with riboflavin, thiamin, or ascorbic acid supplements – or a combination of these – while another 175 acted as a "control" group.[107]

A similar story unfolded in the mid-1940s after a series of dietary investigations of Indian residential schools discovered widespread malnutrition.[108] The initial surveys by dieticians from the Red Cross and the federal Nutrition Division found almost universally poor conditions at these schools, yet attempts to improve their food service through education for the staff proved totally ineffective. After years of follow-up surveys showed little improvement at the schools, Nutrition Division director L.B. Pett began planning an ambitious research project that would use Aboriginal students as experimental subjects. According to Pett, the purpose of his long-term study would be "to investigate certain questions already raised regarding Indians":

(1) Are conditions observed in Northern Manitoba found elsewhere in Canada? (2) What type of food service in residential schools will economically provide the best maintenance of health *and* carry over desirable food habits to the reserve? (3) Will foods fortified with vitamins and minerals provide demonstrable results over the course of 5 years? (4) Can health educational methods be introduced effectively in these schools? etc.[109]

The result was, starting in 1948, a series of five-year experiments on the effects of different nutritional interventions into the diets of close to one thousand Aboriginal students at six residential schools across the country. Tests included a double-blind, randomized study to "compare the effect on gums and on haemoglobin, of ascorbic acid (vitamin C) supplements in the form of tablets" at the Shubenacadie School in Nova Scotia and an examination of the effectiveness of "Newfoundland Flour Mix" – a product that could not be legally sold outside of Newfoundland under Canada's laws against food adulteration because it contained added thiamin, ribo-flavin, niacin, and bone meal – at the St. Mary's School in Kenora, Ontario, where there was a high incidence of riboflavin deficiencies among the students.[110]

In the context of the scientific uncertainty of the 1940s, in other words, Aboriginal populations increasingly provided nutrition experts with a means of testing out their theories about the effectiveness of certain dietary interventions and the links between dietary standards and physical mani-festations of malnutrition. Or, put another way, scientists such as Pett increasingly came to view Aboriginal bodies as "experimental materials" and residential schools and Aboriginal communities as "laboratories" that could be used to pursue a number of different political and professional interests. And while these experiments had started even before the war ended, the sheer scale of Pett's residential school experiments indicates that by the early postwar period, nutrition research – for Aboriginal peoples, at least – was actually blocking reforms of the very land, natural resource, education, and welfare policies that had led to hunger and mal-nutrition in the first place.

Conclusion

By the late 1940s, it had become readily apparent that nutrition was a far less reliable ally than critics of Canada's liberal social and economic order had anticipated during the early years of the war. In the context of a per-ceived national wartime malnutrition crisis, the kinds of optimal dietary standards developed during the 1930s had been easily translated into powerful tools of social criticism. Not only did the confident use of the 1939 and 1942 Canadian Dietary Standards make it possible to calculate malnutrition rates across the entire population in a way that connected food intake with an increasingly broad range of possible medical outcomes, but it also proved to be a particularly effective means of defining a scien-tifically grounded national social minimum to be underwritten by the state. But as it turned out, this scientific consensus depended on an in-creasingly tenuous compromise regarding the social, political, and scientific uses of nutrition. The collapse of this compromise following the publication of the McHenry Report simply highlighted the limitations of nutritional knowledge during this period. Optimal health remained the ambitious cultural and physical goal of public health campaigns such as Canada's Food Rules well into the 1950s; however, the persistence of genuine hunger and malnutrition abroad in the early postwar period meant that warnings of the kind of "hidden hunger" that had guided wartime nutrition policy had become far less effective as policy drivers. Although Orr's social vision of optimal nutrition had been premised on enabling all individuals to meet their potential for growth, strength, intelligence, and health through large-scale nutritional planning, the Red Cross school lunch study showed quite clearly that the long-term benefits of improved nutrition were extremely difficult and expensive to measure. As a result, even verifiable cases of malnutrition – as were discovered among Canada's Aboriginal peoples during the 1940s – came to be viewed more as opportunities for testing nutritional theories in a controlled setting than as evidence of the need for larger structural political and economic changes.

Conclusion

Arriving on the heels of the Great Depression, the onset of the Second World War helped bring significant changes, not only in the way Canadians bought, prepared, and consumed their daily meals, but also in the way they conceived of the broader politics, culture, and science of food. Many experienced the war as a transition period between the hunger and want that had characterized the 1930s and the promise of a more secure and abundant postwar future. Despite being required to cut back on their consumption of sugar, butter, coffee, tea, and other foods to below Depression-era levels through rationing and other controls, many Canadians took advantage of the dramatic economic growth that characterized the war years as an opportunity to simply catch up. Millions used their improved household income to eat more and better food than they had at any time in recent memory. And as the war began to wind down, many looked to postwar reconstruction as an opportunity to protect and build on these wartime gains and to create a system of social and economic security that would provide a buffer against the return of the lean and hungry years of the 1930s. Food was an essential component of this vision of the postwar future: given Canadians' shared wartime sacrifices and experiences, any suggestion that they could or should make do with less food was no longer viewed as fair or acceptable. Food security, in other words, was increasingly viewed as the heart of any successful system of postwar social security.

This lesson was made particularly clear to L.B. Pett, the director of the Nutrition Division of the Department of National Health and Welfare, after he was subjected to national ridicule in the early weeks of 1948. Pett's troubles grew out of an article published on 14 January in the *Ottawa Citizen* examining the contents of a low-cost shopping list that the Nutrition Division had produced during the previous year. The list outlined a weekly menu for a typical family of five based on a food budget of $16.36 per week, or roughly 15.5 cents per person per meal. The "Pett Diet," as critics later dubbed it, was heavy on starches and root vegetables – including 16.5 pounds of potatoes and 11.5 loaves of bread – and included little in the way of "frills." It allowed for no spices or coffee while recommending quantities of meat, butter, sugar, and tea well below wartime ration allotments – 50 percent less in the case of meat.[1] Although austere even by wartime standards, this shopping list was not unusual. Nutrition experts working for governments and social service agencies had long been producing similar lists intended to show how low-income and unemployed families could secure a nutritionally adequate diet with limited resources. But social conditions were, by then, also changing rapidly. The price of food and other necessities rose sharply in 1947 after controls were removed from most consumer goods; a wave of strikes in nearly every major industry swept the nation as organized labour fought to maintain its wartime gains; and efforts to introduce new social security measures after the 1944 introduction of the Family Allowances program stalled, leaving many wondering about the sincerity of the government's wartime promises of a better postwar life. In this context, the Pett Diet became a lightning rod for Canadians' dissatisfaction with the return to postwar "normalcy."

The public response to the Pett Diet – and to the idea that an official government body would suggest that Canadians might need to return to the kinds of monotonous and unpalatable diets of the 1930s – was overwhelmingly negative. The *Citizen* reported that local housewives almost universally found it to be "impractical, improbable and unreal." Responses ranged from "That's all very well, but I'd still like to have my family speaking to me," to "Do you think I could give [my husband] cracked wheat, sugar and milk and toast for breakfast an' not end up in the divorce court?" After wondering how, exactly, a family was supposed to eat 11.5 loaves of bread using only 26 ounces of butter, Mrs. A. Villeneuve of Carlington, Ontario, remarked that at least the diet sheet "gave us a good laugh – nearly as good as a comic strip."[2] When the story broke nationally and was republished in newspapers everywhere from Edmonton to Saskatoon to Toronto, the response was similarly incredulous. Mocking editorial cartoons were printed in the Montreal papers *Le Monde Ouvrier* and *The Gazette,* and the Nutrition Division was "flooded with indignant telephone calls and denunciatory letters."³ When questioned by reporters, Pett defended the budget by suggesting that his own family had tried it out at home for a month. He agreed that his budget "made for something approaching austerity," but he "insisted it was no hardship." And in response to critics who pointed out that his budget even lacked such basic items as coffee, Pett was quoted as suggesting that "nobody 'had' to drink coffee."⁴

The controversy over the Pett Diet captures a number of the key transformations that the politics and culture of food and nutrition had undergone over the course of the war. The discovery of a national malnutrition crisis in the late 1930s and early 1940s brought nutrition experts like Pett new, previously unavailable professional opportunities and an increasingly prominent public role in everything from developing agricultural policies and planning military ration scales to taking part in national debates over social security and reconstruction. Nutrition surveys and the official dietary standards that underpinned their findings, moreover, became increasingly embraced by the political left as the basis for establishing a scientifically determined and state-funded national social minimum. By 1948, however, it had become clear that nutrition was not necessarily the force of progressive social change that many had anticipated. As social activists in Ontario had already learned in the aftermath of the McHenry Report and the broader controversy over unemployment relief, nutrition could be marshalled both to challenge and to defend the economic and political status quo. Pett had fought to create a national school lunch program throughout the war and early postwar years, but many of his critics were unaware of this backroom battle. They therefore viewed his weekly food budget as simply another reactionary defence of federal social and economic policies that sought to return Canada to a pre-war economic system – one that to their minds had been characterized by depression and unemployment and that had led, by 1948, to significant inflation in the cost of necessities such as food.

Fundamentally, the controversy over the Pett Diet was an extension of the broader protests during this period by the Housewives Consumer Association and other critics of the Liberals' decontrol policies. The war had seen the state enter Canadian kitchens in an unprecedented manner following the introduction of a wide-ranging program of economic controls on the price and distribution of food and nearly every other consumer good. Food rationing and price controls were the primary face of the wartime command economy for most Canadians and, contrary to expectations of policy makers, both of these programs proved to be extremely popular, particularly among women. In part, this was due to a perception that economic controls protected the interests of consumers against rising infla- tion and shortages by establishing a marketplace governed by a basic level of fairness and the principle of "equality of sacrifice" rather than by the whims of shopkeepers. It also empowered ordinary women to insist on their social and economic rights as consumers and citizens by providing them with a forum to participate in the governance of the moral economy of the marketplace through work for organizations such as the Consumer Branch of the Wartime Prices and Trade Board. In this way, the wartime command economy helped increase public support for greater postwar state intervention in the national economy and provided a means to enact a number of very different political visions of gender, citizenship, and consumption centred on the fair and equal distribution of food and other necessities. When the federal government began its process of "orderly decontrol" – which by January 1948 had seen the removal of price controls from nearly all foods and other consumer goods – thousands of women took part in the protests by the HCA and other organizations demanding more, not less, state intervention in the postwar marketplace.

It was no coincidence, then, that the Pett Diet controversy erupted only one day before the government announced the temporary reimpos- ition of price controls on butter and meat in response to what the *Gazette* described as the "vehement protests of consumers."[5] For critics of the Pett Diet like J. Paul of Saskatoon, the solution to the problem of poor nutrition and the rising cost of food was "not to lower our standard of living, but to bring foods down to a level within the reach of everyone in the lowest income brackets."[6] This sentiment was echoed by Pett's col- league – and the former Medical Officer of the Nutrition Division – F.W. Hanley. In an opinion piece in the *Ottawa Citizen*, Hanley argued that the real problem with the Pett Diet was that it was disconnected from the realities of Canadians' food preferences, in that it would only work "if no child were so presumptuous as to ask occasionally for tarts instead of turnips, or for a little honey or bananas." Furthermore, it was out of sync with the economic realities of most households. When it was created in 1941, wrote Hanley, the Nutrition Division had been part of a state project to improve Canadians' access to nutritionally important protective foods. But, he added,

> now, with the reduction of the very mainstay of proper nutrition, consumer purchasing power, all such plans become distinctly less than possibilities. It

would seem, in fact, that much energy must now be directed into the parlor game of "scientific minimum food budgets," and that the division's function has deteriorated to help screen from the public the real failure of the government to even maintain, let alone improve, the nutritional standards of Canadians.[7]

Hanley's editorial highlighted the continued political divisions among nutrition professionals, divisions that by the end of the war had facilitated the collapse of the scientific consensus around the optimal dietary standards that had been responsible for the discovery of Canada's wartime malnutrition crisis in the first place. Hanley's column also highlighted the extent to which nutrition and the goal of a scientifically determined social minimum had, by 1948, ceased to be viewed as effective tools of social and political change. This process, moreover, would only accelerate following the introduction, later that year, of a new Canadian Dietary Standard that simultaneously embodied the principles of optimal and minimal nutrition requirements.

As the criticisms from Hanley and others suggest, the Pett Diet controversy exemplified the political and cultural limits of nutrition programs in the early postwar period. When the Canadian Council on Nutrition publicized its findings of widespread malnutrition early in the war, many Canadians saw this as simply a confirmation of what they already knew – that during the Depression they were not getting enough to eat. But as it turned out, popular educational materials like Canada's Official Food Rules went much further. As Canadians were regularly reminded by Pett, E.W. McHenry, and other prominent nutrition professionals, malnutrition was not simply the consequence of not eating *enough* food but, for a large number of Canadians, of not eating the *right* foods. The Pett Diet was simply echoing the message that nutrition was a problem of education rather than income in that it suggested that families with very tight food budgets could meet their basic nutrition requirements through a monotonous, starchy, and flavourless diet. The overwhelmingly negative response to the Pett Diet made it clear that Canadians tended to feel otherwise. The *Citizen* summed up the response of local housewives:

Most Ottawa families, austerity or no austerity want to eat more than $16.36 a week allows. The children want snacks after school and adults like to eat something before retiring at night. Under the health department scheme, the ladies agree, families would be quarrelling and bickering within one week.[8]

In other words, it was not enough to be adequately nourished. Canadians felt that they had made considerable sacrifices during the war, both at home and overseas, and now they were demanding a better standard of living than they had been accustomed to before the war. And as their wartime consumption patterns suggest, most of them wanted to see an improvement in both the quantity and quality of foods available to them. Canadians' postwar culinary vision looked much less like the austere Pett Diet and much more like what they saw on the glossy pages of popular magazines like *Chatelaine* and *Canadian Home Journal* and in bestsellers like *Kate Aitken's Canadian Cookbook*. This was apparent even in wartime community cookbooks, many of which presented War Cake and Victory Icing as only temporary replacements for their genuine counterparts, not as permanent changes in Canadian eating habits. For many Canadians, it was the promise of a better world, an improved standard of living, and protections against the return of Depression-era hunger and poverty that gave meaning to their wartime sacrifices. Critics of the Pett Diet made it clear they had little patience for any suggestion that they give up hard-fought wartime gains in their diets or in their incomes.

In many ways, the place of food in a larger popular vision of a new postwar Canada defined by plenty and abundance – framed largely in contrast to the hunger and want of the Depression – fit within a changing vision of Canada's place in the world. Throughout the war, Canadians were well aware of the essential role that Canadian food, soldiers, and munitions played in the battles being waged overseas. They therefore rallied around the idea that, as a land of plenty, Canada had a duty to provide relief and support for its overseas allies. Canadians who could not enlist to fight overseas or who were not working on farms or in war plants often applied considerable time, energy, and resources to doing everything from planting victory gardens to salvaging fats and bones, volunteering in a local active service canteen, or packing Red Cross POW parcels. Food was often central to these efforts because it provided an important source of comfort and nourishment for Canada's soldiers and allies as well as a powerful symbol of the full-scale patriotic mobilization of the home front. And as images of actual starvation in Allied countries like the Netherlands, India, and China were disseminated during the final years of the war, food became an even more potent symbol of Canada's new international role. As a June 1946 advertisement in the *Globe and Mail* warned readers, "Hunger Makes Hitlers."[9] The message that Canada and the newly formed United Nations had a duty to help build a new international order free from the chaos and hunger of the 1930s was often repeated during the war and early postwar years through a range of government propaganda campaigns, the most notable of which were the National Film Board documentaries *A Friend for Supper* (1944), *Food: Secret of the Peace* (1945), and *Suffer Little Children* (1946). As one of the promotional sheets for *Suffer Little Children* reminded filmgoers, "a hungry world can never be a peaceful world. How can the sick and hungry children we saw in those films grow into good citizens for tomorrow's world without proper care today?"[10] In other words, given its role as one of the world's leading food exporters – with its fields and cities untouched by the destruction that had been inflicted on Europe and Asia – Canada needed to lead the way in preventing starvation and hunger overseas.

Food relief became an important focus of the Canadian government's policy agenda during the early postwar years as officials sought to expand markets for surplus Canadian agricultural goods. But the message that ordinary Canadians also needed to contribute to the prevention of hunger and starvation overseas also resonated for the thousands who, building on their wartime experiences, took part in a variety of voluntary campaigns aimed at providing food relief to liberated countries. Efforts ranged from local canned-food drives and conservation campaigns to national fundraising efforts by the Red Cross and new international relief organizations such as UNRRA (1943), CARE Canada (1945), UNICEF (1946), and World Vision (1954). As was the case with similar programs during the war, however, these postwar voluntary and relief activities could not be separated from broader social and political changes that were occurring on the domestic front. As Liberal Justice Minister and future Prime Minister Louis St-Laurent reminded Canadians in a May 1946 radio speech calling for continued support for food rationing and conservation, overseas food relief was not simply a humanitarian issue. It was also a political one, because starving people "have reached the limit of endurance, and could, tomorrow, driven by desperation, fall prey to the revolutionary tide."[11] In other words, just as wartime voluntary campaigns built on larger gendered visions of nation, citizenship, and empire to rally Canadians behind a range of patriotic causes, the postwar context of a growing Cold War divide between East and West, communism and capitalism, gave the struggle to provide relief to war-torn Europe and Asia a decidedly political angle. These campaigns not only frequently built on a similar combination of the maternalism, nationalism, and internationalism that had driven their wartime counterparts but also often tended to be similarly directed at countries and causes that reflected Canada's broader foreign policy interests. Even by the late 1940s, these interests were increasingly being articulated through the Cold War rhetoric of combatting the growth of Soviet influence and supporting the spread of liberal economic and political institutions abroad.[12]

Canadians might have recognized that they were more fortunate than the citizens of the liberated countries of Europe and Asia. Besides participating in overseas relief campaigns, they were generally willing to tolerate the continued rationing of meat, butter, and sugar in order to assist their overseas allies for nearly three years beyond the end of the conflict. That said, the contrast between Canada's abundance and overseas hunger was clearly not enough to assure Canadians that their own country was on the right course. As the controversy over the Pett Diet and the HCA's nationwide consumer protests made clear, many continued to believe that their wartime gains were still fragile and could easily be lost as a result of the kind of runaway inflation and mass unemployment that had followed the previous war. With food making up more than one-third of the typical Canadian household budget, it was often on the kitchen table that the success or failure of reconstruction could most easily be judged, and food consumption remained central to Canadians' visions of postwar social and economic security and to their expectations regarding their postwar future. Postwar debates over the Pett Diet and decontrol, more generally, reflected continued uncertainty about the best road to postwar affluence and plenty.

The war had changed Canadians' expectations regarding their basic standard of living. At the same time, it had created a broad consensus that the state had a key role to play in ensuring that these expectations would be met through more direct intervention in the economy. Whether it was through continued state controls on the price and distribution of food and other necessities; the establishment of an employment-based national social minimum as outlined in the Marsh Report; or the Liberal vision of a return to a pre-war market economy modified by a combination of targeted Keynesian economic interventions such as family allowances, a generous Veterans Charter, and greater employment protections for employed male breadwinners, Canadians of every political stripe were united by a common vision of a more affluent future defined in opposition to Depression-era hunger and want. The crucible of war, in other words, had not only fostered the articulation of new visions of the place of food, nutrition, and consumption in Canadian politics and culture but also, temporarily at least, acted to destabilize pre-war conceptions of gender, citizenship, and nation. Of course, in the end, it would be the interests of the returned soldier and the male breadwinner – not the empowered female citizen-consumer – that defined the road to postwar plenty. But the failure of these alternative visions of postwar reconstruction does not make them any less important. It is sometimes easy for historians to interpret these postwar calls for the return of direct state intervention in the marketplace as simply a blip in a larger path towards the unimpeded mass consumerism associated with the postwar economic boom. Nonetheless, it is clear that the Second World War had not only transformed Canadians eating habits after a decade of austerity but also created a space for imagining and attempting to enact a different politics and culture of food and nutrition.

Notes

Introduction

1 Library and Archives Canada (LAC), National Council of Women Fonds, MG 28, I25, Vol. 80, File 13, S.P. Day, Report of the Community Nutrition Council of Kingston, 1942.

2 Anne Fromer, "Is Food the Answer to Increased Production?" *Saturday Night,* 12 December 1942, 42-43.

3 The title of C.P. Stacey's classic study, *Arms, Men and Governments,* perhaps best sums up the focus of much of the historical literature on Canada's Second World War, although there has been a growing interest in the past three decades on women, industrial workers, and immigrants. See Stacey, *Arms, Men and Governments: The War Policies of Canada, 1939-1945* (Ottawa: Queen's Printer, 1970); and G.E. Britnell and V.C. Fowke, *Canadian Agriculture in War and Peace, 1935-1950* (Palo Alto, CA: Stanford University Press, 1962).

4 LAC, Wartime Information Board (WIB), RG 36-31, Vol. 27, WIB Information Brief 54, "Men, Food, Munitions: How Has Canada Helped Most?" 4 March 1945.

→ 5 Lizzie Collingham, *The Taste of War: World War Two and the Battle for Food* (Toronto: Allen Lane, 2011), 1-4.

6 W.L. Mackenzie King, *Canada and the War: Three Years of War* (Ottawa: King's Printer, 1942).

7 In 1941, 94 percent of British wheat flour imports originated in Canada, along with 76 percent of bacon, 63 percent of pork, 20 percent of cheese, 16 percent of egg, and 99 percent of apple imports. See LAC, Department of Agriculture, RG 17, Vol. 3426, File 1500-80, "Proportion of Canadian Food in the British Diet"; LAC, RG 17, Vol. 3426, File 1500-79, "History of the War Effort of the Federal Department of Agriculture"; and Britnell and Fowke, *Canadian Agriculture,* 108.

8 Christopher Robb Waddell, "The Wartime Prices and Trade Board: Price Control in Canada in World War II" (PhD diss., York University, 1981), 129-31; Britnell and Fowke, *Canadian Agriculture,* 126-29, 210; LAC, RG 17, Vol. 3426, File 1500-79, History of the War Effort of the Federal Department of Agriculture.

9   See, for instance, Andrew Stewart, "Will Food Win the War?" *Behind the Headlines* 2, 9
    (1942): 1-24; Hiram McCann, "Food Will Win the War" *Saturday Night*, 11 July 1942, 12;
    and R.E.K. Pemberton, "Make Food Canada's Chief Offensive Weapon" *Saturday Night*,
    6 March 1943, 6.

10 On the political economy of hunger, for instance, see Collingham, *Taste of War*; Nick
    Cullather, *The Hungry World: America's Cold War Battle against Poverty in Asia* (Cambridge:
    Harvard University Press, 2010); Evan Fraser and Andrew Rimas, *Empires of Food: Feast,
    Famine, and the Rise and Fall of Civilizations* (New York: Simon and Schuster, 2010); James
    Vernon, *Hunger: A Modern History* (Cambridge: Harvard University Press, 2007); Mike
    Davis, *Late Victorian Holocausts: El Nino Famines and the Making of the Third World*
    (London: Verso Books, 2002); Belinda Davis, *Home Fires Burning: Food, Politics, and
    Everyday Life in World War I Berlin* (Chapel Hill: University of North Carolina Press, 2000).

11 The social, cultural, and spiritual meanings of food consumption have long been well
    established by anthropologists. See, for example, Carole Counihan, *The Anthropology of
    Food and Body: Gender, Meaning, and Power* (New York: Routledge, 1999); Mary Douglas,
    "Standard Social Uses of Food: Introduction," in *Food in the Social Order: Studies of Food
    and Festivities in Three American Communities*, ed. Mary Douglas (New York: Russell Sage
    Foundation, 1984), 1-39; Mary Douglas and Jonathan Gross, "Food and Culture: Measuring
    the Intricacy of Rules Systems," *Social Science Information* 20, 1 (1981): 1-35; Roland Barthes,
    "Toward a Psychosociology of Contemporary Food Consumption," in *Food and Culture:
    A Reader*, eds. Carole Counihan and Penny Van Esterik (New York: Routledge, 1997),
    20-27; Marshall Sahlins, *Culture and Practical Reason* (Chicago: University of Chicago
    Press, 1976); and Pierre Bourdieu, *Distinction: A Social Critique of the Judgment of Taste*,
    trans. Richard Nice (Cambridge: Harvard University Press, 1984).

12 On the social, political, and cultural changes on Canada's home front, see, for instance,
    Jennifer Stephen, *Pick One Intelligent Girl: Employability, Domesticity, and the Gendering
    of Canada's Welfare State, 1939-1947* (Toronto: University of Toronto Press, 2007); Serge
    Durflinger, *Fighting from Home: The Second World War in Verdun, Quebec* (Vancouver:
    UBC Press, 2006); Magda Fahrni, *Household Politics: Montreal Families and Postwar
    Reconstruction* (Toronto: University of Toronto Press, 2005); Jeffrey Keshen, *Saints, Sinners,
    and Soldiers: Canada's Second World War* (Vancouver: UBC Press, 2004); Peter S. McInnis,
    Harnessing Labour Confrontation: Shaping the Postwar Settlement in Canada, 1943-1950
    (Toronto: University of Toronto Press, 2002); Michael D. Stevenson, *Canada's Greatest
    Wartime Muddle: National Selective Service and the Mobilization of Human Resources during
    World War II* (Montreal and Kingston: McGill-Queen's University Press, 2001); Ruth Roach
    Pierson, *"They're Still Women after All": The Second World War and Canadian Womanhood*
    (Toronto: McClelland and Stewart, 1986); and J.L. Granatstein, *Canada's War: The Politics
    of the Mackenzie King Government, 1939-1945* (Toronto: Oxford University Press, 1975).

13 On inflation during the First World War, see Craig Heron and Myer Siemiatycki, "The
    Great War, the State, and Working-Class Canada," in *The Workers' Revolt in Canada, 1917-
    1925*, ed. Craig Heron (Toronto: University of Toronto Press, 1998), 11-42; and David
    Monod, *Store Wars: Shopkeepers and the Culture of Mass Marketing, 1890-1939* (Toronto:
    University of Toronto Press, 1996), 130-31.

14 *Report of the Wartime Prices and Trade Board, September 3, 1939, to March 31, 1943* (Ottawa:
    King's Printer, 1943), 3.

15 The most influential and frequently cited works on this topic are Keshen's *Saints, Sinners
    and Soldiers*; and "One for All or All for One: Government Controls, Black Marketing,

and the Limits of Patriotism, 1939-1947," *Journal of Canadian Studies* 29, 4 (1994): 111-43.

16 Mustafa Koc, Jennifer Sumner, and Tony Winson, eds., *Critical Perspectives in Food Studies* (Toronto: Oxford University Press, 2012), 385.

17 See, for instance, E. Melanie DuPuis, *Nature's Perfect Food: How Milk Became America's Drink* (New York: NYU Press, 2002); Sidney W. Mintz, *Sweetness and Power: The Place of Sugar in Modern History* (New York: Penguin, 1986); Mark Kurlansky, *Salt: A World History* (Toronto: Vintage Canada, 2002); Vernon, *Hunger*; Susanne Freidberg, *Fresh: A Perishable History* (Cambridge: Belknap Press, 2009); Jeffrey Pilcher, *Que Vivan Los Tamales! Food and the Making of Mexican Identity* (Albuquerque: University of New Mexico Press, 1998); and Laura Shapiro, *Perfection Salad: Women and Cooking at the Turn of the Century* (New York: Modern Library, 2001).

18 For excellent overviews of the recent work being done on food history around the globe, see Jeffrey Pilcher, ed., *The Oxford Handbook of Food History* (Toronto: Oxford University Press, 2012); and Peter Scholliers and Kyri W. Claflin, eds., *Writing Food History: A Global Perspective* (New York: Berg Publishers, 2012); as well as the special "Radical Foodways" issue of *Radical History Review* 110 (Spring 2011). For recent works on the history of food and war during the twentieth century, see, for instance, Collingham, *Taste of War*; Ina Zweiniger-Bargielowska, Rachel Duffett, and Alain Drouard, eds., *Food and War in Twentieth Century Europe* (Surrey: Ashgate Publishing, 2011); Frank Trentmann and Flemming Just, eds., *Food and Conflict in Europe in the Age of the Two World Wars* (New York: Palgrave, 2006); and one of the early inspirations for this project, Amy Bentley's *Eating for Victory: Food Rationing and the Politics of Domesticity* (Urbana and Chicago: University of Illinois Press, 1998).

19 On agricultural staples, for example, see Douglas McCalla, *Planting the Province: The Economic History of Upper Canada* (Toronto: University of Toronto Press, 1993); and Marjorie Griffin Cohen, *Women's Work, Markets, and Economic Development in Nineteenth-Century Ontario* (Toronto: University of Toronto Press, 1988). On industrialization and the family economy, see Bettina Bradbury, *Working Families: Age, Gender, and Daily Survival in Industrializing Montreal* (Toronto: Oxford University Press, 1993); and Meg Luxton, *More Than a Labour of Love: Three Generations of Women's Work in the Home* (Toronto: Women's Press, 1980). On food and Aboriginal peoples, see Mary-Ellen Kelm, *Colonizing Bodies: Aboriginal Health and Healing in British Columbia, 1900-50* (Vancouver: UBC Press, 1998); and Maureen Lux, *Medicine That Walks: Disease, Medicine, and Canadian Plains Native People, 1880-1940* (Toronto: University of Toronto Press, 2001).

20 See, for example, Yvon Desloges, *À Table en Nouvelle France* (Québec: Les Éditions du Septentrion, 2009); Elizabeth Driver, *Culinary Landmarks: A Bibliography of Canadian Cookbooks, 1825-1949* (Toronto: University of Toronto Press, 2008); Charles-Alexandre Théorêt, *Maudite poutine! Histoire approximative d'un fameux mets* (Montréal: Éditions Héliotrope, 2007); Dorothy Duncan, *Canadians at Table: A Culinary History of Canada* (Toronto: Dundurn Press, 2006); Fiona Lucas, *Hearth and Home: Women and the Art of Open Hearth Cooking* (Toronto: James Lorimer, 2006); Devonna Edwards, *Wartime Recipes from the Maritimes, 1939-1945* (Halifax: Nimbus Publishing, 2001); and Carol Ferguson and Margaret Fraser, *A Century of Canadian Home Cooking: 1900 through the 1990s* (Toronto: Prentice-Hall Canada, 1992).

21 Recent Canadian works include Franca Iacovetta, Valerie Korinek, and Marlene Epp, eds., *Edible Histories, Cultural Politics: Towards a Canadian Food History* (Toronto: University

of Toronto Press, 2011); and Nathalie Cooke, ed., *What's to Eat? Entrées in Canadian Food History* (Montreal and Kingston: McGill-Queen's University Press, 2009). For international works, see Pilcher, *Que Vivan Los Tamales;* John Burnett, *Plenty and Want: A Social History of Food in England from 1815 to the Present Day,* 3rd ed. (London: Routledge, 1989); Harvey Levenstein, *Revolution at the Table: The Transformation of the American Diet* (Berkeley: University of California Press, 1988); and Donna Gabaccia, *We Are What We Eat: Ethnic Foods and the Making of Americans* (Cambridge: Harvard University Press, 1998).

22 Steve Penfold, *The Donut: A Canadian History* (Toronto: University of Toronto Press, 2008); Diane Tye, *Baking as Biography: A Life Story in Recipes* (Montreal and Kingston: McGill-Queen's University Press, 2010). Other exceptions include Ester Reiter, *Making Fast Food: From the Frying Pan into the Fryer* (Montreal and Kingston: McGill-Queen's University Press, 1996); W.H. Heick, *A Propensity to Protect: Butter, Margarine, and the Rise of Urban Culture in Canada* (Waterloo: Wilfrid Laurier University Press, 1991); and Tasnim Nathoo and Aleck Samuel Ostry, *The One Best Way? Breastfeeding History, Politics, and Policy in Canada* (Waterloo: Wilfrid Laurier University Press, 2009).

23 In the Canadian context, see Caroline Durand, "Le laboratoire domestique de la machine humaine: La nutrition, la modernité et l'Etat québécois, 1860-1945"(PhD diss., McGill University, 2011); Nathoo and Ostry, *The One Best Way?*; Aleck Ostry, *Nutrition Policy in Canada, 1870-1939* (Vancouver: UBC Press, 2006); and Ruby Heap, "From the Science of Housekeeping to the Science of Nutrition: Pioneers in Canadian Nutrition and Dietetics at the University of Toronto's Faculty of Household Science, 1900-1950," in *Challenging Professions: Historical and Contemporary Perspectives on Women's Professional Work,* ed. Elizabeth Smyth et al. (Toronto: University of Toronto Press, 1999), 162-63. For recent works in critical nutrition studies, see, for instance, Jessica J. Mudry, *Measured Meals: Nutrition in America* (Albany: SUNY Press, 2009); Vernon, *Hunger*; Nick Callather, "The Foreign Policy of the Calorie," *American Historical Review* 112, 2 (2007): 1-60; John Coveney, *Food, Morals, and Meaning: The Pleasure and Anxiety of Eating* (London: Routledge, 2000); and Rima Apple, *Vitamania: Vitamins in American Culture* (New Brunswick: Rutgers University Press, 1996).

24 On the broader demographic trends, see Kris Inwood with John Cranfield, "The Great Transformation: A Long-Run Perspective on Physical Well-Being in Canada," *Economics and Human Biology* 5, 2 (July 2007): 204-28; and Peter W. Ward and Patricia C. Ward, "Infant Birth Weight and Nutrition in Industrializing Montreal," *American Historical Review* 89, 2 (April 1984): 324. On the wartime changes in Canadians' food consumption patterns, see Nutrition Division, *Canadian Food and Nutrition Statistics, 1935 to 1956* (Ottawa: Queen's Printer, 1959).

25 See, for instance, E.V. McCollum's *A History of Nutrition: The Sequence of Ideas in Nutrition Investigations* (Boston: Houghton Mifflin, 1957); Vernon, *Hunger*; Apple, *Vitamania*; Levenstein, *Revolution at the Table.*

26 For an excellent overview, see Charlotte Biltekoff, "Critical Nutrition Studies," in *The Oxford Handbook to Food History,* ed. Jeffrey Pilcher (New York: Oxford University Press, 2012), 172-90, as well as the works cited in note 23.

27 See James Struthers's work in "How Much Is Enough? Creating a Social Minimum in Ontario, 1930-44," *Canadian Historical Review* 71, 1 (1991): 39-83; and *The Limits of Affluence: Welfare in Ontario, 1920-1970* (Toronto: University of Toronto Press, 1994) as well as Gail Wills, *A Marriage of Convenience: Business and Social Work in Toronto, 1918-1957* (Toronto: University of Toronto Press, 1995).

28 An excellent account of the American context of these changes is J.L. Anderson, *Industrializing the Corn Belt: Agriculture, Technology, and Environment, 1945-1972* (DeKalb: Northern Illinois University Press, 2008). For the Canadian context, see Anthony Winson, *The Intimate Commodity: Food and the Development of the Agro-Industrial Complex in Canada* (Toronto: Garamond Press, 1992); Clinton L. Evans, *The War on Weeds: In the Prairie West* (Calgary: University of Calgary Press, 2002); John Varty, "Growing Bread: Technoscience, Environment, and Modern Wheat at the Dominion Grain Research Laboratory, Canada, 1912-1960" (PhD diss., Queen's University, 2005); and Thomas R. Murphy, "The Structural Transformation of New Brunswick Agriculture from 1951-1981" (MA thesis, University of New Brunswick, 1983).

29 See, for instance, Freidberg, *Fresh*; John Soluri, *Banana Cultures: Agriculture, Consumption, and Environmental Change in Honduras and the United States* (Austin: University of Texas Press, 2005); William Cronon, *Nature's Metropolis: Chicago and the Great West* (New York: W.W. Norton, 1992); and Levenstein, *Revolution at the Table.*

30 Levenstein, *Paradox of Plenty: A Social History of Eating in Modern America* (Berkeley: University of California Press, 1993), 101. On the corporate consolidation of the Canadian food industry in the interwar period, see Winson, *The Intimate Commodity*; Ian MacLachlan, *Kill and Chill: Restructuring Canada's Beef Commodity Chain* (Toronto: University of Toronto Press, 2001); Charles Davies, *Bread Men: How the Westons Built an International Food Empire* (Toronto: Key Porter Books, 1987); Richard Feltoe, *Redpath: The History of a Sugar House* (Toronto: Dundurn Press, 1991); and Michael Bliss, *A Canadian Millionaire: The Life and Business Times of Sir Joseph Flavelle, Bart., 1858-1939* (Toronto: Macmillan, 1978).

31 Richard Harris, *Creeping Conformity: How Canada Became Suburban, 1900-1960* (Toronto: University of Toronto Press, 2004); Monod, *Store Wars*; Sylvie Taschereau, "Behind the Store: Montréal Shop-Keeping Families between the Wars," in *Intermediate Spaces: Sites of Identity Formation in 19th and 20th Century Montreal*, ed. Bettina Bradbury and Tamara Myers (Vancouver: UBC Press, 2005), 235-58; and "L'arme favorite de l'épicier indépendant: Éléments d'une histoire sociale du crédit (Montréal, 1920-1940)," *Journal of the Canadian Historical Association/Revue de la Société Historique du Canada* 4, 1 (1993): 265-92; and Keith Walden, "Speaking Modern: Language, Culture, and Hegemony in Grocery Window Displays, 1887-1920," *Canadian Historical Review* 70, 3 (September 1989): 285-310.

32 See, for instance, Levenstein, *Paradox of Plenty*; Laura Shapiro, *Something from the Oven: Reinventing Dinner in 1950s America* (New York: Viking, 2004); and Warren Belasco, *Appetite for Change: How the Counterculture Took on the Food Industry* (New York: Pantheon Books, 1989).

33 For the best recent accounts of food during the Great Depression, see Lara Campbell, *Respectable Citizens: Gender, Family, and Unemployment in Ontario's Great Depression* (Toronto: University of Toronto Press, 2009) and Stacey Zembrzycki, "'We Didn't Have a Lot of Money, but We Had Food': Ukrainians and Their Depression-Era Food Memories," in *Edible Histories*, ed. Iacovetta, Korinek, and Epp, 131-39. On the Depression, more generally, see Katrina Srigley, *Breadwinning Daughters: Young Working Women in a Depression-Era City, 1929-1939* (Toronto: University of Toronto Press, 2010); Denyse Baillargeon, *Making Do: Women, Family, and Home in Montreal during the Great Depression*, trans. Yvonne Klein (Waterloo: Wilfrid Laurier University Press, 1999); Barry Broadfoot, *Ten Lost Years, 1929-1939: Memories of Canadians Who Survived the Depression* (Toronto: Doubleday, 1973); Struthers, *Limits of Affluence* and *No Fault of Their Own: Unemployment*

and the Canadian Welfare State, 1914-1941 (Toronto: University of Toronto Press, 1983); and L.M. Grayson and Michael Bliss, eds., *The Wretched of Canada: Letters to R.B. Bennett, 1930-1935* (Toronto: University of Toronto Press, 1971).

34 LAC, RG 17, Vol. 3434, File 1724, Anna M. Speers, "A Report on Nutrition and the Production and Distribution of Food," Ottawa, May 1945. For a longer-term perspective, see Joy Parr, *Domestic Goods: The Material, the Moral, and the Economic in the Postwar Years* (Toronto: University of Toronto Press, 1999).

35 See Graham Broad, "Shopping for Victory," *The Beaver,* April-May 2005, 40-45; and Parr, *Domestic Goods,* 27-31.

36 As Parr suggests, consumption during the 1940s looked a lot more like "self production" – "the process by which the household was sheltered and sustained" – than the simple using and discarding of commodities that is often implied by the terms consumption and consumerism. Parr, *Domestic Goods,* 6.

37 For an excellent analysis of consumption and consumerism, see Frank Trentmann, "Beyond Consumerism: New Historical Perspectives on Consumption," *Journal of Contemporary History* 39, 3 (2004): 373-401, and Frank Trentmann, ed., *The Oxford Handbook of the History of Consumption* (Oxford: Oxford University Press, 2012). On the history of consumption, consumerism, and consumer culture in Canada, see Donica Belisle, *Retail Nation: Department Stores and the Making of Modern Canada* (Vancouver: UBC Press, 2011) and "Toward a Canadian Consumer History," *Labour/Le Travail* 52 (2003): 181-206; Beatrice Craig, *Backwoods Consumers and Homespun Capitalists: The Rise of a Market Culture in Eastern Canada* (Toronto: University of Toronto Press, 2009); Bettina Liverant, "The Promise of a More Abundant Life: Consumer Society and the Rise of the Managerial State," *Journal of the Canadian Historical Association* 19, 1 (2009): 229-51; Penfold, *The Donut;* Michael Dawson, *Selling British Columbia: Tourism and Consumer Culture, 1890-1970* (Vancouver: UBC Press, 2005); and Cynthia Wright, "'Feminine Trifles of Vast Importance': Writing Gender into the History of Consumption," in *Gender Conflicts: New Essays in Women's History,* ed. Franca Iacovetta and Mariana Valverde (Toronto: University of Toronto Press, 1992), 229-60.

38 Lizabeth Cohen, *A Consumers' Republic: The Politics of Mass Consumption in Postwar America* (New York: Vintage, 2003); Parr, *Domestic Goods*; Fahrni, *Household Politics.* On shifting perceptions of consumer citizenship and the politics of food during the 1930s and 1940s, see also Joseph Tohill, "A Consumers' War: Price Control and Political Consumerism in the United States and Canada during World War II" (PhD diss., York University, 2012); Julie Guard, "A Mighty Power against the Cost of Living: Canadian Housewives Organize in the 1930s," *International Labor and Working-Class History* 77, 1 (Spring 2010): 27-47; "Canadian Citizens or Dangerous Foreign Women? Canada's Radical Consumer Movement, 1947-1950," in *Sisters or Strangers? Immigrant, Ethnic, and Racialized Women in Canadian History,* ed. Marlene Epp, Franca Iacovetta, and Frances Swyripa (Toronto: University of Toronto Press, 2004), 161-89; Meg Jacobs, "'How About Some Meat?': The Office of Price Administration, Consumption Politics, and State Building from the Bottom up, 1941-1946," *Journal of American History* 84, 3 (1997): 910-41; and Trentmann and Just, *Food and Conflict in Europe.*

39 Stephen, *Pick One Intelligent Girl;* Stevenson, *Canada's Greatest Wartime Muddle;* Daniel J. Robinson, *The Measure of Democracy: Polling, Market Research, and Public Life, 1930-1945* (Toronto: University of Toronto Press, 1999); Donald H. Avery, *The Science of War: Canadian Scientists and Allied Military Technology during the Second World War* (Toronto:

University of Toronto Press, 1998); Doug Owram, *The Government Generation: Canadian Intellectuals and the State* (Toronto: University of Toronto Press, 1986); Gary Evans, *John Grierson and the National Film Board: The Politics of Wartime Propaganda* (Toronto: University of Toronto Press, 1984); J.L. Granatstein, *The Ottawa Men: The Civil Service Mandarins, 1935-1957*, 2nd ed. (Toronto: University of Toronto Press, 1998).

40 Dominique Marshall, *The Social Origins of the Welfare State: Quebec Families, Compulsory Education, and Family Allowances, 1940-1955*, trans. Nicola Doone Danby (Waterloo: Wilfrid Laurier University Press, 2006); Shirley Tillotson, *Contributing Citizens: Modern Charitable Fundraising and the Making of the Welfare State* (Vancouver: UBC Press, 2008). See also, for instance, Campbell, *Respectable Citizens*; Fahrni, *Household Politics*; Stephen, *Pick One Intelligent Girl*; and Margaret Jane Hillyard Little, *'No Car, No Radio, No Liquor Permit': The Moral Regulation of Single Mothers in Ontario, 1920-1997* (Toronto: Oxford University Press, 1998).

41 On the changing politics of the period and the transformation of the welfare state, see Alvin Finkel, *Social Policy and Practice in Canada: A History* (Waterloo: Wilfrid Laurier University Press, 2006); Dennis Guest, *The Emergence of Social Security in Canada*, 3rd ed. (Vancouver: UBC Press, 2003); Nancy Christie, *Engendering the State: Family, Work, and Welfare in Canada* (Toronto: University of Toronto Press, 2000); Granatstein, *Canada's War*.

42 Sonya O. Rose, *Which People's War: National Identity and Citizenship in Britain, 1939-1945* (New York: Oxford University Press, 2003), 149.

43 Desmond Morton, *A Military History of Canada*, 5th ed. (Toronto: McClelland and Stewart, 2007), 185.

44 The best overview of these changes remains Pierson, *"They're Still Women After All."*

45 For an alternative interpretation of Pierson's question as to whether the war was emancipatory, see Keshen, "Revisiting Canada's Civilian Women during World War II," *Histoire sociale/Social History* 30, 60 (1997): 239-66. For more recent perspectives, see Stephen, *Pick One Intelligent Girl*; Helen Smith and Pamela Wakewich, "The Politics of 'Selective' Memory: Re-visioning Canadian Women's Wartime Work in the Public Memory," *Oral History* 34, 2 (Autumn 2006): 56-68; Helen Smith and Pamela Wakewich, "'Beauty and the Helldivers': Representing Women's Work and Identities in a Warplant Newspaper," *Labour/Le Travail* 44 (Fall 1999): 71-107; and Carolyn Gossage, *Greatcoats and Glamour Boots: Canadian Women at War, 1939-1945.* (Toronto: Dundurn Press, 2001).

46 For some excellent analyses of women's domestic labour in the kitchen in Canada, see, for example, Meg Luxton, Harriet Rosenberg, and Sedef Arat-Koe, eds., *Through the Kitchen Window: The Politics of Home and Family* (Toronto: Garamond Press, 1990); Luxton, *More Than a Labour of Love*; Cynthia Commacchio, *The Infinite Bonds of Family: Domesticity in Canada, 1850-1940* (Toronto: University of Toronto Press, 1999); and Veronica Strong-Boag, *The New Day Recalled: Lives of Girls and Women in English Canada, 1919-1939* (Toronto: Penguin Books, 1988).

47 On the social construction of wartime masculinity in Canada, see Michael Brendan Baker, "Who's on the Home Front? Canadian Masculinity in the NFB's Second World War Series 'Canada Carries On,'" in *Making It Like a Man: Canadian Masculinities in Practice*, ed. Christine Ramsay (Waterloo: Wilfrid Laurier University Press, 2011), 39-52; and Paul Jackson, *One of the Boys: Homosexuality in the Military during World War II* (Montreal and Kingston: McGill-Queen's University Press, 2004). On masculinities during the middle decades of the twentieth century more generally, see, for instance, Wayne Martino and Christopher J. Greig, *Canadian Men and Masculinities: Historical and Contemporary Perspectives* (Toronto:

Canadian Scholars' Press, 2012); Mary-Ellen Kelm, "Manly Contests: Rodeo Masculinities at the Calgary Stampede," *Canadian Historical Review* 90, 4 (2009): 711-51; Christopher Dummitt, *The Manly Modern: Masculinity in Postwar Canada* (Vancouver: UBC Press, 2007); Dummitt, "Finding a Place for Father: Selling the Barbecue in Postwar Canada," *Journal of the Canadian Historical Association* 9 (1998): 209-23; Craig Heron, "Boys Will Be Boys: Working-Class Masculinities in the Age of Mass Production," *International Labor and Working-Class History* 69, 1 (2006): 6-34; Robert Rutherdale, "Fatherhood, Masculinity, and the Good Life during Canada's Baby Boom, 1945-1965," *Journal of Family History* 24, 3 (1 July 1999): 351-73; and Joy Parr, *The Gender of Breadwinners: Women, Men, and Change in Two Industrial Towns, 1880-1950* (Toronto: University of Toronto Press, 1990).

48 See Keshen, *Saints, Sinners, and Soldiers*; Durflinger, *Fighting from Home*. See also Mary F. Williamson and Tom Sharp, eds., *Just a Larger Family: Letters of Marie Williamson from the Canadian Home Front, 1940-1944* (Waterloo: Wilfrid Laurier University Press, 2011); Stephen High, ed., *Occupied St. John's: A Social History of a City at War, 1939-1945* (Montreal and Kingston: McGill-Queen's University Press, 2010); Sylvia Crooks, *Homefront and Battlefront: Nelson B.C. in World War II* (Vancouver: Granville Island Publishing, 2005); Gunda Lambton, *Sun in Winter: A Toronto Wartime Journal, 1942 to 1945* (Montreal and Kingston: McGill-Queen's University Press, 2003); and Stephen Kimber, *Sailors, Slackers, and Blind Pigs: Halifax at War* (Toronto: Doubleday, 2002). On the history of the everyday experience of the First World War, see Robert Rutherdale, *Hometown Horizons: Local Responses to Canada's Great War* (Vancouver: UBC Press, 2005); and Desmond Morton, *Fight or Pay: Soldiers' Families in the Great War* (Vancouver: UBC Press, 2004).

49 Wilfred Eggleston, "Canada at the End of the War," *Queen's Quarterly* 12 (1945): 360.

50 At its 1945 peak, there were 2,124,189 Red Cross members; when combined with the nationwide membership of the Junior Red Cross, total membership actually exceeded three million members – more than one-quarter of Canada's total population. See Canadian Red Cross Society (CRCS), *Annual Report for 1945* (Toronto, 1946).

51 On the changing currents of public opinion gathering and research, see Robinson, *The Measure of Democracy*; Evans, *John Grierson*; William R. Young, "Academics and Social Scientists versus the Press: The Policies of the Bureau of Public Information and the Wartime Information Board, 1939-1945," *Historical Papers/Communications historiques* 13, 1 (1978): 217-40; and Young, "Mobilizing English Canada for War: The Bureau of Public Information, the Wartime Information Board, and a View of the Nation during the Second World War," in *The Second World War as a National Experience*, ed. Sidney Aster (Ottawa: Canadian Committee for the History of the Second World War, 1981).

Chapter 1: "Eat Right, Feel Right – Canada Needs You Strong"

1 LAC, Department of National Health and Welfare, RG 29, Vol. 110, File 180-26-22, Metropolitan Life Insurance Company, "Especially these days ... a man needs a good meal" [1942]. See also the ad in the *Canadian Home Journal* (September 1942), 21.

2 On the sequence of major discoveries in the science of nutrition, see E.V. McCollum, *A History of Nutrition: The Sequence of Ideas in Nutrition Investigations* (New York: Houghton Mifflin, 1957); and Kenneth J. Carpenter's four-part series, "A Short History of Nutrition," which starts in the March 2003 edition (133, 3) of *Journal of Nutrition* and culminates in the November 2003 edition (133, 11).

3 See, for instance, Jessica J. Mudry, *Measured Meals: Nutrition in America* (Albany: SUNY Press, 2009); James Vernon, *Hunger: A Modern History* (Cambridge: Harvard University Press, 2007); Nick Callather, "The Foreign Policy of the Calorie," *American Historical Review* 112, 2 (2007): 1-60; John Coveney, *Food, Morals, and Meaning: The Pleasure and Anxiety of Eating* (London: Routledge, 2000); Rima Apple, *Vitamania: Vitamins in American Culture* (New Brunswick: Rutgers University Press, 1996); Harvey Levenstein, *Revolution at the Table: The Transformation of the American Diet* (Berkeley: University of California Press, 1988); and Laura Shapiro, *Perfection Salad: Women and Cooking at the Turn of the Century* (New York: Modern Library, 2001).

4 For a timeline, see Kenneth J. Carpenter, "A Short History of Nutritional Science: Part 3 (1912-1944)," *Journal of Nutrition* 133, 10 (October 2003): 3028.

5 Levenstein's *Revolution at the Table* remains one of the best – and most readable – overviews of these developments.

6 See, for instance, Lara Campbell, *Respectable Citizens: Gender, Family, and Unemployment in Ontario's Great Depression* (Toronto: University of Toronto Press, 2009); Denyse Baillargeon, *Making Do: Women, Family, and Home in Montreal during the Great Depression*, trans. Yvonne Klein (Waterloo: Wilfrid Laurier University Press, 1999); Barry Broadfoot, *Ten Lost Years, 1929-1939: Memories of Canadians Who Survived the Depression* (Toronto: Doubleday, 1973); James Struthers, *The Limits of Affluence: Welfare in Ontario, 1920-1970* (Toronto: University of Toronto Press, 1994); Struthers, *No Fault of Their Own: Unemployment and the Canadian Welfare State, 1914-1941* (Toronto: University of Toronto Press, 1983); and L.M. Grayson and Michael Bliss, eds., *The Wretched of Canada: Letters to R.B. Bennett, 1930-1935* (Toronto: University of Toronto Press, 1971).

7 For a background to Canadian nutrition policy and practice in the prewar period, see Caroline Durand, "Le laboratoire domestique de la machine humaine: La nutrition, la modernité et l'Etat québécois, 1860-1945" (PhD diss., McGill University, 2011); Aleck Samuel Ostry, *Nutrition Policy in Canada, 1870-1939* (Vancouver: UBC Press, 2006); Ruby Heap, "From the Science of Housekeeping to the Science of Nutrition: Pioneers in Canadian Nutrition and Dietetics at the University of Toronto's Faculty of Household Science, 1900-1950," in *Challenging Professions: Historical and Contemporary Perspectives on Women's Professional Work*, ed. Elizabeth Smyth et al. (Toronto: University of Toronto Press, 1999), 141-70; Tara D. Corless, "'Lunch Boxes on the March': Women, Family-Feeding, and the Nova Scotia Nutrition Programme, 1935-1959" (MA thesis, Dalhousie, Saint Mary's, and Mount Saint Vincent Universities, 1998); and Alana J. Hermiston, "'If It's Good for You, It's Good for the Nation!' The Moral Regulation of Nutrition in Canada, 1930-1945" (PhD diss., Carleton University, 2005).

8 L.B. Pett, "Nutrition as a National Problem," *Canadian Welfare* 18, 1 (1 April 1942), 21-29; E.W. McHenry, "Nutrition in Toronto," *Canadian Public Health Journal* (hereafter *CPHJ*) 30, 1 (January 1939): 4-13; E. Gordon Young, "A Dietary Survey in Halifax," *CPHJ* 32, 5 (May 1941): 236-40; George Hunter and L. Bradley Pett, "A Dietary Survey in Edmonton," *CPHJ* 32, 5 (May 1941): 259-65; J. Ernest Sylvestre and HonoréNadeau, "Enquête sur l'alimentation habituelle des familles de petits-salariés dans la ville de Québec," *CPHJ* 32, 5 (May 1941): 241-50; Jean M. Patterson and E.W. McHenry, "A Dietary Investigation in Toronto Families Having Annual Incomes between $1,500-$2,400," *CPHJ* 32, 5 (May 1941): 251-58.

9 McHenry, "Nutrition in Toronto," 5.

10 Young, "A Dietary Survey in Halifax," 236-40.

11 Hunter and Pett, "A Dietary Survey in Edmonton"; Sylvestre and Nadeau, "Enquête sur l'alimentation habituelle."

12 See Patterson and McHenry, "A Dietary Investigation in Toronto."

13 Hunter and Pett, "A Dietary Survey in Edmonton," 265. See also L.B. Pett, "Food Makes a Difference," *CPHJ* 33, 12 (December 1942): 565-70; and Pett, "What's Wrong with Canada's Diet?" *National Health Review* 10, 36 (January 1942): 1-7. Similarly dire warnings were made in the United States as well, where Surgeon General Thomas Parran warned that 40 percent of the population was underfed. See Mudry, *Measured Meals*, 61.

14 Campbell, *Respectable Citizens*; Julie Guard, "A Mighty Power against the Cost of Living: Canadian Housewives Organize in the 1930s," *International Labor and Working-Class History* 77 (2010): 27-47; Struthers, *Limits of Affluence* and *No Fault of Their Own*; and Gale Wills, *A Marriage of Convenience: Business and Social Work in Toronto, 1918-1957* (Toronto: University of Toronto Press, 1995).

15 Leonard Marsh et al., *Health and Unemployment: Some Studies of Their Relationship* (New York: Oxford University Press, 1938); Harry Cassidy, *Unemployment and Relief in Ontario: 1929-1932* (Toronto: J.M. Dent, 1932). On the transformation of the social sciences in Canada during this period, see Marlene Shore, *The Science of Social Redemption: McGill, the Chicago School, and the Origins of Social Research in Canada* (Toronto: University of Toronto Press, 1987); and Doug Owram, *The Government Generation: Canadian Intellectuals and the State* (Toronto: University of Toronto Press, 1986). On transformation of social scientific research more generally, see Dorothy Ross, *The Origins of American Social Science* (Cambridge: Cambridge University Press, 1991).

16 See, for instance, the Canadian Prepatory Committee of the British Commonwealth Scientific Conference's "Report of the Subcommittee on Nutrition," *National Health Review* 4, 15 (October 1936): 59.

17 Department of Pensions and National Health, *Annual Report for the Year Ending March 31, 1938* (Ottawa: 1938); League of Nations, *The Problem of Nutrition*, vol. III: *Nutrition in Various Countries* (Geneva: 1936), 215. For a background to this issue, see Ostry, *Nutrition Policy in Canada*.

18 Coveney, *Food, Morals, and Meaning*, xv. For similar Foucaultian perspectives on nutrition, see Callather, "The Foreign Policy of the Calorie"; and Vernon, *Hunger*.

19 Bruce Curtis, *The Politics of Population: State Formation, Statistics, and the Census of Canada, 1840-1875* (Toronto: University of Toronto Press, 2001), 26.

20 Harvey Levenstein, *Paradox of Plenty: A Social History of Eating in Modern America* (Berkeley: University of California Press, 1993), 58.

21 John Boyd Orr, *Food, Health, and Income: Report on a Survey of Adequacy of Diet in Relation to Income*, 2nd ed. (London: Macmillan, 1937).

22 See Vernon, *Hunger*; Levenstein, *Paradox of Plenty*; Coveney, *Food, Morals, and Meaning*; David F. Smith, ed., *Nutrition in Britain: Science, Scientists, and Politics in the Twentieth Century* (London: Routledge, 1997); and Harmke Kamminga and Andrew Cunningham, eds., *The Science and Culture of Nutrition, 1840-1940* (Amsterdam: Editions Rodopi, 1995).

23 I. Leitch, "The Evolution of Dietary Standards," *Nutrition Abstracts and Reviews* 11, 4 (April 1942): 509-21; L.B. Pett, C.A. Morrell, F.W. Hanley, "The Development of Dietary Standards," *Canadian Journal of Public Health* (hereafter *CJPH*) 36 (June 1945): 232-39.

24 Orr, *Food, Health, and Income*, 39.

25 Ibid., 11.
26 For a good background to McHenry's work at the University of Toronto's School of Hygiene, see P.A. Bator and A.J. Rhodes, *Within Reach of Everyone: A History of the University of Toronto School of Hygiene and the Connaught Laboratories,* vol. I: *1927-1955* (Toronto: Canadian Public Health Association, 1990), 90-96.
27 LAC, RG 29, Vol. 958, File 387-9-1, E.W. McHenry, "Dietary Standards for Use in Canada," 15 March 1938.
28 On the margins of safety adopted by the CCN, see LAC, RG 29, Vol. 959, File 387-9-1, Frederick F. Tisdall to C.A. Morrell, 1 October 1940. More generally, Morrell summed up the general attitude within the nutrition profession in a 1940 letter to McHenry: "I do not believe that one ought to consider so-called *minimal* requirements as being properly individual requirements at all. It is surely necessary to do more than to protect an individual from scurvy. In my opinion vitamin requirements are 'optimal,' i.e., an excess over these amounts produces no beneficial effects." LAC, RG 29, Vol. 959, File 387-9-1, C.A. Morrell to E.W. McHenry, 21 September 1940.
29 LAC, RG 29, Vol. 958, File 387-9-1, John Boyd Orr to C.A. Morrell, 14 May 1938.
30 McHenry, "Nutrition in Toronto," 5.
31 Perhaps one of the best, most comprehensive examinations of nutritional inequalities within families remains the chapter "Feeding a Family" in Ellen Ross, *Love and Toil: Motherhood in Outcast London, 1870-1918* (Oxford: Oxford University Press, 1993), 27-55. A good example of such inequality in Canada can be found in Denyse Baillargeon's excellent *Making Do: Women, Family, and Home in Montreal during the Great Depression* (Waterloo: Wilfrid Laurier University Press, 1999), 106-10. For an excellent overview of the sociological and anthropological literature on gender and nutritional inequality, see Alan Beardsworth and Theresa Keil, *Sociology on the Menu: An Invitation to the Study of Food and Society* (London: Routledge, 1996), 77-87.
32 McHenry, "Nutrition in Toronto," 9.
33 Patterson and McHenry, "A Dietary Investigation in Toronto," 257.
34 McHenry, "Nutrition in Toronto," 8.
35 Ibid., 11.
36 LAC, RG 29, Vol. 958, File 387-9-1, Marjorie Bell to R.E. Wodehouse, 6 April 1938, and Marjorie Bell to C.A. Morrell, 17 June 1941. On gender relations within the profession more generally, see Heap, "From the Science of Housekeeping"; Wills, *A Marriage of Convenience*; and the much more detailed discussion of the conflict between Bell and McHenry in Chapter 5 of this book.
37 Hunter and Pett, "A Dietary Survey in Edmonton," 265.
38 Sylvestre and Nadeau, "Enquête sur l'alimentation habituelle," 250.
39 LAC, RG 29, Vol. 959, File 387-9-1, "Recommendations of the Canadian Dietetic Assn. for Requirements of Director and Secretary for the Canadian Council on Nutrition," 27 June 1941; and Charlotte P. Black to C.A. Morrell, 4 July 1941. See also LAC, National Council of Women Fonds, MG 28 I25, Vol. 80, File 13, Marjorie Bell to Mrs. Edgar Hardy, 27 June 1941; and "A Woman's Specialty," *Toronto Star,* 8 July 1941, 6.
40 LAC, RG 29, Vol. 960, File 387-9-1, E.W. McHenry to C.A. Morrell, 31 October 1941.
41 The Assistant Director, Marion Harlow, was trained in home economics and had been a nutritional supervisor and instructor of public health nurses, as well as head nutritionist for the Victorian Order of Nurses. The four field workers hired had a similar background and had worked as front-line dieticians or nutritionists. "Who's Who in Ottawa?" *Canadian*

Home Economics Newsletter 1, 1 (November 1943): 4; Heap, "From the Science of Housekeeping," 162-63.

42 See Ostry, *Nutrition Policy in Canada*; Durand, "Le laboratoire domestique de la machine humaine"; Cynthia R. Comacchio, *Nations Are Built of Babies: Saving Ontario's Mothers and Children* (Montreal: McGill-Queen's University Press, 1993); and Katherine Arnup, *Education for Motherhood: Advice for Mothers in Twentieth-Century Canada* (Toronto: University of Toronto Press, 1994).

43 Doug Owram, "Two Worlds: The Canadian Civil Service in 1939," in *A Country of Limitations: Canada and the World in 1939,* ed. Norman Hillmer, Robert Bothwell, Roger Sarty, and Claude Beauregard (Ottawa: Canadian Committee for the History of the Second World War, 1996); Owram, *The Government Generation*; J.L. Granatstein, *The Ottawa Men: The Civil Service Mandarins, 1935-1957,* 2nd ed. (Toronto: University of Toronto Press, 1998).

44 LAC, RG 29, Vol. 935, File 386-6-4, J. Ernest Sylvestre, "Provincial Nutrition Committee Preliminary Progress Report in Carrying Out the National Nutrition Programme" [1943]. On the history of nutrition education in Quebec in the years prior to the war, see Durand, "Le laboratoire domestique de la machine humaine"; and Yolande Cohen, "De la nutrition des pauvres malades: L'histoire du *Montreal Diet Dispensary* de 1910 à 1940," *Histoire social/ Social history* 41, 81 (2008): 133-63.

45 Ibid.

46 The exception would be PEI, which depended in large part on the work of nutrition professionals from the Red Cross and other charitable organizations.

47 Ostry, *Nutrition Policy in Canada,* 86, 96, 103.

48 Problems with the reliability of vital statistics from the period due to uneven collection practices throughout the country make generalizations in this area difficult, and there is significant disagreement among historians. Cynthia Comacchio, for instance, suggests that a range of diseases were often underreported during the 1930s and that health outcomes were likely far worse than those suggested by Ostry. See Comacchio, *Nations Are Built of Babies,* 158-59, 212-15. On the international debate over the impact of malnutrition during the 1930s, see Charles Webster, "Healthy or Hungry Thirties?" *History Workshop Journal* 13, 1 (1982): 110-29.

49 "Vitamin D Levels OK for Most: Most Canadians Need 600 IU of Vitamin D Daily, Triple Current Recommendation," *CBC News,* 11 November 2010, accessed 5 July 2011, http://www.cbc.ca/news/health/story/2010/11/29/vitamin-d-diet-calcium.html.

50 See, for instance, Jan Golinski, *Making Natural Knowledge: Constructivism and the History of Science* (Chicago: University of Chicago Press, 2005); John V. Pickstone, *Ways of Knowing: A New History of Science, Technology, and Medicine* (Chicago: University of Chicago Press, 2001); Bruno Latour, *Pandora's Hope: Essays on the Reality of Science Studies* (Cambridge: Harvard University Press, 1999); and Andrew Pickering, ed., *Science as Practice and Culture* (Chicago: University of Chicago Press, 1992).

51 Bruno Latour, *Science in Action: How to Follow Scientists and Engineers through Society* (Cambridge: Harvard University Press, 1987).

52 Orr, *Food, Health, and Income,* 7.

53 Ibid., 8.

54 Paul Weindling, "The Role of International Organizations in Setting Nutritional Standards in the 1920s and 1930s," in Kamminga and Cunningham, *The Science and Culture of Nutrition,* 319-32; Timothy Boon, "Agreement and Disagreement in the Making of *World of Plenty,*" in Smith, *Nutrition in Britain,* 166-67.

55 Hunter and Pett, "A Dietary Survey in Edmonton," 265.
56 Patterson and McHenry, "A Dietary Investigation in Toronto," 251.
57 Coveney, *Food, Morals, and Meaning*, 62.
58 L.B. Pett, "Food Rules," in *Wartime Recipes and Food Rules* (Edmonton: Woodland Dairy, 1942).
59 R.M. Farquharson, "Startling Army Revelations – So What Now!" *Canadian Home Journal* (February 1942), 8-9, 23-24. See also L.B. Pett, "Nutrition as a National Problem," *Canadian Welfare* 18, 1 (April 1942): 21-29; and Germaine Bernier, "L'alimentation rationnelle et les petits salaires," *Le Devoir*, 11 October 1941. For a postwar account of military rejections, see W.R. Feasby, ed., *Official History of the Canadian Medical Services, 1939-1945* (Ottawa: Department of National Defence, 1953).
60 "The Need for Action in Nutrition," *CPHJ* (1941): 317-18.
61 For an overview, see Ruth Roach Pierson, *"They're Still Women after All": The Second World War and Canadian Womanhood* (Toronto: McClelland and Stewart, 1986); Jennifer A. Stephen, *Pick One Intelligent Girl: Employability, Domesticity, and the Gendering of Canada's Welfare State, 1939-1947* (Toronto: University of Toronto Press, 2007); and Michael D. Stevenson, *Canada's Greatest Wartime Muddle: National Selective Service and the Mobilization of Human Resources during World War II* (Montreal and Kingston: McGill-Queen's University Press, 2001).
62 Stephen, *Pick One Intelligent Girl*.
63 L.B. Pett, "A Canadian Nutrition Program," *CPHJ* (1942): 320-24.
64 Pett, "Food Makes a Difference," 567.
65 E.W. McHenry, "Nutrition and Child Health" *CPHJ* 33, 4 (April 1942): 152-56; L.B. Pett, "Applied Nutrition," *CJPH* 34, 1 (January 1943): 1-5; Pett, "Food Makes a Difference"; W.A. Crandall, "Vitamins: A Review of Present Knowledge," *National Health Review* 9, 35 (October 1941): 222-28; E.W. McHenry, "Some Observations on Canadian Nutrition," *CPHJ* 31, 12 (December 1940): 584-88; C.A. Morell, "Nutrition in Canada," *National Health Review* (April 1940): 84-86.
66 Craig Heron, "Boys Will Be Boys: Working-Class Masculinities in the Age of Mass Production," *International Labor and Working-Class History* 69, 1 (2006): 8. On wartime masculinities in Canada during the Second World War, see Michael Brendan Baker, "Who's on the Home Front? Canadian Masculinity in the NFB's Second World War Series 'Canada Carries On,'" in *Making It Like a Man: Canadian Masculinities in Practice*, ed. Christine Ramsay (Waterloo: Wilfrid Laurier University Press, 2011), 39-52; and Paul Jackson, *One of the Boys: Homosexuality in the Military during World War II* (Montreal and Kingston: McGill-Queen's University Press, 2004). On Canadian masculinities during the middle decades of the twentieth century more generally, see, for instance, Wayne Martino and Christopher J. Greig, *Canadian Men and Masculinities: Historical and Contemporary Perspectives* (Toronto: Canadian Scholars' Press, 2012); Mary-Ellen Kelm, "Manly Contests: Rodeo Masculinities at the Calgary Stampede," *Canadian Historical Review* 90, 4 (2009): 711-51; Christopher Dummitt, *The Manly Modern: Masculinity in Postwar Canada* (Vancouver: UBC Press, 2007); and Joy Parr, *The Gender of Breadwinners: Women, Men, and Change in Two Industrial Towns, 1880-1950* (Toronto: University of Toronto Press, 1990).
67 Pett, "Food Makes a Difference," 565.
68 "The Need for Action in Nutrition," *CPHJ* 32, 6 (June 1941): 317-18.
69 Nutrition was, therefore, very much part of a larger trend towards normalizing discourses within medicine and psychology during this period. See Mona Gleason, *Normalizing the*

Ideal: Psychology, Schooling, and the Family in Postwar Canada (Toronto: University of Toronto Press, 1999); Mary Louise Adams, *The Trouble with Normal: Postwar Youth and the Making of Heterosexuality* (Toronto: University of Toronto Press, 1997); and Stephen, *Pick One Intelligent Girl.* On the origins of normal as a scientific constant, see Ian Hacking, *The Taming of Chance* (Cambridge: Cambridge University Press, 1990).

70 LAC, RG 29, Vol. 960, File 387-9-1, Canadian Dietary Standards, April 1942.
71 LAC, RG 29, Vol. 960, File 387-9-1, Grace Sharpe, Canadian Dietetic Assn, to L.B. Pett, 19 December 1941.
72 L.B. Pett, "Vitamin Requirements of Human Beings," *Vitamins and Hormones* 13 (1955): 217. On the background to the creation of the RDAs, see Levenstein, *Paradox of Plenty,* 64-66; and Susan Levine, *School Lunch Politics: The Surprising History of America's Favorite Welfare Program* (Princeton: Princeton University Press, 2008), 60-65.
73 L.B. Pett et al., *Nutrition in Industry* (Montreal: ILO, 1946).
74 LAC, RG 17, Vol. 3670, file N-9-12, L.B. Pett,"Outline of the Canadian Nutrition Program," 1942.
75 See "Canada's Food Rules," *Canadian Nutrition Notes* 2, 7 (1946): 1-2.
76 LAC, RG 17, Vol. 3670, File N-9-12, "Canada's Official Food Rules."
77 LAC, RG 17, Vol. 3670, File N-9-12A, Agenda Item 5, Canadian Council on Nutrition, 9th Meeting, 8 May 1944.
78 "Canada's Food Rules," 1-2.
79 "Nutrition Campaign," *Saturday Night,* 2 January 1943, 1.
80 L.B. Pett, "Feeding the Nation," *Public Affairs* 6, 2 (1942), 56.
81 "Canada's Food Rules," 1-2.
82 Levenstein, *Paradox of Plenty,* 70-71; Levine, *School Lunch Politics,* 66-68. On the background to the Basic Seven and other American food advice, see Anne Shaw, "A Brief History of Food Guides in the United States," *Nutrition Today* 27, 6 (1992): 6-12; and Marion Nestle, *Food Politics: How the Food Industry Influences Nutrition and Health* (Berkeley: University of California Press, 2002), 1-92.
83 This was somewhat at odds with the policies of other federal bodies, such as the Department of National War Services' advisory Committee on Co-operation in Canadian Citizenship, which, according to historian Ivana Caccia, sought to use a more inclusive approach in its policies towards immigrant and ethnic groups as a means of better securing their support for the broader war effort. See Caccia, *Managing the Canadian Mosaic in Wartime: Shaping Citizenship Policy, 1939-1945* (Montreal and Kingston: McGill-Queen's University Press, 2010); and Norman Hillmer, *On Guard for Thee: War, Ethnicity, and the Canadian State, 1939-1945* (Ottawa: Canadian Committee for the History of the Second World War, 1988).
84 "Food Fads and Fallacies," *Canadian Nutrition Notes* 3, 3 (March 1947): 1-4.
85 "Canada's Food Rules," 1-2. Others within the CCN like F.F. Tisdall had long been making a similar argument about the economic and nutritional potential of eating more Canadian foodstuffs. See "Eat Native Foods, Says Nutritionist," *Montreal Gazette,* 17 May 1940, 7.
86 R.P. Vivian, "Bakery Products and Nutrition," *Canadian Baker* (May 1945), 18.
87 Weindling, "The Role of International Organizations"; Boon, "The Making of *World of Plenty.*"
88 City of Vancouver Archives (CVA), Phyllis Ross Fonds, 592-E-3, File 9, Phyllis Ross, "Food and Nutrition in a World at War," Montreal Nutrition Conference, 1943.
89 Boon, "The Making of *World of Plenty.*"

90   LAC, RG 29, Vol. 961, File 387-9-1, Appendix II, Memorandum for Technical Committee Meeting, 5 May 1947.
91   Nutrition Division, *Healthful Eating* (Ottawa: Queen's Printer, 1949).
92   Pett et al., *Nutrition in Industry*, 33.
93   LAC, RG 29, Vol. 941, File 387-2-1, "Nutrition Manual for Use in Junior Red Cross Branches"; LAC, RG 29, Vol. 936, File 386-6-9, BC Provincial Board of Health, "What Have You Done about Nutrition? A True Story Related by Miss A. Haughland, Terrace Elementary School." For "Check Your Food by the Colour Test" and other wartime educational materials, see UBC Library, Rare Books and Special Collections (UBCL RBSC) L.B. Pett, Miscellaneous Files.
94   "Gallup Poll Checks Canada's Diet," *Toronto Daily Star*, 6 January 1943, 5.
95   CVA, Vancouver Health Department Fonds, Senior Nutritionist's subject files, 145-E-3, File 7, Department of National Health and Welfare, "Report on a Nutrition Survey in British Columbia by the Nutrition Division," Ottawa: April 1946.
96   LAC, RG 29, Vol. 929, File 386-3-9, Grace Duggan, Chief Nutritionist, Nutrition Division, to Mrs. Allan (Rosamond) Stevenson, National Director, Canadian Red Cross Society Nutrition Services, 27 April 1946.
97   For wartime estimates of the ability of families to purchase nutritionally adequate foods, see Frederick F. Tisdall, Alice C. Willard, and Marjorie Bell, *Report on Study of Relief Food Allowances and Costs* (City of Toronto, November 1941); Toronto Welfare Council, *The Cost of Living, Revised 1944: A Study of the Cost of a Standard of Living in Toronto Which Should Maintain Health and Self-Respect* (Toronto: 1944); Leonard Marsh, *Report on Social Security For Canada, 1943* (Toronto: University of Toronto Press, 1975).
98   Levenstein, *Paradox of Plenty*, 62-63; Lizzie Collingham, *The Taste of War: World War Two and the Battle for Food* (Toronto: Allen Lane, 2011), 363-67.
99   Mrs. Allan Stevenson, National Director, Nutrition Services, Canadian Red Cross Society, "Evaluation of Educational Techniques for Adults," in Division of Nutrition, Department of National Health and Welfare, *Proceedings of the Nutrition Conference, 6-8 June 1945* (Ottawa: 1945), 61-65.
100 LAC, RG 29, Vol. 929, File 386-3-9, Mabel Patrick, Professor of Household Economics, University of Alberta, to L.B. Pett, 29 April 1946; LAC, RG 29, Vol. 961, File 387-9-1, Mrs. J. Anderson, Manitoba Department of Health and Public Welfare, to L.B. Pett, 19 July 1948.
101 UBCL RBSC, L.B. Pett, Miscellaneous Files, "Men without Milk," *Liberty Magazine* (n.d.).
102 CVA, Vancouver Health Department Fonds, 145-E-3, File 7, Department of National Health and Welfare, "Report on a Nutrition Survey in British Columbia by the Nutrition Division" (Ottawa: 1946).
103 See P.E. Moore, H.D. Kruse, and F.F. Tisdall, "Nutrition in the North: A Study of the State of Nutrition of the Canadian Bush Indian," *The Beaver*, March 1943, 21-23; and the final report on the study, P.E. Moore, H.D. Kruse, F.F. Tisdall, and R.S.C. Corrigan, "Medical Survey of Nutrition among the Northern Manitoba Indians," *Canadian Medical Association Journal* 54 (March 1946): 223-33. For a detailed analysis, see Ian Mosby, "Administering Colonial Science: Nutrition Research and Human Biomedical Experimentation in Aboriginal Communities and Residential Schools, 1942-1952," *Histoire sociale/Social History* 46, 91 (May 2013): 145-72.
104 LAC, RG 29, Vol. 2986, File 851-6-1, "Indians in North Forsake Health-Giving Native Diet," 14 January 1948.

105 See Dominique Marshall, *The Social Origins of the Welfare State: Quebec Families, Compulsory Education, and Family Allowances, 1940-1955*, trans. Nicola Doone Danby (Waterloo: Wilfrid Laurier University Press, 2006), 76; and Hugh Shewell, *"Enough to Keep Them Alive": Indian Welfare in Canada, 1873-1965* (Toronto: University of Toronto Press, 2004).

106 In a June 1942 letter to the Metropolitan Life Insurance Company, Pett put the situation quite bluntly, noting that his budget "is so limited for actual publicity purposes that we shall have to depend on free space and the kindness of commercial organizations." LAC, RG 29, Vol. 110, File 180-26-22, L.B. Pett to N.L. Burnette, Assistant Secretary, Metropolitan Life Insurance Company, 29 June 1942.

107 "Advertising and Promotion Data for Nutrition Drive Available," *Food in Canada* 3, 1 (January 1943): 39.

108 *Eat Right to Work and Win* (Toronto: Swift Canadian, 1942).

109 LAC, RG 17, Vol. 3670, File N-9-12, Seventh Meeting, Canadian Council on Nutrition, 26 November 1942.

110 On the marketing of nutrition during the interwar years, see Apple, *Vitamania*, 13-32; and Levenstein, *Revolution at the Table*, 147-60.

111 *Globe and Mail*, 5 February 1943, 13; *Globe and Mail*, 4 February 1943, 14.

112 Department of Pensions and National Health, *The Canadian Nutrition Programme* (Ottawa: Queen's Printer, July 1942). See also the statement from Pett in the May 1942 edition of *Food in Canada*.

113 See the back page of *Food in Canada* 2, 6 (June 1942).

114 LAC, RG 17, Vol. 3670, File N-9-12, Seventh Meeting, Canadian Council on Nutrition, 26 November 1942.

115 Hiram McCann, "Canada's Faulty Diet Is Adolf Hitler's Ally," *Saturday Night*, 14 June 1941, 8; Rosamond Stevenson, "Food for Health in Peace and War," *Canadian Red Cross Junior* (hereafter *CRCJ*) 19, 8 (October 1940): 18; Florence McLaughlin, "Round Table – Health versus Apathy," *CRCJ* 24, 4 (April 1944): 4; LAC, RG 29, Vol. 960, File 387-9-1, Draft Statement by Mackenzie King on Nutrition, 1942.

116 LAC, Department of National Defense, RG 24, Vol. 17948, File 914-1, White Spot Restaurants, "Straw Men (Don't Let This Happen to Canadians)."

117 Janet Keith, "Do You Want to Be Captain of Your Team?" *CRCJ* 23, 1 (January 1943): 2; Keith, "Do You Want To Be Good-Looking?" *CRCJ* 22, 12 (December 1942): 2.

118 Dr. Ernest Couture, "Urgence d'une alimentation rationnelle pour nos jeunes gens," *CRCJ* 24, 6 (June 1944): 14-15.

119 LAC, RG 29, Vol. 935, File 386-6-5, Kingston Nutrition Council, Radio Script, "Little Red Riding Hood."

120 Feasby, *Official History of the Canadian Medical Services*, 148.

121 Life Insurance Companies of Canada and Canadian Medical Association (CMA), *What They Eat to Be Fit Is Good for the Health of All Canadians*, 1943.

122 "Edith Adams 8th Annual Cook Book, 1942," *Vancouver Sun*, in Elizabeth Driver, *Edith Adams Omnibus* (Vancouver: Whitecap Books, 2005).

123 CMA, *Food for Health in Peace and War* (Ottawa: 1941).

124 Comacchio, *Nations Are Built of Babies*, 133. See also Arnup, *Education for Motherhood*; and Margaret Jane Hillyard Little, *"No Car, No Radio, No Liquor Permit": The Moral Regulation of Single Mothers in Ontario, 1920-1997* (Toronto: Oxford University Press, 1998). In the American context, see Molly Ladd-Taylor and Lauri Umansky, eds., *"Bad" Mothers: The Politics of Blame in Twentieth-Century America* (New York: NYU Press, 1998); and

Rebecca Jo Plant, *Mom: The Transformation of Motherhood in Modern America* (Chicago: University of Chicago Press, 2010).

125 Patricia Anne Solberg, *Nutrition Education as Presented in Provincial Programmes of Study* (Ottawa: Canadian Education Association, March 1949).

126 LAC, RG 29, Vol. 941, File 387-2-1, "The Canadian Red Cross Society Nutrition Program, 1929-1944." See also Canadian Red Cross Society, *Annual Report for the Year 1945* (Ottawa: 1946).

127 LAC, RG 29, Vol. 941, File 387-2-1, "Meeting of National Red Cross Nutrition Committee – 31 July 1942."

128 Canadian Red Cross, Ontario Division, *War Economy Nutrition* (Toronto: n.d.).

129 Vancouver Council of Social Agencies, *Practical Nutrition for Wartime Living* (Vancouver: n.d.).

130 Health Service of the Federated Agencies of Montreal, *Food and the Family Income: Low Cost Recipes* (Montreal: J.B. Lippincott, 1941).

131 Vancouver Council, *Practical Nutrition*.

132 L.B. Pett, "A New Dietary Standard For Canada, 1949," *CMAJ* 61 (November 1949): 452.

Chapter 2: The Kitchen and the State

1 James Struthers, "A Profession in Crisis: Charlotte Whitton and Canadian Social Work in the 1930s," in *The "Benevolent" State: The Growth of Welfare in Canada*, ed. Allan Moscovitch and Jim Albert (Toronto: Garamond Press, 1987), 111-25; Judith Roberts-Moore, "Charlotte Whitton: Pioneering Social Worker and Public Policy Activist," in *Framing Our Past: Canadian Women's History in the Twentieth Century*, ed. Sharon A. Cook, Lorna R. McLean, and Kate O'Rourke (Montreal and Kingston: McGill-Queen's University Press, 2001), 232-39; Patricia T. Rooke and R.L. Schnell, *No Bleeding Heart: Charlotte Whitton – A Feminist on the Right* (Vancouver: UBC Press, 1987).

2 Charlotte Whitton, "What's the Matter with Us?" *Chatelaine*, December 1944, 12-13.

3 See Jeffrey Keshen, *Saints, Sinners, and Soldiers: Canada's Second World War* (Vancouver: UBC Press, 2004); Keshen, "One for All or All for One: Government Controls, Black Marketing and the Limits of Patriotism, 1939-1947," *Journal of Canadian Studies* 29, 4 (1994): 111-43. See also Serge Marc Durflinger, *Fighting from Home: The Second World War in Verdun, Quebec* (Vancouver: UBC Press, 2006); and Graham Broad, "Shopping for Victory," *The Beaver* May 2005, 40-45.

4 See, for instance, Lizabeth Cohen, *A Consumers' Republic: The Politics of Mass Consumption in Postwar America* (New York: Vintage Books, 2003); Frank Trentmann, ed., *The Making of the Consumer: Knowledge, Power, and Identity in the Modern World* (New York: Berg, 2006); Dana Frank, *Purchasing Power: Consumer Organizing, Gender, and the Seattle Labor Movement, 1919-1929* (Cambridge: Cambridge University Press, 1994); and Victoria de Grazia and Ellen Furlough, eds., *The Sex of Things: Gender and Consumption in Historical Perspective* (Berkeley: University of California Press, 1996). In the Canadian context, see, for instance, Joy Parr, *Domestic Goods: The Material, the Moral, and the Economic in the Postwar Years* (Toronto: University of Toronto Press, 1999); Magda Fahrni, *Household Politics: Montreal Families and Postwar Reconstruction* (Toronto: University of Toronto Press, 2005); Julie Guard, "Canadian Citizens or Dangerous Foreign Women? Canada's Radical Consumer Movement, 1947-1950," in *Sisters or Strangers? Immigrant, Ethnic, and*

Racialized Women in Canadian History, ed. Marlene Epp, Franca Iacovetta and Frances Swyripa (Toronto: University of Toronto Press, 2004), 161-89; and Joseph Tohill, "A Consumers' War: Price Control and Political Consumerism in the United States and Canada during World War II" (PhD diss., York University, January 2012). For recent literature on social and economic citizenship, see Alice Kessler Harris, *In Pursuit of Equity: Women, Men, and the Quest for Economic Citizenship in 20th-Century America* (Oxford: Oxford University Press, 2001); and the special issue on economic citizenship in *Social Politics: International Studies in Gender, State, and Society* 10, 2 (Summer 2003).

5 Cooperative Commonwealth Federation (CCF), *Women in Peace as in War Protect Your Home* (Ottawa: 1945).

6 See, for instance, articles like Anne Fromer, "Is Food the Answer to Increased Production?" *Saturday Night*, 12 December 1942, 42-43; *Foods for Home Defence* (Ottawa: Department of Agriculture, 1942); and the National Film Board documentaries *A Friend for Supper* (1944) and *Food: Secret of the Peace* (1945).

7 For the best background, see G.E. Britnell and V.C. Fowke, *Canadian Agriculture in War and Peace, 1935-1950* (Palo Alto, CA: Stanford University Press, 1962).

8 *Report of the Wartime Prices and Trade Board, April 1, 1943 to December 31, 1943* (Ottawa: King's Printer, 1944); Britnell and Fowke, *Canadian Agriculture*, 125.

9 Dominion Bureau of Statistics, *Cost of Living Index Numbers for Canada, 1913-1946* (Ottawa: Department of Trade and Commerce, 1947).

10 WIB, *Canadian Food and Agriculture in the War* (Ottawa: 25 May 1944); Nutrition Division, *Canadian Food and Nutrition Statistics, 1935 to 1956* (Ottawa: Department of National Health and Welfare, 1959); Britnell and Fowke, *Canadian Agriculture*, 150-51.

11 Christopher Robb Waddell, "The Wartime Prices and Trade Board: Price Control in Canada in World War II" (PhD diss., York University, 1981), 129-31; Britnell and Fowke, *Canadian Agriculture*, 126-29.

12 *Report of the Wartime Prices and Trade Board, September 3, 1939, to March 31, 1943* (Ottawa: King's Printer, 1943), 59.

13 "Gallup and Fortune Polls," *Public Opinion Quarterly* 6, 2 (Summer 1942), 309.

14 See Graham Broad, "Shopping for Victory," *The Beaver*, April–May 2005, 40-45; and Parr, *Domestic Goods*, 27-31.

15 For the best accounts of the mechanics of price control, see Tohill, "A Consumer's War"; and Waddell, "The Wartime Prices and Trade Board."

16 LAC, RG 64, Vol. 6, File 145, Radio Speech by Donald Gordon, 26 January 1942.

17 See Michael D. Stevenson, *Canada's Greatest Wartime Muddle: National Selective Service and the Mobilization of Human Resources during World War II* (Montreal and Kingston: McGill-Queen's University Press, 2001); and Jennifer Stephen, *Pick One Intelligent Girl: Employability, Domesticity, and the Gendering of Canada's Welfare State, 1939-1947* (Toronto: University of Toronto Press, 2007).

18 See LAC, RG 64, Vol. 60, File 3, History of the Enforcement Administration to 31 December 1945; and LAC, RG 64, Vol. 63, File 21, History of the W.P.T.B. Regional Office Prince Edward Island.

19 See *Report of the Wartime Prices and Trade Board, September 3, 1939, to March 31, 1943* (Ottawa: King's Printer, 1943), 66; *Report of the Wartime Prices and Trade Board, January 1, 1946, to December 31, 1946* (Ottawa: King's Printer, 1947), 52-53; and LAC, RG 64, Vol. 60, File 3, History of the Enforcement Administration to 31 December 1945.

20 LAC, RG 64, Vol. 6, File 145, Radio Address By Donald Gordon, 28 November 1941.

21 LAC, RG 64, Vol. 6, File 145, "Women's Help Wanted" – Address by Mr. Donald Gordon, Chairman of the Wartime Prices and Trade Board, before the Women's Canadian Club, Toronto, 6 March 1945.
22 On the history of the 'Mrs. Consumer' concept, see chapter 13, "Selling Mrs. Consumer," in Susan Strasser, *Never Done: A History of American Housework* (New York: Henry Holt, 2000), 242-62; and Victoria de Grazia, "Establishing the Modern Consumer Household," in de Grazia and Furlough eds., *The Sex of Things*, 151-61.
23 LAC, RG 64, Vol. 60, File 3, A Brief Summary of the Origin and Development of the Consumer Branch.
24 Joseph Schull, *The Great Scot: A Biography of Donald Gordon* (Montreal and Kingston: McGill-Queen's University Press, 1979), 76. On the composition of the civil service and women's positions within it during this period, see J.L. Granatstein, *The Ottawa Men: The Civil Service Mandarins, 1935-1957*, 2nd ed. (Toronto: University of Toronto Press, 1998), 4; and Doug Owram, "Two Worlds: The Canadian Civil Service in 1939," in *A Country of Limitations: Canada and the World in 1939*, ed. Norman Hillmer et al. (Ottawa: Canadian Committee on the History of the Second World War, 1996).
25 This was, surprisingly, the most popular English-language soap opera during the war. Schull, *The Great Scot*, 76.
26 See LAC, RG 64, Vol. 22, File 252, History of the Information Branch; and Waddell, "Price Control," 569-70.
27 "Three Million Price Cops," *Food in Canada* 2, 5 (May 1942): 4; LAC, RG 64, Vol. 6, File 145, Speech By Donald Gordon at the Retailers' Wartime Conference, Toronto, 5 April 1943.
28 Byrne Hope Sanders, "The Food Manufacturer, the Grocery Retailer, and the Consumer," *Food in Canada* 2, 8 (August 1942): 14-16; LAC, RG 64, Vol. 6, File 145, Radio Address by Donald Gordon, 28 November 1941.
29 LAC, RG 64, Vol. 60, File 3, A Brief Summary of the Origin and Development of the Consumer Branch.
30 Ibid.
31 "Three Million Price Cops," *Food in Canada* 2, 5 (May 1942): 4; Lillian D. Millar, "Price Control Depends Largely on the Women," *Saturday Night*, 10 October 1942, 20; Lillian D. Millar, "Has This Structure of a Million Women Post-War Potentialities?" *Saturday Night*, 8 July 1944, 22-23.
32 LAC, RG 64, Vol. 60, File 3, A Record of Consumer Branch Work in the Field of Consumer Problems and the Principal Problems Which Arose with Some Comments on Methods.
33 LAC, RG 64-A-4, Series 1240, Vol. 1445, Minutes of Regular Meeting of the [Victoria] WRAC Board and Liaison Officers, 8 September 1943.
34 LAC, RG 64, Vol. 60, File 3, A Record of Consumer Branch Work.
35 LAC, RG 64-A-4, Series 1240, Vol. 1448, File A10-29-12, Louis Dallamore, Report on Consumer Questionnaire Panels – First Series: Preserves Coupons, 14 June 1946.
36 LAC, RG 64-A-4, Series 1240, Vol. 1445, File A10-29, "Price Study Panels," n.d.; LAC, RG 64-A-4, Series 1240, Vol. 1445, File A10-29-1, Mrs. W.P.M. Kennedy, "Price Panel Operation in Toronto," n.d.; Tohill, "A Consumer's War," 249.
37 LAC, RG 64, Vol. 60, File 3, A Brief Summary of the Origin and Development of the Consumer Branch.
38 LAC, RG 64-A-4, Series 1240, Vol. 1446, File A10-29-6, Christine White, "Report of Visit to Montreal," 2 November 1942. For a similar perspective from a shopper in Toronto, see

Mary F. Williamson and Tom Sharp, eds., *Just a Larger Family: Letters of Marie Williamson from the Canadian Home Front, 1940-1944* (Waterloo: Wilfrid Laurier University Press, 2011), 245.

39 LAC, RG 64, Vol. 6, File 145, CBC Transcript, "Price Control Anniversary Continuity," 1 December 1942.
40 LAC, RG 36-31, Vol. 22, WIB Field Reports, 39, 12 January 1944.
41 LAC, RG 64-A-4, Vol. 1445, File A10-29-2, Meeting Minutes, Montreal Women's Regional Advisory Committee (WRAC), 21 March 1944.
42 LAC, RG 64, Vol. 60, File 3, History of the Enforcement Administration to 31 December 1945.
43 "Big Majority Behind 'Ceiling' Is Surprise," *Toronto Daily Star*, 3 December 1941, II, 1; Daniel J. Robinson, *The Measure of Democracy: Polling, Market Research, and Public Life, 1930-1945* (Toronto: University of Toronto Press, 1999), 71; Hadley Cantril and Mildred Strunk, *Public Opinion, 1935-1946* (Princeton: Princeton University Press, 1951), 1004.
44 LAC, RG 64, Vol. 1566, Controls for Victory, Canadian Affairs Pictorial, 4, 1943; LAC, RG 64, Vol. 26, File 276, History of Meat and Meat Products Administration.
45 LAC, RG 17, Vol. 3709, File W-5-42A, Conference of Agricultural Press and Representatives of Department of Agriculture and Wartime Prices and Trade Board, 17 April 1943.
46 *Public Opinion Quarterly* (Winter 1943), 748.
47 Keshen, "One For All," 112; Waddell, "Price Control," 225.
48 William R. Young, "Academics and Social Scientists versus the Press: The Policies of the Bureau of Public Information and the Wartime Information Board, 1939-1945," *Historical Papers/Communications historiques* 13, 1 (1978): 236.
49 See also William R. Young, "Mobilizing English Canada For War: The Bureau of Public Information, the Wartime Information Board, and a View of the Nation during the Second World War," in *The Second World War as a National Experience,* ed. Sidney Aster (Ottawa: CCHSWW, 1981); and Gary Evans, *John Grierson and the National Film Board: The Politics of Wartime Propaganda* (Toronto: University of Toronto Press, 1984).
50 See, for instance, LAC, RG 64, Series 1040, Vol. 1194, File 19-6-1, J.M. Rodrigue Villeneuve, OMI, Archbishop of Quebec, to K.W. Taylor, Food Administrator, 14 May 1943.
51 "Sugar Allotment Declared Unfair," *Globe and Mail*, 19 May 1943; "Average Canning Sugar Allotment 10 lbs," *Globe and Mail*, 20 May 1943; "Rap Ottawa over 'Hoax,' Unequal Sugar Rationing and Ceiling Price Breach," *Toronto Telegram*, 2 July 1943. See also LAC, RG 64, Vol. 22, File 252, WPTB Information Branch, Weekly News Digest, 17-22 May to 5-10 July 1943.
52 LAC, RG 64, Vol. 22, File 252, WPTB Information Branch, Weekly News Digest, 17-22 May 1943.
53 LAC, RG 64-A-4, Vol. 1445, File A10-29-2, Meeting Minutes, Saskatchewan WRAC, 11 April 1944.
54 "Sugar for Canning Season Up to 23 Pounds per Person," *Globe and Mail*, 2 May 1944; LAC, RG 64, Vol. 22, File 252, WPTB Information Branch, Weekly News Digest, 23-28 April 1945.
55 LAC, RG 64, Vol. 23, File 256, WPTB Information Branch, Report 2 – Canadian Opinion in May 1945 – Nation-Wide Attitudes Towards Inflation, Price, Distribution and Supply – 7 July 1945.
56 But as Daniel Robinson has argued, wartime opinion polling by the Canadian Institute of Public Opinion, which was responsible for much of the WIB and WPTB Information

Branch's wartime polls, frequently underpolled francophones. That said, polls also tended to under-represent women and the poor, two of the strongest supporters of price control and rationing. See Robinson, *The Measure of Democracy,* 7-8.

57 York University Archives (YUA), Maurice Duplessis Fonds, 1980-008/001, Reel 7, 'Schema – Discours' [n.d.], 2; Reel 3, speech by Maurice Duplessis [n.d., no title], 14, cited in Fahrni, *Household Politics,* 112.

58 Schull, *The Great Scot,* 114; LAC, RG 64, Vol. 22, File 252, History of the Information Branch.

59 Waddell, "Price Control," 542.

60 Ibid., 526-27.

61 LAC, RG 64, Vol. 63, File 22, History of the WPTB Nova Scotia Regional Office.

62 LAC, RG 64, Vol. 63, File 24, Historique de l'activite du bureau regional de Quebec de la Commission des Prix et du Commerce en Temps de Guerre.

63 See LAC, RG 64, Vol. 60, File 3, History of the Enforcement Administration to 31 December 1945.

64 LAC, RG 64, Vol. 22, WPTB Information Branch, Weekly News Digest, 14-19 June 1943. See also WPTB Information Branch, Weekly News Digest, 26-31 July 1943.

65 See Keshen, *Saints, Sinners, and Soldiers,* 71.

66 "Fruits and Vegetables Very High, Going Higher," *Globe and Mail,* 5 May 1943; "Council Asks Prices Probe," *Globe and Mail,* 27 April 1943; "Price Confusion," *Hamilton Spectator,* 7 July 1943.

67 LAC, RG 64-A-4, Series 1240, Vol. 1446, File A10-29-6, Christine White to Byrne Sanders, 5 May 1943. See also C.H. Herbert, *Is the Cost-of-Living Index Phoney?* (Montreal: La Patrie, n.d.).

68 Waddell, "Price Control," 261.

69 "Gov't Asks Miners to Resume Work," *Vancouver Sun,* 2 October 1945, 1.

70 LAC, RG 64, Vol. 613, File 19-3, Alex Fage to W.L. Mackenzie King, 15 October 1945.

71 LAC, RG 64, Vol. 638, File 19-32-4, "A Canadian Who Believes in Canada First, Last, and Always" to the WPTB, 21 September 1945.

72 LAC, RG 64, Vol. 613, File 19-3, Donald Gordon to J.L. Ilsley, 10 March 1943.

73 LAC, RG 29, Vol. 929 File 386-3-2, Minutes of the meeting of the Advisory Committee on Nutrition to the Foods Administration, 17 March 1943.

74 LAC, RG 64, Vol. 613, File 19-3-1, S.R. Wadden to Donald Gordon, 4 March 1943. See also RG 64, Vol. 63, File 22, WPTB, History of the Nova Scotia Regional Office.

75 LAC, RG 64, Vol. 613, File 19-3, Donald Gordon to J.L. Ilsley, 10 March 1943.

76 LAC, RG 64, Vol. 615, File 19-3-3, Memorandum, H.R. Delany, Chief of Consumer Section, Approvals Division, to Sugar Administration, 10 March 1944, and H.I. Ross to R.C. Carr, 27 May 1943; LAC, RG 64, Vol. 615, File 19-3-4, Memorandum 63 to Local Ration Boards, 25 September 1943; LAC, RG 64, Vol. 613, File 19-3, Christine White, "Special Report: Concerning Supplementary Rations for Railwaymen and Other Industrial Workers," 29 October 1945.

77 LAC, RG 64, Vol. 1195, File 19-6-4, Instructions to Local Committee on Extra Meat Rations for Coal Mine Workers [n.d.]; LAC, RG 64, Vol. 14, File 193, History of the WPTB in Alberta.

78 LAC, RG 36-31, Vol. 27, WIB Information Brief 57, The Home Front: Verdict on Wartime Controls, 16 April 1945.

79 LAC, RG 64, Vol. 23, File 256, WPTB Information Branch, Report 3A, Resume of Canadian Opinion on Rationing, 1 October 1945.

80 LAC, RG 36-31, Vol. 27, WIB Information Brief 55, Sending Food Abroad: A Review of Public Attitudes, 19 March 1945.

81 "Public Opinion Polls," *Public Opinion Quarterly* 8, 1 (Spring 1944): 159; LAC, RG 64, Vol. 23, File 256, WPTB Information Branch, Report 2, Canadian Opinion in May 1945: Nation-Wide Attitudes Towards Inflation, Price, Distribution, and Supply, 7 July 1945.

82 "Showdown Looms in Butcher Strike as Violence Flares," *Montreal Gazette*, 27 September 1945, 1; "Butchers Open Today; Appeal to Ottawa for Trial of Voluntary System," *Montreal Gazette*, 29 September 1945, 1.

83 "The Quarter's Polls," *Public Opinion Quarterly* 9, 3 (Autumn 1945): 376. On public attitudes towards the Montreal butcher's strike, see Chapter 5 in Magda Fahrni, "Under Reconstruction: The Family and the Public in Postwar Montreal, 1944-1949" (PhD diss., York University, 2001).

84 LAC, RG 36-31, Vol. 27, WIB Information Brief 57, The Home Front: Verdict on Wartime Controls, 16 April 1945; LAC, RG 64, Vol. 23, File 256, WPTB Information Branch, Report 3, Nation-Wide Attitudes Towards Inflation, Price, Distribution, and Supply, 31 August 1945.

85 LAC, RG 64, Vol. 22, File 252, History of the Information Branch. See also Young, "Academics and Social Scientists," 234-35.

86 LAC, RG 64, Vol. 60, File 2, Christine S. White, "History of the Development of the Labour Relations Department of the Consumer Branch," 8 October 1946.

87 Ibid.

88 LAC, RG 64-A-4, Series 1240, Vol. 1446, File A10-29-6, Report of Development Work with Labour Organizations, 26 May 1944.

89 LAC, RG 64, Vol. 22, File 252, WPTB Information Branch, Weekly News Digest, 30 August–4 September 1943; J.L. Granatstein, *Canada's War: The Politics of the Mackenzie King Government, 1939-1945* (Toronto: Oxford University Press, 1975), 186; Tohill, "A Consumer's War"; Waddell, "The Wartime Prices and Trade Board."

90 Dominion Bureau of Statistics (DBS), *Cost of Living Index Numbers For Canada, 1913-1946*; Britnell and Fowke, *Canadian Agriculture*, 365-82.

91 See Keshen, "One for All"; and Keshen, *Saints, Sinners, and Soldiers*, 94-120.

92 According to Keshen, there were only 1,201 convictions for WPTB rule violations in 1942, 3,663 in 1943, 4,170 in 1944, and 4,481 in 1945. See Keshen, "One for All," 114.

93 See, for instance, LAC, RG 64, Vol. 63, File 22, History of the WPTB Nova Scotia Regional Office and *Report of the Wartime Prices and Trade Board, January 1, 1945 to December 31, 1945* (Ottawa: King's Printer, 1946), 56.

94 Cantril and Strunk, *Public Opinion*, 342; Mildred A. Schwartz, *Public Opinion and Canadian Identity* (Berkeley: University of California Press, 1967), 96.

95 On public utilities, see Robinson, *The Measure of Democracy*, 81.

96 On the changing politics of the period and the transformation of the welfare state, see, for instance, Alvin Finkel, *Social Policy and Practice in Canada: A History* (Waterloo: Wilfrid Laurier University Press, 2006); Dennis Guest, *The Emergence of Social Security in Canada*, 3rd ed. (Vancouver: UBC Press, 2003); Nancy Christie, *Engendering the State: Family, Work, and Welfare in Canada* (Toronto: University of Toronto Press, 2000); and Granatstein, *Canada's War*.

97 See E.P. Thomson, "The Moral Economy of the English Crowd in the 18th Century," *Past and Present* 50 (1971), 76-136. On the continuation of this idea through to the twentieth century in the Canadian context, see "Markets of the Mind," in Christopher Armstrong and H.V. Nelles, *Monopoly's Moment: The Organization and Regulation of Canadian Utilities, 1830-1930* (Philadelphia: Temple University Press, 1986), 323.

98 LAC, RG 64, Vol. 638, File 19-32-4, L.A. Fitzgerald to W.L. Mackenzie King, 14 September 1945.

99 All quotes are from LAC, RG 64-A-4, Vol. 1448, File A10-29-12, WPTB Research Division, Report 3: Consumer Questionnaire Analysis, 8 February 1946.

100 LAC, RG 64, Vol. 60, File 3, A Record of Consumer Branch Work in the Field of Consumer Problems and the Principal Problems Which Arose with Some Comments on Methods.

101 LAC, RG 64-A-4, Vol. 1445, File A10-29-2, Minutes of Northern Ontario WRAC Meeting, 16 March 1944.

102 LAC, RG 64-A-4, 1445, File A10-29-2, Minutes of Northern Ontario WRAC Meeting, 31 May 1944.

103 LAC, RG 64, Vol. 1445, File A10-29-1, W.P.M. Kennedy, "Price Panel Operation in Toronto," n.d.

104 Kessler-Harris, *In Pursuit of Equity*, 6.

105 LAC, RG 64-A-4, Vol. 1445, File A10-29-1, Minutes of Montreal WRAC Meeting, 20 June 1944.

106 LAC, RG 64, Vol. 1447, File A10-29-1, Report of Annual Conference of the [Montreal Region] Women's Regional Advisory Committee, 7-8 November 1944.

107 "Three Million Price Cops," *Food in Canada* 2, 5 (May 1942): 4.

108 "Price Rise Effective on Tuesday," *Globe and Mail*, 27 September 1946.

109 "Ottawa Women Start Boycott[,] Cut Milk Purchase 50 Per Cent," *Toronto Star*, 1 October 1946; "Housewives Mass to Hit Milk Price," *Toronto Star*, 2 October 1946.

110 Schull, *The Great Scot*, 99.

111 *Report of the Wartime Prices and Trade Board, January 1, 1945, to December 31, 1945* (Ottawa: King's Printer, 1946). On decontrol, see also Keshen, "All for One"; Waddell, "Price Control"; and Schull, *The Great Scot*.

112 *Report of the Wartime Prices and Trade Board, January 1, 1945, to December 31, 1945* (Ottawa: King's Printer, 1946); *Report of the Wartime Prices and Trade Board, January 1, 1946, to December 31, 1946* (Ottawa: King's Printer, 1947).

113 Schwartz, *Public Opinion*, 98.

114 See Cohen, *A Consumers' Republic*, 103; *Report of the Wartime Prices and Trade Board, January 1, 1946, to December 31, 1946* (Ottawa: King's Printer, 1946).

115 "Boycott Proposed as Price Protest," *Globe and Mail*, 9 February 1947; "Week's Boycott of Beef Urged by Housewives," *Toronto Star*, 19 July 1946; "One-Day Protest Strike Planned at Vancouver," *Toronto Star*, 24 April 1947; "Organized Butter Boycott Is Likely," *Globe and Mail*, 1 May 1947; "Housewives Ask Better Control to Check Prices," *Hamilton Spectator*, 31 May 1947. For a background to the 1947 protests, see Julie Guard, "Canadian Citizens or Dangerous Foreign Women? Canada's Radical Consumer Movement, 1947-1950," in *Sisters or Strangers? Immigrant, Ethnic, and Racialized Women in Canadian History*, ed. Marlene Epp, Franca Iacovetta, and Frances Swyripa (Toronto: University of Toronto Press, 2004), 165-73; and Joan Sangster, *Dreams of Equality: Women on the Canadian Left, 1920-1950* (Toronto: McClelland and Stewart, 1989), 187.

116 CBC Digital Archives, "Don't Be a Sucker, Don't Buy 8 Cent Bars," http://www.cbc.ca/archives/categories/economy-business/consumer-goods/consumer-goods-general/dont

-be-a-sucker-dont-buy-8-cent-bars.html; "'We'll Eat Worms First' Students Spurn 8-Cent Bar," *Toronto Star*, 3 May 1947; "Little Hope Held for 5-Cent Bar," *Hamilton Spectator*, 1 May 1947.

117 On the history of the HCA, see Julie Guard, "Women Worth Watching: Radical Housewives in Cold War Canada," in *Whose National Security? Canadian State Surveillance and the Creation of Enemies*, ed. D. Buse, G. Kinsman, and M. Steedman (Toronto: Between the Lines, 2000), 73-88; Julie Guard, "The Politics of Milk: Canadian Housewives Organize in the 1930s," in *Edible Histories, Cultural Politics: Towards a Canadian Food History*, ed. Franca Iacovetta, Valerie Korinek, and Marlene Epp (Toronto: University of Toronto Press, 2011); Guard, "Canadian Citizens or Dangerous Foreign Women?"; Sangster, *Dreams of Equality*; and Parr, *Domestic Goods*, 84-100.

118 Guard, "The Politics of Milk."

119 See LAC, RG 64, Series 1040, Vol. 1192, File 19-6, M. Dawes, Secretary, Housewives Consumer Association, Toronto, to J.G. Taggart, WPTB Foods Administrator, September 1942; and C.E. Nix, Secretary, Consumers' League, Edmonton, to Donald Gordon, 23 September 1942.

120 Guard, "Canadian Citizens or Dangerous Foreign Women?" 171.

121 "Restore Price Controls, Demand from Women," *Globe and Mail*, 1 April 1947; "Women Demand Bracken Present Their Price Brief," *Globe and Mail*, 2 April 1947.

122 "Rolling Pin," *Toronto Star*, 25 June 1947; Guard, "Canadian Citizens or Dangerous Foreign Women?" 174.

123 Parr, *Domestic Goods*, 93.

124 On the history of the CAC, see Parr, *Domestic Goods*, 84-100; Guard, "Canadian Citizens or Dangerous Foreign Women?" 179-81; and Fahrni, *Household Politics*, 114-19.

125 "Changes Mind: Abbott to See Housewife Group," *Toronto Star*, 17 April 1948.

126 See Schwartz, *Public Opinion*, 98; and Statistics Canada, *Historical Statistics of Canada, Section K: Price Indexes*, http://www.statcan.gc.ca/pub/11-516-x/pdf/5500100-eng.pdf, accessed 8 December 2010.

127 For a good background, see Gary Marcuse and Reginald Whitaker, *Cold War Canada: The Making of a National Insecurity State, 1945-1957* (Toronto: University of Toronto Press, 1996).

128 Dan Azoulay, "'Ruthless in a Ladylike Way': CCF Women Confront the Postwar 'Communist Menace,'" *Ontario History*, 89, 1 (March 1997): 23-52; and Guard, "Canadian Citizens or Dangerous Foreign Women?" 178-81.

129 Christine White, "War Controls So Good Labor Wants Return," *Saturday Night*, 12 July 1947, 14.

130 Cohen, *A Consumers' Republic*, 8.

131 Fahrni, *Household Politics*, 7.

Chapter 3: Mobilizing Canada's "Housoldiers" and "Kitchen Commandos" for War

1 *Cariboo Observer*, 27 March 1943, 4.

2 On the First World War home front, see Sarah Glassford and Amy Shaw, eds., *A Sisterhood of Suffering and Service: Women and Girls of Canada and Newfoundland during the First World War* (Vancouver: UBC Press, 2012); Robert Rutherdale, *Hometown Horizons: Local Responses to Canada's Great War* (Vancouver: UBC Press, 2005); and Desmond Morton, *Fight or Pay: Soldiers' Families in the Great War* (Vancouver: UBC Press, 2004).

3 Helen G. Campbell, "Home Defense," *Chatelaine*, November 1939, 57.

4 Katherine Caldwell Bayley, "We Women Man the Food Front: Canada's Kitchens on Active Service," *Canadian Home Journal*, November 1939, 63.

5 *Economy Recipes for Canada's "Housoldiers"* (Montreal and Toronto: Canada Starch, 1943); *Chatelaine*, November 1942, 71. See also "The Call to 'Kitchen Commandos,'" *Toronto Star*, 11 January 1943.

6 Lara Campbell, *Respectable Citizens: Gender, Family, and Unemployment in Ontario's Great Depression* (Toronto: University of Toronto Press, 2009), 28.

7 See, for instance, Katherine Arnup, *Education for Motherhood: Advice for Mothers in Twentieth-Century Canada* (Toronto: University of Toronto Press, 1994); and Cynthia Comacchio, *The Infinite Bonds of Family: Domesticity in Canada, 1850-1940* (Toronto: University of Toronto Press, 1999).

8 For recent works, see Denyse Baillargeon, *Making Do: Women, Family, and Home in Montreal During the Great Depression*, trans. Yvonne Klein (Waterloo: Wilfrid Laurier University Press, 1999); Lara Campbell, *Respectable Citizens*; and Katrina Srigley, *Breadwinning Daughters: Young Working Women in a Depression-Era City, 1929-1939* (Toronto: University of Toronto Press, 2010).

9 Joy Parr, *Domestic Goods: The Material, the Moral, and the Economic in the Postwar Years* (Toronto: University of Toronto Press, 1999); Jeffrey Keshen, *Saints, Sinners, and Soldiers: Canada's Second World War* (Vancouver: UBC Press, 2004); Graham Broad, "Shopping for Victory," *The Beaver* 85, 2 (April-May 2005): 40-45. On women's domestic labour in the kitchen in the pre- and post-war periods, see Dianne Dodd, "Women and Domestic Technology: Household Drudgery, 'Democratized Consumption,' and Patriarchy," in *Framing Our Past: Canadian Women's History in the Twentieth Century*, ed. Sharon Anne Cook, Lorna R. McLean, and Kate O'Rourke (Montreal and Kingston: McGill-Queen's University Press, 2001), 101-10; Margaret Hobbs and Ruth Roach Pierson, "A Kitchen That Wastes No Steps: Gender, Class, and the Home Improvement Plan, 1936-1940," *Histoire Sociale/Social History* 21 (May 1988): 9-38; Meg Luxton, Harriet Rosenberg, and Sedef Arat-Koe, eds., *Through the Kitchen Window: The Politics of Home and Family* (Toronto: Garamond Press, 1990); Meg Luxton, *More Than a Labour of Love: Three Generations of Women's Work in the Home* (Toronto: The Women's Press, 1980); Cynthia Commacchio, *The Infinite Bonds of Family: Domesticity in Canada, 1850-1940* (Toronto: University of Toronto Press, 1999); and Veronica Strong-Boag, *The New Day Recalled: Lives of Girls and Women in English Canada, 1919-1939* (Toronto: Penguin Books, 1988).

10 On the imagery of food and wartime social stability, in particular, see Amy Bentley, *Eating for Victory: Food Rationing and the Politics of Domesticity* (Urbana and Chicago: University of Illinois Press, 1998).

11 As Melissa Debakis and others have argued, images of women workers were themselves fraught with the same contradictions, often being both "complicitous with and resistant to dominant wartime constructions of femininity." Dabakis, "Gendered Labor: Norman Rockwell's Rosie the Riveter and the Discourses of Wartime Womanhood," in *Gender and American History since 1890*, ed. Barbara Melosh (London: Routledge, 1993), 201. See also Helen Smith and Pamela Wakewich, "'Beauty and the Helldivers': Representing Women's Work and Identities in a Warplant Newspaper," *Labour/Le Travail* 44 (Fall 1999): 71-107; as well as discussions in Ruth Roach Pierson, *"They're Still Women After All": The Second World War and Canadian Womanhood* (Toronto: McClelland and Stewart, 1986); and Sonya

O. Rose, *Which People's War: National Identity and Citizenship in Britain, 1939-1945* (New York: Oxford University Press, 2003).

12 LAC, Department of Agriculture, RG 17, Vol. 3698, File W-5-4-29, Press Release: Wartime Garden Survey, 28 April 1944. On the origins of the name and practice of victory gardening, see, Bentley, *Eating For Victory*, 114-18.

13 Edwinna von Baeyer, "The Home Gardener of the 1880s," in *Consuming Passions: Papers Presented at the 101st Annual Conference of the Ontario Historical Society* (Willowdale: 1990), 208. See also Bentley, *Eating for Victory*; and Char Miller, "In the Sweat of Our Brow: Citizenship in American Domestic Practice during WWII – Victory Gardens," *Journal of American Culture* 26, 3 (2003): 395-409.

14 LAC, RG 17, Vol. 3706, File 250, William Bowie, Executive Director of the Community Garden League of Greater Montreal, to the Department of Agriculture, 8 January 1943; LAC, RG 17, Vol. 3374, File 1500, Elizabeth Constance Mackenzie to H. Barton, Deputy Minister of Agriculture, 2 November 1942; Lorraine Johnson, "Revisiting Victory: Gardens Past, Gardens Future," in *The Edible City: Toronto's Food from Farm to Fork* (Toronto: Coach House Press, 2009), 58-65; Elizabeth Bailey Price, "What Women Are Thinking: The Women's Institute," *Chatelaine,* September 1941, 65-67.

15 *Chatelaine,* September 1944, 24.

16 LAC, RG 17, Vol. 3709, File W-5-45, Agricultural Supplies Board and Economics Division of the Department of Agriculture, Report on Production of Vegetables in Wartime Gardens, March 1944.

17 LAC, RG 17, Vol. 3709, File W-5-45, Report on Victory Gardens, 15 September 1943.

18 A notable exception is Lara Campbell in *Respectable Citizens,* 30-31. On working-class gardening (although not relief gardening) during the Depression, see Joy Parr, *The Gender of Breadwinners: Women, Men, and Change in Two Industrial Towns, 1880-1950* (Toronto: University of Toronto Press, 1990), 191.

19 LAC, RG 17, Vol. 3709, File W-5-45, Report on Victory Gardens, 15 September 1943.

20 "A Victory Garden," *Canadian Red Cross Junior,* December 1942, 9.

21 Canadian Red Cross Society (CRCS), *Annual Report for the Year 1943* (Toronto: 1944).

22 On shifting perceptions of masculine domesticity during the middle decades of the twentieth century, see, for instance, Christopher Dummitt, "Finding a Place for Father: Selling the Barbecue in Postwar Canada," *Journal of the Canadian Historical Association* 9 (1998): 209-23; Craig Heron, "Boys Will Be Boys: Working-Class Masculinities in the Age of Mass Production," *International Labor and Working-Class History* 69, 1 (2006): 6-34; Robert Rutherdale, "Fatherhood, Masculinity, and the Good Life during Canada's Baby Boom, 1945-1965," *Journal of Family History* 24, 3 (1999): 351-71; and Rutherdale, "Fatherhood and Masculine Domesticity during the Baby Boom: Consumption and Leisure in Advertising and Life Stories," in *Family Matters: Papers in Post-Confederation Canadian Family History,* ed. Lori Chambers and Ed Montigny (Toronto: Canadian Scholars' Press, 1998), 309-33.

23 Philip Ragan, *He Plants for Victory* (Ottawa: NFB, 1943), animated short, 89s, http://www.nfb.ca/film/he_plants_for_victory.

24 See, for instance, Nova Scotia Department of Agriculture, *Gardening for Vim and Vitamins* (Halifax: 1943).

25 *Chatelaine,* June 1945, 75. As both Campbell and Parr suggest, the popular imagery of victory gardening was often contradicted by the reality in working-class gardens, in particular,

where men and women had long worked side by side. Lara Campbell, *Respectable Citizens*, 31; Parr, *The Gender of Breadwinners*, 191.

26 WPTB and Agricultural Supplies Board, *Home Vegetable Gardening and Home Canning of Vegetables in Wartime* (Ottawa: King's Printer, 1942). See also LAC, RG 17, Vol. 3706, File 249, Memorandum for the Special Committee on Community Gardens and Home Canning, 1 February 1943.

27 LAC, RG 17, Vol. 3374, File 1500, E. Barton, Deputy Minister of Agriculture, to Mildred Low, 14 April 1943.

28 LAC, RG 17, Vol. 3698, File W-5-4-29, Memorandum from Ernest MacGinnis, Secretary, Agricultural Committee, BC Department of Agriculture, 25 March 1944.

29 *Cariboo Observer*, 12 June 1943, 3; 27 March 1943, 4.

30 LAC, RG 44, Vol. 8, File "Salvage – Complaints," J.T. Thorson to R.B. Hanson, 14 April 1942, cited in Keshen, *Saints, Sinners, and Soldiers*, 38.

31 "No Longer Fear of Fat Famine in Dominion," *Globe and Mail*, 31 October 1944; G.E. Britnell and V.C. Fowke, *Canadian Agriculture in War and Peace, 1935-1950* (Palo Alto, CA: Stanford University Press, 1962), 341-46.

32 "Behind the Lines," *Hamilton Spectator*, 1 March 1944.

33 "Dominion Government Launches New Drive," *Cariboo Observer*, 5 December 1942, 1.

34 LAC, Department of National War Services, RG 44, Vol. 10, History of the Voluntary and Auxiliary Services Division, Appendix 6: Reports of Citizens' Committee and Co-ordinating Councils.

35 See "The Call to 'Kitchen Commandos,'" *Toronto Star*, 11 January 1943; and "The Housewife and the U Boat," *Toronto Star*, 3 December 1943.

36 J.W. Van Loon, "Children Invest over $200,000 in War Savings Stamps and Aid in Extensive Salvage Campaign," *Hamilton Spectator*, 24 December 1943.

37 "More Fats Now Being Collected," *Globe and Mail*, 30 March 1943.

38 Britnell and Fowke, *Canadian Agriculture*, 341-46; LAC, RG 64, Vol. 26, File 276, Wartime Prices and Trade Board, History of Meat and Meat Products Administration; "More Fats Now Being Collected," *Globe and Mail*, 30 March 1943; See also LAC, RG 44, Vol. 11, History of the Voluntary and Auxiliary Services Division.

39 LAC, RG 44, Vol. 11, History of the Voluntary and Auxiliary Services Division.

40 Keshen, *Saints, Sinners, and Soldiers*, 146.

41 For a good background to charitable fundraising in the twentieth century, see Shirley Tillotson, *Contributing Citizens: Modern Charitable Fundraising and the Making of the Welfare State* (Vancouver: UBC Press, 2008). And for an excellent case study of the Red Cross, see Sarah Glassford, "Marching as to War: The Canadian Red Cross Society, 1885-1939" (PhD diss., York University, 2007). Also see Sarah Glassford's essay for the website *WartimeCanada.ca*, "Volunteering in the First and Second World War," http://wartimecanada.ca/essay/volunteering/volunteering-first-and-second-world-war.

42 "Packing a Box for a Soldier? This Is What They'd Like to Get," *Chatelaine*, January 1941, 45; Irene Todd, "More about Women and the War: The Parcels They Mail," *Chatelaine*, July 1941, 13.

43 Janine Roelens-Grant, ed., *Fighting for Home and Country: Women Remember World War II* (Guelph: Federated Women's Institutes of Ontario, 2004), 90.

44 Blanch J. Pownall, "Box for Overseas," *Chatelaine*, November 1941, 16.

45 Catherine C. Cole, "'Every Kitchen Is an Arsenal': Women's War on the Home Front in Northern Alberta," in K.W. Tingley, *For King and Country: Alberta in the Second World*

War (Edmonton: Provincial Museum of Alberta, 1995), 255-68; LAC, RG 44, Vol. 11, History of the Voluntary and Auxiliary Services Division. See Jenni Mortin, *A Prairie Town Goes to War* (Shelbourne: George A. Vanderburgh, 2003), for a case study of Dilke, Saskatchewan's, local Comforts Committee's efforts to provide food and other comforts to soldiers overseas.

46 See the Canadian Red Cross Society [hereafter CRCS], Annual Reports, 1942 to 1945; and CRCS, *Prisoners: Wounded, Missing, Sick (December 1942),* in LAC, RG 17, Vol. 3419, File 1500-43-2.

47 Donna Alexander Zwicker, "Volunteer War Service in Alberta, 1939-1945," in Tingley, *For King and Country*, 271.

48 Government of Nova Scotia, *Nova Scotia Helps the Fighting Man* (Halifax: 1943), in CRCS Archives, Box 16, File 2.

49 LAC, RG 44, Vol. 10, History of the Voluntary and Auxiliary Services Division, Appendix 6: Reports of Citizens' Committee and Co-ordinating Councils; CRCS, *Annual Report for 1942* (Toronto: 1943).

50 The end of Earl Birney's 1949 novel *Turvey* includes a wonderful scene where, as a ship filled with returning soldiers docks in Halifax, the sight of bananas being brought out for the returning troops by a fruit wholesaler brings "renewed bellowing from the ship's rail and a general rushing and pushing to get as near the almost forgotten fruit as possible." Birney, *Turvey* (Toronto: McClelland and Stewart, 1963[1949]), 276.

51 Government of Nova Scotia, *Nova Scotia Helps the Fighting Man*; LAC, RG 44, Vol. 10, History of the Voluntary and Auxiliary Services Division, Appendix 6.

52 Linda Granfield, *Brass Buttons and Silver Horseshoes: Stories from Canada's British War Brides* (Toronto: McClelland and Stewart, 2002), 48.

53 See Chapter 3 of Bentley, *Eating for Victory*, 59-84.

54 See, for instance, Radford Crawley, *Call for Volunteers* (Ottawa: NFB, 1941), documentary short, 9m 29s, http://www.nfb.ca/film/call_for_volunteers; Katherine Caldwell Bayley, "The Cooking Class Serves a Dinner Like Mother Used to Make in Honour of Soldier Guests"; and Mona Parr, "Best Food Foremost When Guests Are from the Army" *Canadian Home Journal,* July 1942, 34, 37.

55 Benedict Anderson, *Imagined Communities: Reflections on the Origin and Spread of Nationalism,* rev. ed. (London: Verso, 2006), 7.

56 Crawley, *Call for Volunteers.*

57 This number does not even include the large number of hostels and leave centres, almost all of which included their own food and recreation services. See LAC, RG 44, Vol. 11, History of the Voluntary and Auxiliary Services Division.

58 Ibid.

59 Government of Nova Scotia, *Nova Scotia Helps the Fighting Man*; LAC, RG 44, Vol. 11, History of the Voluntary and Auxiliary Services Division.

60 LAC, RG 44, Vol. 28, File "Rationed Food in Urban Canteens."

61 Government of Nova Scotia, *Nova Scotia Helps the Fighting Man*. See also *Active Service Canteen Toronto, 1939-1945* (Toronto: 1945), in LAC, RG 44, Vol. 11, History of the Voluntary and Auxiliary Services Division.

62 *Active Service Canteen Toronto, 1939-1945* (Toronto, 1945); LAC, RG 44, Vol. 10, History of the Voluntary and Auxiliary Services Division, Appendix 6.

63 From the Women's Voluntary Service Newspaper, *Volunteer Voice*, December 1943.

64 LAC, RG 44, Vol. 10, History of the Voluntary and Auxiliary Services Division, Appendix 6.

65 See Pierson, *"They're Still Women after All,"* 32-33; Keshen, *Saints, Sinners and Soldiers,* 203.

66 Tarah Brookfield, "Protection, Peace, Relief, and Rescue: Canadian Women's Cold War Activism at Home and Abroad, 1945-1975" (PhD diss., York University, 2008); Susan Armstrong-Reid and David Murray, *Armies of Peace: Canada and the UNRRA Years* (Toronto: University of Toronto Press, 2008).

67 LAC, RG 44, Vol. 11, History of the Voluntary and Auxiliary Services Division.

68 As Shirley Tillotson's work on the history of modern charitable fundraising in Canada shows, many Community Chests and other social service charitable fundraising organizations actually found themselves exceeding pre-war donations and their own fundraising targets. See Tillotson, *Contributing Citizens,* 153-54.

69 LAC, RG 44, Vol. 11, History of the Voluntary and Auxiliary Services Division.

70 LAC, RG 44, Vol. 10, History of the Voluntary and Auxiliary Services Division, Appendix 6.

71 Linda Ambrose, *For Home and Country: The Centennial History of the Women's Institutes in Ontario* (Toronto: Federated Women's Institutes of Ontario, 1996); Roelens-Grant, *Fighting for Home and Country,* 147.

72 CRCS, *Annual Report for 1945* (Toronto: 1946).

73 For an excellent account of the early work of the Red Cross, see Glassford, "Marching as to War."

74 CRCS, *Annual Report for 1941* (Toronto: 1942); and McKenzie Porter, *To All Men: The Story of the Canadian Red Cross* (Toronto: McClelland and Stewart, 1960), 75.

75 Porter, *To All Men,* 73.

76 CRCS, *Annual Report for 1942* (Toronto: 1943).

77 CRCS, *Annual Report for 1945* (Toronto: 1946).

78 See the 1943 and 1945 Red Cross Annual Reports.

79 Roelens-Grant, *Fighting for Home and Country,* 147.

80 Ibid., 149.

81 F.F. Tisdall, "Further Report on Canadian Red Cross Food Parcels for British Prisoners-of-War," *Canadian Medical Association Journal* 50 (February 1944): 135-38. Pilot biscuits, for those unfamiliar, were a form of hardtack: a very hard, long-lasting cracker. They were most commonly used as sailors' rations and were a staple of Newfoundland cuisine.

82 P.H. Gordon, *Fifty Years in the Canadian Red Cross* (Regina: Canadian Red Cross, 1967), 72.

83 Tisdall, "Food Parcels for British Prisoners-of-War"; LAC, RG 44, Vol. 10, History of the Voluntary and Auxiliary Services Division, Appendix 6.

84 CRCS, *Annual Report for 1945* (Toronto: 1946); Tisdall, "Food Parcels for British Prisoners-of-War"; CRCS, *Prisoners: Wounded, Missing, Sick.*

85 Tisdall, "Food Parcels for British Prisoners-of-War." For press coverage, see, for example, Lotta Dempsey, "Food for Our Prisoners of War," *Chatelaine,* February 1942, 8-9. Mary Etta MacPherson, "As the Editor Sees It," *Chatelaine,* March 1944, 72.

86 "Food Is the Main Interest of Prisoners of War," *Saturday Night,* 10 February 1945, 13.

87 LAC, RG 44, Vol. 11, History of the Voluntary and Auxiliary Services Division.

88 Ibid.

89 Jennifer Stephen, *Pick One Intelligent Girl: Employability, Domesticity, and the Gendering of Canada's Welfare State, 1939-1947* (Toronto: University of Toronto Press, 2007); and, *"They're Still Women after All."*

90 Byrne Hope Sanders, "As an Editor Sees It," *Chatelaine,* August 1941, 1.

91 LAC, Department of Health and Welfare, RG 29, Vol. 936, File 386-6-9, Mrs. Marion Spencer to Nutrition Services, 7 March 1942.

92 LAC, RG 29, Vol. 935, File 386-6-5, Mrs. William D. Tucker to the Minister of Health, 8 January 1942.
93 LAC, National Council of Women Fonds, MG 28, I25, Vol. 82, File 12, 6823, SP Day, Secretary, Report on the Community Nutrition Council of Kingston, 1942.
94 LAC, RG 29, Vol. 930, File 386-3-10, Quebec Federation of Home and School Associations Research Committee, Report on School Lunches.
95 LAC, MG 28, I25, Vol. 80, File 13, Report on the "Food for Health – Health for Victory" Nutrition Campaign, January and February 1942.
96 LAC, RG 29, Vol. 961, File 387-9-1, M.J. Vann, "Methods of Nutrition Education for Adults and Their Effectiveness – Manitoba's Experience," June 1945.
97 LAC, Department of National War Services, RG 35, Vol. 18, Wartime History of Women's Voluntary Services Division.
98 Katharine Bentley Beauman, *Green Sleeves: The Story of WVS/WRVS* (London: Seeley Service, 1977).
99 LAC, RG 35, 18, Wartime History of Women's Voluntary Services Division.
100 LAC, RG 17, Vol. 3709, File W-5-45, Report on Victory Gardens, 15 September 1943.
101 LAC, RG 64, Vol. 60, A Brief Summary of the Origin and Development of the Consumer Branch WPTB.
102 LAC, RG 44, Vol. 10, History of the Voluntary and Auxiliary Services Division, Appendix 6.
103 LAC, RG 64-A-4, Series 1240, Vol. 1447, File A10-29-8, Byrne Sanders Memorandum, 23 June 1942.
104 Carolyn Gossage, *Greatcoats and Glamour Boots: Canadian Women at War, 1939-1945,* rev. ed. (Toronto: Dundurn Press, 2001), 16.
105 LAC, MG 28, I25, Vol. 85, File 10, *Volunteer Voice,* December 1943.
106 Priscilla Galloway, ed., *Too Young to Fight: Memories from Our Youth during World War II* (Toronto: Stoddart Publishing, 1999), 178.
107 Parr, *Domestic Goods,* 85.

Chapter 4: Tealess Teas, Meatless Days, and Recipes for Victory

1 "Butter Substitutes," *Globe and Mail,* 15 January 1943, 9.
2 This estimate is based on an analysis of Elizabeth Driver's excellent and exhaustive *Culinary Landmarks: A Bibliography of Canadian Cookbooks, 1825-1949* (Toronto: University of Toronto Press, 2008).
3 See, for instance, Arlene Voski Avakian, ed., *From Betty Crocker to Feminist Food Studies: Critical Perspectives on Women and Food* (Amherst: University of Massachusetts Press, 2005); Sherrie A. Inness, *Secret Ingredients: Race, Gender, and Class at the Dinner Table* (New York: Palgrave, 2006); Jessamyn Neuhaus, *Manly Meals and Mom's Home Cooking: Cookbooks and Gender in Modern America* (Baltimore: Johns Hopkins University Press, 2003); and Janet Theophano, *Eat My Words: Reading Women's Lives through the Cookbooks They Wrote* (New York: Palgrave, 2002). In the Canadian context, see Franca Iacovetta and Valerie J. Korinek, "Jell-O Salads, One-Stop Shopping, and Maria the Homemaker: The Gender Politics of Food" (190-230) and Marlene Epp, "The Semiotics of Zwieback: Feast and Famine in the Narratives of Mennonite Refugee Women" (314-40), both in *Sisters or Strangers? Immigrant, Ethnic, and Racialized Women in Canadian History,* ed. Marlene Epp,

Franca Iacovetta, and Frances Swyripa (Toronto: University of Toronto Press, 2004); and see also Franca Iacovetta, Marlene Epp, and Valerie Korinek, eds., *Edible Histories, Cultural Politics: Towards a Canadian Food History* (Toronto: University of Toronto Press, 2012).

4 See the Department of Agriculture's *Foods for Home Defence* (Ottawa: King's Printer, 1942) and *Wartime Sugar Savers* (Ottawa: King's Printer, 1943).

5 See "Brief Reports from Ottawa Agencies of Activities and Material for Consumers," in *Proceedings of the Nutrition Conference, Called by the Division of Nutrition, Dept. of National Health and Welfare* (Ottawa: June 1945), 49-52. See also "Nutrition Experts Prepare Helpful Wartime Recipes," *Calgary Herald*, 18 September 1942, 7; and "Desserts avec moins de sucre," *Le Devoir*, 12 November 1943, 5.

6 *Canadian Home Journal*, December 1939 and August 1940.

7 Mona Parr, "For Fun, Festivity, and Food – Apples," *Canadian Home Journal*, December 1939, 38; Catherine Bayley, "It's Patriotic and Pleasant to Eat Canadian Lobster," *Canadian Home Journal*, July 1940, 28-29.

8 H.G. Campbell, "A Patriotic Christmas Dinner," *Chatelaine*, December 1940, 58-62.

9 "Aliments pour le temps de guerre," in *Le Devoir*, 9 September 1941, 5, and 16 September 1941, 5; "Notre table aux temps des fêtes: Un Noël patriotique," *Le Devoir*, 18 December 1941, 5; "Notre table aux temps des fêtes," *Le Devoir*, 19 December 1941, 5; "Menu de Noël," *Le Devoir*, 22 December 1941, 5.

10 Robert Rutherdale, *Hometown Horizons: Local Responses to Canada's Great War* (Vancouver: UBC Press, 2005); Desmond Morton, *Fight or Pay: Soldiers' Families in the Great War* (Vancouver: UBC Press, 2004).

11 *Maclean's*, 15 June 1941, 3.

12 CBC Digital Archives, "Food Facts and Fashions," radio program, originally aired 12 June 1942, http://www.cbc.ca/archives/categories/war-conflict/second-world-war/on-every-front-canadian-women-in-the-second-world-war/homemaking-during-wartime.html. These changes were ostensibly made to streamline the production of cans and canned foods with the goal of reducing waste and freeing up productive capacity for the war effort.

13 LAC, RG 64, Vol. 1194, File 19-6-1, "WPTB Order 532: Meatless Days in Public Eating Places," 13 July 1945; LAC, RG 64, Vol. 26, File 276, History of Meat and Meat Products Administration.

14 Complaints were regularly voiced at WRAC meetings, and this did much to spur the rule change. See LAC, RG 64-A-4, Vol. 1445, File A10-29-2, Montreal WRAC Meeting Minutes, 19 October 1943; LAC, RG 64, Vol. 1447, File A-10-29-8, Memorandum on Use of Rationed Commodities outside the Home, 11 September 1943; LAC, RG 64, Vol. 22, File 252, WPTB Information Branch Weekly News Digest, 25-30 October 1943.

15 Media Arts Department, Sheridan College of Applied Arts and Technology, *The Home Front: An Oral History of World War Two* (Oakville: 1970), 43.

16 Ann Adam, "Today's Food," *Globe and Mail*, 2 January 1943.

17 "1943 Cookbook Edition," *Daily Standard-Freeholder*, 29 May 1943; *Edith Adams Wartime 9th Annual Cook Book* (Vancouver: Vancouver Sun, 1943); Helen Campbell, "Tealess Teas," *Chatelaine*, February 1943, 46.

18 *Globe and Mail*, 12 May 1943, 8; *Vancouver Sun*, 23 February 1943, 6.

19 See *Chatelaine*, October 1939, 76, and November 1942, 25.

20 Mona Parr, "You'll Be Feeding Your Family for Fitness Following Canada's Official Food Rules," *Canadian Home Journal*, January 1943, 28; Ann Adam, "Today's Food," *Globe and Mail*, 6 January 1943 and 20 January 1943.

21 See *Ottawa Citizen*, 18 February 1942, 19; and Driver, *Culinary Landmarks*, 860-61.

22 Amy Bentley, *Eating for Victory: Food Rationing and the Politics of Domesticity* (Chicago and Urbana: University of Illinois Press, 1998), 9-29.

23 *Eat Right to Work and Win* (Toronto: Swift Canadian, 1942; Chicago: Swift, 1942).

24 "1943 Cookbook Edition," *Daily Standard-Freeholder*, 29 May 1943, 1.

25 "They're Talking About," *Chatelaine*, March 1944; Priscilla Galloway, ed., *Too Young to Fight: Memories from Our Youth during World War II* (Toronto: Stoddart Publishing, 1999), 20; Mary Peate, *Girl in a Sloppy Joe Sweater: Life on the Canadian Home Front during World War Two* (Montreal: Optimum Publishing International, 1988), 97-98; *Food in Canada* 2, 9 (September 1942). On the history of saccharine, see Carolyn Thomas de la Peña, *Empty Pleasures: The Story of Artificial Sweeteners from Saccharin to Splenda* (Chapel Hill: University of North Carolina Press, 2010).

26 LAC, RG 64, Vol. 84, File 84, Meat Rationing Handbook for Retail Meat Dealers (Ottawa: WPTB, 1943); RG 64, Vol. 1192, File 19-6, Conference of Agricultural Press and Representatives of Department of Agriculture and WPTB, 17 April 1943.

27 LAC, RG 64-A-4, Vol. 1446, File A10-29-6, Christine White to Byrne Sanders, 5 May 1943.

28 By the end of 1943, those wishing to purchase evaporated milk were actually required to present a medical prescription or a doctor's formula to their local ration board. See Tasnim Nathoo and Aleck Ostry, *The One Best Way? Breastfeeding History, Politics, and Policy in Canada* (Waterloo: Wilfrid Laurier University Press, 2009), 97-98.

29 "This Week's Best War-Time Recipes," *Windsor Daily Star*, 14 March 1942, 9.

30 "Butter Substitutes," *Globe and Mail*, 15 January 1943, 9; Vancouver Sun, *Edith Adams Wartime 9th Annual Cook Book*.

31 Driver, *Culinary Landmarks*, 62, 830-31, 859.

32 *Cook to Win* (Calgary: Wesley United Church, 1943).

33 *Victory Cookbook* (Regina: Friendship Circle, Knox United Church, ca. 1945); *East York Schools Win the War Cook Book* (Toronto: Toronto Star, ca. 1939-45); *Willing War Workers Cook Book* (St. Stephen, NB: St. Croix Printing and Publishing, 1942).

34 *Canadian Favourites: CCF Cookbook* (Ottawa: 1944).

35 Canadian War Museum, Military History Research Center, FCWM Oral History Project, interview with Private William Patrick, 18 October 2000.

36 W.B. MacKinnon, "Are You Fit to Win a War?" *Maclean's*, January 1943, 14, 33-34; "Responsibilities of Dieticians in the RCAF," *Canadian Hotel Review*, July 1943, 14.

37 LAC, RG 17, Vol. 3434, File 1724, Anna M. Speers, *A Report on Nutrition and the Production and Distribution of Food* (Ottawa: May 1945); WIB, *Canadian Food and Agriculture in the War* (Ottawa: 25 May 1944); Nutrition Division, *Canadian Food and Nutrition Statistics, 1935 to 1956* (Ottawa: Queen's Printer, 1959), 26-29; G.E. Britnell and V.C. Fowke, *Canadian Agriculture in War and Peace, 1935-1950* (Palo Alto, CA: Stanford University Press, 1962), 150-51.

38 Statistics Canada, "Section E: Wages and Working Conditions," *Historical Statistics of Canada*, last modified 22 October 2008, http://www.statcan.gc.ca/pub/11-516-x/sectione/4147438-eng.htm#2. See also Peter S. McInnis, *Harnessing Labour Confrontation: Shaping the Postwar Settlement in Canada, 1943-1950* (Toronto: University of Toronto Press, 2002), 19-46; and Jeffrey Keshen, *Saints, Sinners, and Soldiers: Canada's Second World War* (Vancouver: UBC Press, 2004), 41-70.

39 "Restaurants Are Big Business Now," *Canadian Hotel Review*, October 1948, 24-25, 34-36, 94; Statistics Canada, "Section V: Internal Trade," *Historical Statistics of Canada*, last modified 22 October 2008, http://www.statcan.gc.ca/pub/11-516-x/sectionv/4057758-eng.htm#1.

40 LAC, RG 64, Vol. 26, File 276, History of Meat and Meat Products Administration; Britnell and Fowke, *Canadian Agriculture*, 250.

41 Nutrition Division, *Canadian Food and Nutrition Statistics*, 8.

42 The importance of these foods was widely confirmed by the Canadian Council on Nutrition (CCN) and the Dominion Bureau of Statistics (DBS) consumption studies conducted during this period. For the best breakdown of the relative importance of these items as a percentage of the typical family budget, see DBS, *Family Income and Expenditure in Canada, 1937-38: A Study of Urban Wage-Earner Families, including Data on Physical Attributes* (Ottawa: King's Printer, 1941), 44-70. See also Speers, *A Report on Nutrition*. On the margarine ban, see W.H. Heick, *A Propensity to Protect: Butter, Margarine, and the Rise of Urban Culture in Canada* (Waterloo: Wilfrid Laurier University Press, 1991).

43 For a background, see Alan Beardsworth and Theresa Keil, *Sociology on the Menu: An Invitation to the Study of Food and Society* (London: Routledge, 1996); Roland Barthes, "Toward a Pychosociology of Contemporary Food Consumption," in *Food and Culture: A Reader*, ed. Carole Counihan and Penny Van Esterik (New York: Routledge, 1997), 20-27; Mary Douglas, "Deciphering a Meal," in *Food and Culture*, ed. Counihan and Van Esterik, 36-54; Mary Douglas and Jonathan Gross, "Food and Culture: Measuring the Intricacy of Rules Systems," *Social Science Information* 20, 1 (1981): 1-35; Pierre Bourdieu, *Distinction: A Social Critique of the Judgement of Taste*, trans. Richard Nice (Cambridge: Harvard University Press, 1984); Marshall Sahlins, *Culture and Practical Reason* (Chicago: University of Chicago Press, 1976); and Roland Barthes, *Mythologies*, trans. Annette Lavers (New York: Hill and Wang, 1972).

44 For excellent accounts of the central place of meat and sugar in the modern North American and European diet, see Ellen Ross, *Love and Toil: Motherhood in Outcast London, 1870-1918* (Oxford: Oxford University Press, 1993); Sidney W. Mintz, *Sweetness and Power: The Place of Sugar in Modern History* (New York: Penguin, 1986); Chapter 4 in Bentley, *Eating for Victory*; and Beardsworth and Keil, *Sociology on the Menu*.

45 Nutrition Division, *Canadian Food and Nutrition Statistics*, 9, 26-29.

46 See DBS, *Family Income and Expenditure*, 61-62; and W.C. Hopper, "Income and Food Consumption," *Canadian Journal of Economics and Political Science* 9, 4 (November 1943): 487-506.

47 Hopper, "Income and Food Consumption"; Speers, *Report on Nutrition;* LAC, RG 64, Vol. 26, File 276, History of Meat and Meat Products Administration.

48 LAC, RG 64, Vol. 26, File 276, History of Meat and Meat Products Administration.

49 LAC, RG 64, Vol. 22, File 252, WPTB Information Branch: Weekly News Digest, 7 June to 12 July 1943.

50 Canadian Welfare Council, *Managing in the Home on Small Income* (Ottawa: 1938), 17-18.

51 H.G. Campbell, "With a Little Meat," *Maclean's*, May 1943, 27-30.

52 K.C. Bayley, "Variety Meats Give the V-Sign for Vitamins, Value, and Availability," *Canadian Home Journal*, March 1943, 34, 38; H.G. Campbell, "Try Kidney," *Chatelaine*, April 1943, 66-67.

53 "1943 Cookbook Edition," *Daily Standard-Freeholder*, 29 May 1943. For similar "war cake" recipes, see also Mrs. Graham's Canada War Cake in "This Week's Best War-Time Recipes," *Windsor Daily Star*, 14 March 1942, 9; and the recipe for war cake in "Two Good Recipes," *Globe and Mail*, 25 January 1941, 11.

54 See, for instance, the recipe for "Canada's War Time Fruit Cake," which appeared in
    St. Josephat's Ladies Auxiliary, *Tested Recipes* (Edmonton: Ukrainian Ladies' Good Will
    Organization, n.d.).
55 "Reader's Recipes," *Vancouver Sun*, 18 March 1930, 15; *Food and the Family Income: Low
    Cost Recipes* (Montreal: Health Service and Federated Agencies of Montreal, 1942); *Canadian
    Favourites: CCF Cookbook*, 2nd ed. (Ottawa: CCF National Council, 1947), 202.
56 For the best account of Depression-era foodways in Canada, see Lara Campbell, *Respectable
    Citizens: Gender, Family, and Unemployment in Ontario's Great Depression* (Toronto: Uni-
    versity of Toronto Press, 2009), 27-34.
57 Barry Broadfoot, *Six War Years, 1939-1945* (Toronto: Doubleday Canada, 1974), 32. Similar
    sentiments can be found in wartime memoirs such as Peate's *Sloppy Joe Sweater* and Donald
    F. Ripley's *The Home Front: Wartime Life in Camp Aldershot and Kentville, Nova Scotia*
    (Hantsport: Lancelot Press, 1991).
58 Ruth Latta, ed., *The Memory of All That: Canadian Women Remember World War II*
    (Burnstown: General Store Publishing, 1992), 44-45.
59 "1943 Cookbook Edition," *Daily Standard-Freeholder*, 29 May 1943.
60 This change is particularly apparent if one compares the kinds of recipes that appear in
    reader-submitted cookbooks like the *Vancouver Sun*'s annual and the Cornwall *Standard
    Freeholder*'s semi-annual "Cookbook Edition" before and after 1942.
61 For some good examples of scholarship focusing on popular, mass-market cookbooks, see
    Rhona Richman Kenneally, "'There Is a Canadian Cuisine, and It Is Unique in All the
    World': Crafting National Food Culture During the Long 1960s," in *What's to Eat? Entrées
    in Canadian Food History*, ed. Nathalie Cooke (Montreal and Kingston: McGill-Queen's
    University Press, 2009), 167-96; Jessamyn Neuhaus, "The Way to a Man's Heart: Gender
    Roles, Domestic Ideology, and Cookbooks in the 1950s," *Journal of Social History* 32, 3
    (1999): 529-55; and Innes, *Secret Ingredients*.
62 Susan J. Leonardi, "Recipes for Reading: Summer Pasta, Lobster a La Riseholme, and Key
    Lime Pie," *PMLA* 104, 3 (1989): 340-47; Lynne Ireland, "The Compiled Cookbook as
    Foodways Autobiography," *Western Folklore* 40, 1 (1981): 107-14; Laura Shapiro, *Something
    from the Oven: Reinventing Dinner in 1950s America* (New York: Viking, 2004); Elizabeth
    Driver, "Regional Differences in the Canadian Meal? Cookbooks Answer the Question,"
    in Cooke, *What's to Eat?*, 197-212.
63 St. Josephat's Ladies' Auxiliary, *Tested Recipes*.
64 See, for instance, Tina Lohman, *Book of Jewish Recipes* (Toronto: The Jewish Standard,
    1942); the 1940 through 1945 versions of the *Hadassah Souvenir Book and Shopper's Guide*
    (see Driver, *Canadian Favourites*, 978-83, for publication information); *Nordwesten –
    Kochbuch* (Winnipeg: 1945); *Ukrainian English Cookbook* (Winnipeg, 1945); Hadassah,
    Lillian Freiman Chapter, *Cook Book* (Moose Jaw: 1943).
65 Donna R. Gabaccia, *We Are What We Eat: Ethnic Foods and the Making of Americans*
    (Cambridge: Harvard University Press, 1998), 182. On the use of cookbooks in transmitting
    knowledge and practices within individual ethnic communities, see also Janet Theophano's
    chapter "Cookbooks as Collective Memory and Identity," in her *Eat My Words*, 49-84.
66 In the American context, see Gabaccia, *We Are What We Eat*, 144-48.
67 *Chatelaine*, December 1944, 28.
68 "Assaisonnements et légumes peuvent prolonger la ration de viande," *Le Devoir*, 26 Nov-
    ember 1943, 5.

69 Janet March, "Figuring the Meat Situation," *Saturday Night,* 31 October 1942, 42.
70 On the wartime transformation of ideas about ethnicity and citizenship, see Ivana Caccia, *Managing the Canadian Mosaic in Wartime: Shaping Citizenship Policy, 1939-1945* (Montreal and Kingston: McGill-Queen's University Press, 2010); and Norman Hillmer, ed., *On Guard for Thee: War, Ethnicity, and the Canadian State, 1939-1945* (Ottawa: Canadian Committee on the History of the Second World War, 1988).
71 See Driver, *Culinary Landmarks,* 1068.
72 Sherrie Inness, *Dinner Roles: American Women and Culinary Culture* (Iowa City: University of Iowa Press, 2001); Inness, *Secret Ingredients;* Theophano, *Eat My Words;* Neuhaus, "Way to a Man's Heart."
73 Vancouver Sun, *Edith Adams 8th Annual Cook Book* (Vancouver: 1942), in *Edith Adams Omnibus,* ed. Elizabeth Driver (Vancouver: Whitecap Books, 2005), 120; *Economy Recipes for Canada's 'Housoldiers'* (Toronto and Montreal: Canada Starch, 1943).
74 Margaret Laurence, "Foreword," in Marie Holmes, *Food from Market to Table: A Complete Guide to Buying and Cooking for Every Day and Special Occasions* (Toronto: Macmillan, 1940), v.
75 Laurence, "Foreword," vi.
76 Laura Shapiro, *Perfection Salad: Women and Cooking at the Turn of the Century* (New York: Modern Library, 2001). See also Sarah Stage and Virginia B. Vincenti, eds., *Rethinking Home Economics: Women and the History of a Profession* (Ithaca: Cornell University Press, 1997); and Harvey Levenstein, *Revolution at the Table: The Transformation of the American Diet* (Berkeley: University of California Press, 1988).
77 United Farmers of Canada (UFC), *Cook Book* (Saskatoon: Women's Section, United Farmers of Canada, Saskatchewan Section, 1940).
78 Ibid.
79 Paul Magee, "Introduction: Foreign Cookbooks," *Postcolonial Studies* 8, 1 (2005): 3-18.
80 Benedict Anderson, *Imagined Communities: Reflections on the Origin and Spread of Nationalism* (London: Verso, 1991).
81 Jeffrey Pilcher, *Que Vivan Los Tamales! Food and the Making of Mexican Identity* (Albuquerque: University of New Mexico Press, 1998), 67.
82 Arjun Appadurai, "How to Make a National Cuisine: Cookbooks in Contemporary India," *Comparative Studies in Society and History* 30, 1 (1988): 7. For an excellent overview of recent literature in this area, see the chapter "Cuisine and Nation Building" in Pilcher, *Food in World History* (New York: Routledge, 2006), 63-70.
83 Rhona Richman Kenneally, "'There Is a Canadian Cuisine, and It Is Unique in All the World': Crafting National Food Culture during the Long 1960s," in *What's to Eat? Entrées in Canadian Food History,* ed. Nathalie Cooke (Montreal and Kingston: McGill-Queen's University Press, 2009), 167-96. On the lack of such a perspective prior to the 1950s, see Driver, "Regional Differences."
84 *Canadian Favourites,* 2nd ed. (1947). Also see Joan Sangster, *Dreams of Equality: Women on the Canadian Left, 1920-1950* (Toronto: McClelland and Stewart, 1989), 205; and Ivan Avakumovic, *Socialism in Canada: A Study of the CCF-NDP in Federal and Provincial Politics* (Toronto: McClelland and Stewart, 1978), 141.
85 Sangster, *Dreams of Equality.* See also Dan Azoulay, "'Ruthless in a Ladylike Way': CCF Women Confront the Postwar 'Communist Menace,'" *Ontario History* 89, 1 (1997): 23-52; and Dean Beeby, "Women in the Ontario CCF, 1940-1950," *Ontario History* 74, 4 (1982): 258-83.

86 *Canadian Favourites: CCF Cookbook* (Ottawa: CCF National Council, 1944), 3-4; LAC, Co-operative Commonwealth Federation and New Democratic Party fonds, MG 28 IV, I, 198, CCF, "Women in Peace as in War Protect Your Home" (Ottawa: 1945).

87 *Canadian Favourites* (1944), vii.

88 Elizabeth Driver, "Kate and Her Cookbook," in *Kate Aitken's Canadian Cookbook* (Vancouver: Whitecap Books, 2004).

89 Ibid.

90 Iacovetta and Korinek, "Jell-O Salads," 201.

91 Women's Voluntary Service (WVS), *Canadian Cook Book for British Brides* (Ottawa: King's Printer, 1945). For an excellent study of food as a means of understanding the experiences of war brides, see Kendra Horosko, "Deliciously Detailed Narratives: The Use of Food in Stories of British War Brides' Experiences" (MA thesis, University of Victoria, Department of History, 2010).

92 Franca Iacovetta, *Gatekeepers: Reshaping Immigrant Lives in Cold War Canada* (Toronto: Between the Lines, 2006), 137.

93 Nutrition Division, *Canadian Food and Nutrition Statistics*, 9.

94 L.B. Kuffert, *A Great Duty: Canadian Responses to Modern Life and Mass Culture, 1939-1967* (Montreal and Kingston: McGill-Queen's University Press, 2003), 68-69.

95 Harvey Levenstein, *Paradox of Plenty: A Social History of Eating in Modern America* (Berkeley: University of California Press, 1993), 101; Steve Penfold, "Selling by the Carload: The Early Years of Fast Food in Canada," in *Creating Postwar Canada: Community, Diversity, and Dissent, 1945-1975*, ed. Robert Rutherdale and Magda Fahrni (Vancouver: UBC Press, 2008); and Ester Reiter, *Making Fast Food: From the Frying Pan into the Fryer* (Montreal and Kingston: McGill-Queen's University Press, 1996).

96 Kenneally, "There Is a Canadian Cuisine," 181.

97 Iacovetta, *Gatekeepers*, 138.

Chapter 5: The Politics of Malnutrition

1 Margaret Gould, *Family Allowances in Canada: Facts versus Fiction* (Toronto: Ryerson Press, 1945), 30. Also see Dorothy Stepler, "Family Allowances for Canada," *Behind the Headlines* 3, 2 (August 1944). For an opposing viewpoint from the period, see Charlotte Whitton, *The Dawn of Ampler Life: Some Aids to Social Security* (Toronto: Macmillan of Canada, 1943), 2; and Whitton "Security for Canadians," *Behind the Headlines* 3, 6 (1943): 6.

2 L.B. Pett, "Food Rules," in *Wartime Recipes and Food Rules* (Edmonton: Woodland Dairy, 1942).

3 On the gendered divisions within the profession, see Chapter 1 as well as Ruby Heap, "From the Science of Housekeeping to the Science of Nutrition: Pioneers in Canadian Nutrition and Dietetics at the University of Toronto's Faculty of Household Science, 1900-1950," in *Challenging Professions: Historical and Contemporary Perspectives on Women's Professional Work*, ed. Elizabeth Smyth et al. (Toronto: University of Toronto Press, 1999), 141-70; and Gale Wills, *A Marriage of Convenience: Business and Social Work in Toronto, 1918-1957* (Toronto: University of Toronto Press, 1995).

4 Alvin Finkel, *Social Policy and Practice in Canada: A History* (Waterloo: Wilfrid Laurier University Press, 2006), 117.

5 Wills, *A Marriage of Convenience*, 81-82.

6 Ibid., 9-10.

7 Leonard Marsh, *Employment Research: An Introduction to the McGill Programme of Research in the Social Sciences* (Toronto: Oxford University Press, 1935), xi. See also Marlene Shore's *The Science of Social Redemption: McGill, the Chicago School, and the Origins of Social Research in Canada* (Toronto: University of Toronto Press, 1987); Allan Irving, "Canadian Fabians: The Work and Thought of Harry Cassidy and Leonard Marsh, 1930-1945," *Canadian Journal of Social Work Education* 7 (1981): 7-28; and Michiel Horn, *The League for Social Reconstruction: Intellectual Origins of the Democratic Left in Canada, 1930-1942* (Toronto: University of Toronto Press, 1980).

8 See James Struthers, *The Limits of Affluence: Welfare in Ontario, 1920-1970* (Toronto: University of Toronto Press, 1994), and Struthers, *No Fault of Their Own: Unemployment and the Canadian Welfare State, 1914-1941* (Toronto: University of Toronto Press, 1983); Margaret Little, *"No Car, No Radio, No Liquor Permit': The Moral Regulation of Single Mothers in Ontario, 1920-1997"* (Toronto: Oxford University Press, 1998); and Finkel, *Social Policy and Practice.*

9 For a background on Canadian unemployment policies in the 1930s, see Struthers, *No Fault of Their Own*; Finkel, *Social Policy and Practice;* and Dennis Guest, *The Emergence of Social Security in Canada*, 3rd ed. (Vancouver: UBC Press, 2003).

10 Harry Cassidy, *Unemployment and Relief in Ontario, 1929-1932: A Survey Report* (Toronto: J. Dent, 1932), 182-84; F.F. Tisdall et al., "Relief Diets," *Bulletin of the Ontario Medical Association* (December 1933): 15-16; Canadian Prepatory Committee, "Report of the Sub-committee on Nutrition, British Commonwealth Scientific Conference," *National Health Review* 4, 15 (Ottawa: October 1936): 59.

11 LAC, Canadian Council on Social Development Fonds, MG 28-I10, Vol. 52, File 463, Marjorie Bell, "Food Allowance for One Week," April 1937.

12 Leonard Marsh, *Health and Unemployment: Some Studies of Their Relationships* (Montreal: Oxford University Press, 1938).

13 E.W. McHenry, "Nutrition in Toronto," *Canadian Public Health Journal (CPHJ)* 30, 1 (1939): 5.

14 Ibid., 9, 11.

15 Toronto Welfare Council (TWC), *The Cost of Living: Study of the Cost of a Standard of Living in Toronto which Should Maintain Health and Self-respect* (Toronto: 1939), 1-2.

16 "Relief Diet Impairs Health Welfare Council Complains," *Toronto Star*, 10 July 1941, 2.

17 McHenry, "Nutrition in Canada," 432.

18 Ibid., 433-34.

19 See the discussion in Chapter 1; see also LAC, National Health and Welfare, RG 29, Vol. 959, File 387-9-1, Frederick F. Tisdall to C.A. Morrell, 1 October 1940, and C.A. Morrell to E.W. McHenry, 21 September 1940.

20 James Vernon, *Hunger: A Modern History* (Cambridge: Harvard University Press, 2007), 134.

21 John Boyd Orr, *Food, Health, and Income: Report on a Survey of Adequacy of Diet in Relation to Income*, 2nd ed. (London: Macmillan, 1937), 10.

22 League of Nations, *New Technical Efforts towards a Better Nutrition* (Geneva: 1938), 32; League of Nations, *Nutrition: Final Report of the Mixed Committee of the League of Nations on the Relation of Nutrition to Health, Agriculture, and Economic Policy* (Geneva: 14 August 1937), 38.

23 A.E. Grauer, *Public Health: A Study Prepared for the Royal Commission on Dominion–Provincial Relations* (Ottawa: King's Printer, 1939), 2. Also see A.E. Grauer, *Public Assistance and Social Insurance: A Study Prepared for the Royal Commission on Dominion–Provincial Relations* (Ottawa: King's Printer, 1939).

24 Struthers, *The Limits of Affluence*, 138. For its use by organized labour, see, for instance, LAC, Trades and Labor Congress of Canada fonds, MG 28-I103, Vol. 340, File 14, The Canadian Brotherhood of Railway Employees and Other Transport Workers, "Wages and the Cost of Living: A Study of a Current Issue," September 1941.

25 Brigitte Kitchen, "The Introduction of Family Allowances in Canada," in *The "Benevolent" State: The Growth of Welfare in Canada,* ed. Allan Moscovitch and Jim Albert (Toronto: Garamond Press, 1987), 234; LAC, RG 29, Vol. 929, File 386-3-9, Mary Baldwin to L.B. Pett, 22 January 1945.

26 For the best overview, see Struthers, *No Fault of Their Own*, 175-207. See also Finkel, *Social Policy and Practice*, 108-17; and Guest, *Social Security in Canada*, 107-8.

27 For a recent account of the postwar leftward turn, see Finkel, *Social Policy and Practice*, 125-44.

28 On the "culture of reconstruction" during the war, see L.B. Kuffert, *A Great Duty: Canadian Responses to Modern Life and Mass Culture, 1939-1967* (Montreal and Kingston: McGill-Queen's University Press, 2003). On the changing discourse of children's rights during this period, see Dominique Marshall, "Reconstruction Politics, the Canadian Welfare State, and the Ambiguity of Children's Rights, 1940-1950," in *Uncertain Horizons: Canadians and Their World in 1945,* ed. Greg Donaghy (Ottawa: Canadian Committee for the History of the Second World War, 1996), 261-83; and Marshall, *The Social Origins of the Welfare State: Quebec Families, Compulsory Education, and Family Allowances, 1940-1955,* trans. Nicola Doone Danby (Waterloo: Wilfrid Laurier University Press, 2006).

29 On the intellectual background to Marsh's McGill work, see Shore, *The Science of Social Redemption.*

30 Leonard Marsh, *Report on Social Security for Canada* (Toronto: University of Toronto Press, 1975 [1943]), 116.

31 Ibid., 33.

32 Marsh, *Health and Unemployment*, 154.

33 Ibid., 30-31.

34 Ibid., 36-37.

35 Ibid., 38.

36 Ibid., 38-41.

37 Harry M. Cassidy, *Social Security and Reconstruction in Canada* (Toronto: Ryerson Press, 1943), 48.

38 See, for instance, Finkel, *Social Policy and Practice*, 135-42; J.L. Granatstein, *Canada's War: The Politics of the Mackenzie King Government, 1939-1945* (Toronto: Oxford University Press, 1975), 249-93; and James Struthers, "Family Allowances, Old Age Security, and the Construction of Entitlement in the Canadian Welfare State, 1943-1951," in *The Veteran's Charter and Post-World War II Canada,* ed. Peter Neary and J.L. Granatstein (Montreal and Kingston: McGill-Queen's University Press, 1998), 179-204.

39 *Labour Gazette* 42 (October 1942): 1114.

40 For recent works, see Marshall, *The Social Origins;* and Raymond B. Blake, *From Rights to Needs: A History of Family Allowances in Canada, 1929-1992* (Vancouver: UBC Press, 2009).

41 Whitton, *The Dawn of Ampler Life,* 2.
42 Whitton, "Security for Canadians," 6.
43 Whitton, *Dawn of Ampler Life,* 119.
44 Gould, *Family Allowances in Canada,* 6.
45 Stepler, "Family Allowances for Canada," 9-10.
46 Ibid., 13.
47 Ibid., 10.
48 Gould, *Family Allowances in Canada,* 13-4, 38.
49 Ibid., 30.
50 For an overview of the Toronto debate over relief allowances, see James Struthers, "How Much Is Enough? Creating a Social Minimum in Ontario, 1930-44," *Canadian Historical Review* 71, 1 (1991): 39-83; and Wills, *A Marriage of Convenience.* Also see City of Toronto Archives (CTA), Fonds 1040, Box 89, File 11, Bessie Touzel, "Memorandum on History of Relief Standards Discussions 1942-3," 23 June 1942.
51 CTA, Fonds 220, Series 100, File 632, Box 46623, Folio 10, Dr. Gordon Park Jackson, Medical Officer of Health, and A.W. Laver, Commissioner of Public Welfare, to R.C. Day, Mayor of Toronto, 24 October 1939.
52 Touzel, "Memorandum."
53 CTA, Fonds 1040, Box 89, File 12, TWC Brief to the Chair, Committee on Public Welfare, 7 July 1941.
54 "Cross Country," *Maclean's* June 1943, 15; "Relief Diet Impairs Health," 2.
55 It is clear that the tensions among McHenry, Tisdall, Willard, and Bell continued into other aspects of their professional relationship, and in 1943, L.B. Pett recommended against having both Tisdall and McHenry on a WPTB Advisory Committee on Nutrition because it "might present some difficulties." LAC, Wartime Prices and Trade Board, RG 64, Vol. Series 1040, Vol. 894, File 1-25-8, Anna Speers to J.G. Taggart, 3 July 1942.
56 LAC, RG 29, Vol. 959, File 387-9-1, Part 11, F.F. Tisdall, "Suggestions for the work of national importance by the Canadian Council on Nutrition," 17 December 1940.
57 J.H. Ebbs, F.F. Tisdall, and W.A. Scott, "The Influence of Prenatal Diet on the Mother and Child," *Journal of Nutrition* 22 (1941): 515-26.
58 Frederick F. Tisdall, Alice C. Willard, and Marjorie Bell, *Report on Study of Relief Food Allowances and Costs* (Toronto: City of Toronto, November 1941).
59 On declining relief rolls, see Struthers, "How Much Is Enough?" 76.
60 For a detailed account of the development of Ontario's relief policies, see Struthers, *The Limits of Affluence.*
61 E.W. McHenry et al., *A Report on Food Allowances for Relief Recipients in the Province of Ontario* (Toronto: Department of Public Welfare, 1945), 2.
62 Ibid., 23.
63 These calculations are based on the 1944 revision of the *Cost of Living,* which effectively updated the Tisdall–Willard–Bell figures to account for wartime inflation. See TWC, *The Cost of Living, Revised 1944: A Study of the Cost of a Standard of Living in Toronto Which Should Maintain Health and Self-respect* (Toronto: 1944).
64 LAC, RG 17, Vol. 3670, File N-9-12A, Agenda Item 5, Canadian Council on Nutrition, 9th Meeting, 8 May 1944.
65 McHenry et al., *A Report on Food Allowances.*
66 E.W. McHenry, "Recent Trends in Nutrition," *Canadian Journal of Public Health* (hereafter *CJPH*) 35 (April 1944): 154.

67 E.W. McHenry et al., "A Nutrition Survey in East York Township: I. Description of Survey and General Statements of Results," *CJPH* 34, 5 (May 1943): 193-204; E.W. McHenry, Helen P. Ferguson, and H. Jean Leeson, "A Nutrition Survey in East York Township: II. The Influence of the Choice of Dietary Standard upon Interpretation of Data," *CJPH* 35, 2 (February 1944): 66-70; E.W. McHenry and Helen Ferguson, "A Nutrition Survey in East York Township: III. Repetition of Dietary Studies after Two Years," *CJPH* 35, 6 (June 1944): 241-45.

68 McHenry, "Recent Trends," 154.

69 "The Construction and Use of Dietary Standards: A Statement Adopted by the Canadian Council on Nutrition, June 8, 1945," *CJPH* 36 (July 1945): 274.

70 LAC, RG 29, Vol. 961, File 387-9-1, Minutes, 7th Meeting, CCN Executive Committee, 7 January 1945; E.W. McHenry, Memorandum re: Assessment of the State of Nutrition – 11 Nov 1944 – to Be Presented to US Food and Nutrition Board; Minutes, 8th Meeting, CCN Executive Committee, 10 March 1945.

71 On Orr and the FAO, see Timothy Boon, "Agreement and Disagreement in the Making of *World of Plenty*," in *Nutrition in Britain: Science, Scientists and Politics in the Twentieth Century*, ed. David F. Smith (London: Routledge, 1997), 166-67; Lizzie Collingham, *The Taste of War: World War Two and the Battle for Food* (Toronto: Allen Lane, 2011), 483-84.

72 L.B. Pett, C.A. Morrell, and F.W. Hanley, "The Development of Dietary Standards," *CJPH* 36 (June 1945): 234.

73 Ibid., 233.

74 Ibid., 235.

75 Ibid., 234.

76 "A Dietary Standard for Canada," *Canadian Bulletin on Nutrition* 3, 2 (August 1953): 1-19.

77 E.W. Crampton, "Canadian Nutritional Problems, with Reference to the Canadian Dietary Standards," *CJPH* 41, 9 (September 1950): 361.

78 The CCN minutes make it clear that the nutritional floor would be used to calculate minimum relief payments while optimum would be used to calculate agricultural production goals. See LAC, RG 29, Vol. 961, File 387-9-1, Part 22, Minutes, 12th CCN Meeting, 5 May 1947; and Anna Spears to CCN Technical Committee, 6-7 May 1947.

79 "A New Dietary Standard for Canada, 1949," *Canadian Nutrition Notes* 5, 9 (September 1949): 65-72.

80 E.W. McHenry, "The Health Officer and Nutrition," *Canadian Nutrition Notes* 3, 12 (December 1947): 1-2.

81 See L.B. Pett, "Are There Nutritional Problems in Canada?" *CMAJ* 59 (October 1948): 326-28; and E. Gordon Young, "An Appraisal of Canadian Nutriture," *Canadian Bulletin on Nutrition* 3, 1 (July 1953): 1-31.

82 Floyd S. Chalmers, "What Britain Eats," *Maclean's*, March 1942, 7, 34; Denys Val Baker, "Communal Feeding In Wartime Britain," *Food in Canada* 3, 1 (January 1943): 11-12; LAC, RG 17, Vol. 3434, File 1724, Marjorie L. Scott, "Appendix H: Special Distribution of Food in Great Britain," in Anna M. Speers, *A Report on Nutrition and the Production and Distribution of Food* (Ottawa: May 1945).

83 LAC, RG 29, Vol. 930, File 386-3-10, Quebec Federation of Home and School Associations Research Committee, Report on School Lunches.

84 Susan Levine, *School Lunch Politics: The Surprising History of America's Favorite Welfare Program* (Princeton: Princeton University Press, 2008).

85 LAC, RG 29, Vol. 930, File 386-3-10, Memorandum, Hot School Lunch in Ontario.

86 Patricia Anne Solberg, *Nutrition Education as Presented in Provincial Programmes of Study: Canadian Education Association* (March 1949); National Committee for School Health Research, *A Health Survey of Canadian Schools, 1945-1946: A Survey of Existing Conditions in the Elementary and Secondary Schools of Canada* (Toronto: March 1947). See also LAC, RG 29, Vol. 930, File 386-3-10, Quebec Federation of Home and School Associations Research Committee, Report on School Lunches, n.d.; and Nutrition Services, *Survey of Feeding Projects in Canadian Schools,* June 1943.

87 LAC, RG 29, Vol. 930, File 386-3-10, CCN Committee on Nutrition in Schools and School Lunch Committee of the Canada and Newfoundland Education Association (CNEA), "A School Lunch Programme For Canada," July 1944.

88 CCN and CNEA, "A School Lunch Programme"; National Film Board, *Family Allowances: A Children's Charter* (Ottawa: 1945); LAC, RG 29, Vol. 930, File 386-3-10, Pett to G.D.W. Cameron, Deputy Minister of National Health, 3 September 1946.

89 Helen Campbell of *Chatelaine* magazine, for her part, advocated for the proposed plan as the "easiest, quickest way to raise the nutrition standard of the country." H.G. Campbell, "Lessons in Lunches," *Chatelaine,* February 1945, 57-58; "Nutrition in the Schools," *Vancouver Sun,* 23 May 1947, 4; National Committee, *A Health Survey of Canadian Schools.*

90 LAC, RG 29, Vol. 930, File 386-3-10, L.B. Pett to R.E. Wodehouse, 1 February 1944 and 18 October 1944.

91 LAC, RG 29, Vol. 930, File 386-3-10, L.B. Pett to Edna Guest, 24 October 1944, and L.B. Pett to Mrs. C.W. Sinclair, 4 November 1944.

92 LAC, RG 29, Vol. 961, File 387-9-1, Brooke Claxton to Major General Chisholm, 6 February 1945.

93 "Message from the Honourable, Mr. Brooke Claxton, Minister of National Health and Welfare," in *Proceedings of the Nutrition Conference, Called by the Division of Nutrition, Dept. of National Health and Welfare, June 6-8, 1945* (Ottawa: 1945), 15.

94 NFB, *Family Allowances* (Ottawa: 1945).

95 Marsh, *Social Security,* 39.

96 TWC, *The Cost of Living, Revised 1944.*

97 See, for instance, Nancy Christie, *Engendering the State: Family, Work, and Welfare in Canada* (Toronto: University of Toronto Press, 2000), 308; Finkel, *Social Policy and Practice,* 136-38; and Struthers, "Entitlement in the Canadian Welfare State."

98 Dominique Jean, "Family Allowances and Family Autonomy: Quebec Families Encounter the Welfare State, 1945-1955," in *Canadian Family History: Selected Readings,* ed. Bettina Bradbury (Toronto: Copp Clark Pittman, 1988), 430.

99 LAC, RG 29, Vol. 961, File 387-9-1, Brooke Claxton to Major General Chisholm, 6 February 1945.

100 LAC, RG 29, Vol. 941, File 387-2-1, W.S. Stanbury to L.B. Pett, 5 July 1949.

101 LAC, RG 29, Vol. 930, File 386-3-10, Dorothy J. Tyers, "School Lunches in Canada," n.d.

102 On the mixed results of the study, see F.F. Tisdall et al., *The Canadian Red Cross Society's School Meal Study, 1947-1949* (Toronto: CRCS, 1952). See also LAC, RG 29, Vol. 930, File 386-3-10, Report of School Lunch Experiments in Kingston and Orillia, 1945-46.

103 L.B. Pett, "Signs of Malnutrition in Canada," *CMAJ* 63, 1 (July 1950): 10.

104 Walter J. Vanast, "'Hastening the Day of Extinction': Canada, Quebec, and the Medical Care of Ungava's Inuit, 1867-1967," *Études Inuit Studies* 15 (1991): 55-84; P.E. Moore et al. "Medical Survey of Nutrition among the Northern Manitoba Indians," *CMAJ* 54 (March 1946); R.P. Vivian et al., "The Nutrition and Health of the James Bay Indian," *CMAJ* 59,

6 (December 1948): 505-18; John J. Honigmann, "The Logic of the James Bay Survey," *Dalhousie Review* 30, 4 (January 1951).

105 LAC, RG 29, Vol. 936, File 386-6-10, Report by P.E. Moore, 26 March 1942.

106 LAC, Department of Indian Affairs and Northern Development, RG 10, 8585, File 1/1-2-17, House of Commons Special Committee, *Minutes of Proceedings and Evidence*, 24 May 1944. As Mary Ellen Kelm has argued, deciding to "study the problem first and then determine the correct course of action" was a "time-honoured Canadian tradition." See Mary-Ellen Kelm, *Colonizing Bodies: Aboriginal Health and Healing in British Columbia, 1900-50* (Vancouver: UBC Press, 1998), 119.

107 P.E. Moore, H.D. Kruse, and F.F. Tisdall, "Nutrition in the North: A Study of the State of Nutrition of the Canadian Bush Indian," *The Beaver* 273 (March 1943): 21-23; LAC, RG 29, Vol. 2986, File 851-6-1, P.E. Moore to R.S.C. Corrigan, 14 September 1943, and "Minutes of Meeting of Indians and Doctors, Norway House, Manitoba," 20 March 1944; LAC, RG 10, 8585, File 1/1-2-17, House of Commons Special Committee, *Minutes of Proceedings and Evidence*, 24 May 1944; J.V.V. Nicholls, "Ophthalmic Status of Cree Indians," *Canadian Medical Association Journal*, 54, 4 (April 1946): 344-48. For a comprehensive account of these studies, see Ian Mosby, "Administering Colonial Science: Nutrition Research and Human Biomedical Experimentation in Aboriginal Communities and Residential Schools, 1942-1952," *Histoire sociale/Social History* 46, 91 (May 2013): 145-72.

108 On the earliest surveys of residential schools, see LAC, RG 29, Vol. 941, File 387-2-1, and 973, File 388-6-1, reports and correspondence of Mrs. Allan (Rosamond) Stevenson, National Director of Nutrition Services for the Canadian Red Cross Society.

109 LAC, RG 29, Vol. 2989, File 851-6-4 part 1, L.B. Pett to G.D.W. Cameron, 18 October 1948.

110 For a detailed discussion, see Mosby, "Administering Colonial Science," 158-64.

Conclusion

1 Greg Connolley, "Housewives Claim Budget Is Absurd: 'Completely Impractical' Menus Prepared by Health-Welfare Dept," *Ottawa Evening Citizen*, 14 January 1948, 1; Kenneth Cragg, "It's Sound: $16.36 only a Guide and It Works," *Globe and Mail*, 21 January 1948, 13.

2 Mrs. A. Villeneuve, Carlington, ON, "Food for a Family of Five," *Ottawa Citizen*, 21 January 1948, 26; Connolley, "Housewives Claim Budget Is Absurd," and "How to Do It: $16.36 Feeds a Family of 5 for a Week" *Globe and Mail*, 16 January 1946, 1.

3 For editorial cartoons, see *Montreal Gazette*, 16 January 1948, 8; and "La regime alimentaire d'Ottawa," *Le Monde Ouvrier*, 31 January 1948, 3, cited in Magda Fahrni, *Household Politics: Montreal Families and Postwar Reconstruction* (Toronto: University of Toronto Press, 2005), 115. On the national reaction, see "Blaming the Thermometer," *Ottawa Evening Citizen*, 24 January 1948, 28; Cragg, "It's Sound"; "15 Cent Meals," *Saskatoon Star-Phoenix*, 24 January 1948, 24; "Though Dr. Pett Gives Data on Meals Housewives Ridicule $16.36 Budget," *Montreal Gazette*, 16 January 1948, 6; "Ridiculous, Say Housewives – 4 Live on $12.08 A Week But It's Pretty Austere," *Edmonton Journal*, 16 January 1948, 1.

4 "How to Do It: $16.36 Feeds a Family of 5 for a Week" *Globe and Mail*, Toronto, 16 January 1943, 1.

5 "Price Controls Are Restored over Meat and Butter," *The Gazette*, 16 January 1946, 1.

6 "15 Cent Meals," *Saskatoon, Star-Phoenix,* 24 January 1948, 24.

7 F.W. Hanley, "Canada's Ill-Fed Children," *Ottawa Evening Citizen,* 30 January 1948, 32.

8 Connolley, "Housewives Claim Budget Is Absurd."

9 *Globe and Mail,* 10 June 1946.

10 LAC, RG 36-31, Vol. 27, File 15, Promotional Material for Use with the Film "Suffer Little Children" and Discussion Trailer on the World Food Emergency, Issued by the Food Information Committee.

11 LAC, RG 36-31, Vol. 27, File 15, Radio Speech by Louis Saint-Laurent, Minister of Justice, 12 May 1946.

12 For an excellent analysis of postwar relief efforts in Canada, see Tarah Brookfield, *Cold War Comforts: Canadian Women, Child Safety, and Global Insecurity* (Waterloo: Wilfrid Laurier University Press, 2012).

Index

Marshall, Dominique, 14

marshmallows, 142, 157

masculinity, 15-16; and meat, 80-83; and victory gardening, 106-8; and volunteer work, 112; wartime crisis of, 39-41

mayonnaise, 149, 159

McClung, Nellie, 142

McCollum, E.V., 24

McCready, Margaret, 156

McGill University, 156, 165-67, 175

McHenry, E.W., 54, 192, 207, 222n26: and the Canadian Dietary Standard, 29, 186-87; and the nutrition professions, 32-33; Toronto dietary surveys, 31-33, 167-72; and unemployment relief, 181-87, 202, 205

McPhail, Agnes, 156-57

Mead, Margaret, 44-45

meat, 8, 86, 117-18, 150, 160: butchers' strike, 84, 87; canned, 82, 124; coal miners' strike, 16, 80-83; consumption levels, 143, 145; European ration allotments, 75; extenders, 140-41; and the food rules, 21, 44; meatless days, 8, 64, 76, 82, 137; and military ration scales, 143; off-ration access, 75, 82-83; postwar boycotts, 90; prices, 32, 64, 90-91, 206; quality, 115, 145-46; rationing, 5, 63, 73, 80-84, 137-38, 143-46, 149, 204, 210; and wartime controls, 72, 109-11. *See also* beef; bologna; butcher shops; fame animals; heart; hot dogs; lamb; liver; pork; sausage; tongue

Metis peoples, 50, 199

Metropolitan Life Insurance Company, 21, 105

Milbank Memorial Fund, 50

military: bases, 19, 106, 115; Canadian attitudes towards, 3; and food exports, 5, 64; rejection rates, 16, 38-39, 53, 81, 179; ration scales, 34, 54, 140, 143, 205. *See also* Royal Canadian Air Force (RCAF); Royal Canadian Army; soldiers

milk, 10, 117, 143-44, 148, 160: and Canadian foodways, 49; condensed, 141; evaporated, 4; and the Food Rules, 21, 42-48, 59, 139, 196; in France, 75;

and the Pett Diet, 204; powdered, 124; prices, 8, 64, 80, 86, 89-91, 196; and school lunches, 193-95

Milk for Britain Campaign, 120-21

minerals. *See* Canadian Dietary Standard; dietary standards; malnutrition; nutrition

molasses, 77, 147, 159

Monde Ouvrier, Le, 204

Montreal, 19, 34, 73, 91, 105, 157: and black markets, 79; butchers' strike, 84, 87; dietary studies, 26, 166-67; nutrition programs, 34, 58, 127, 147; POW parcel-packing plant, 124; and school lunches, 194, 197; victory gardening, 124; WRAC, 74, 88

Montreal Gazette, 204, 206

Montreal Standard, 139, 157

Moore, Percy, 199-200

Moore's Mills, 142

Moose Jaw, 89, 116

moral economy, 87, 206

morale, 19, 98-100, 108, 111, 114, 123-26, 139

Morrel, C.A., 188-89

mortality rates, 32, 35, 37, 40, 179-80, 182

mothers, 117-19, 141, 172: blame for malnutrition crisis, 16, 31-32, 54-58, 168, 170, 184; malnutrition rates, 25, 162-63, 168-72, 184, 193; mother's allowances, 173; and nutrition education, 34, 42, 46-47, 54; wartime duties of, 5, 21, 58-59, 69, 99-102, 112-13, 126, 152; as war workers, 140

Mrs. Consumer, 68-69, 72, 93, 100, 129, 230n22

mussels, 135

Mussolini, Benito, 97-98

National Committee for School Health Research, 195

National Council of Women, 18, 33-34, 56, 93, 127, 195

National Film Board (NFB), 18, 46-48, 209

National Research Council (US), 41, 176, 189

Printed and bound in Canada by Friesens

Set in Clarendon, News Gothic, and Garamond
by Artegraphica Design Co. Ltd.

Copy editor: Matthew Kudelka

Proofreader: Lana Okerlund